HOW NOT TO BE A LEADEI

'How not to be a Leadership D*ckhead'

AND BUILD A

HIGH PERFORMING TEAM

Steve Sallis

Published by Mabel and Stanley Publishing

Copyright © June 2024 Steve Sallis

All rights reserved

Disclaimer

The tips and advice in this book are drawn from the learnings and experiences of Steve Sallis. The suggestions and advice given do not guarantee specific results and all results will be governed by individual efforts, implementation and unique experiences and circumstances.

The book draws on many quotes gleaned from Steve's personal journey – these are referenced wherever possible, but some may be from origins unknown as they have been accumulated over many years of learning and from a wide variety of sources. Immense gratitude is given to unknown contributors for their wisdom.

SCAN ME
TO VISIT
WWW.LEADERSHIPMINDSET.UK

"You don't build a business, you build the people, and then the people build the business."

This book is dedicated to the 'Leadership Loners' out there who need to be Leadership Lovers.

Reminder: If you give love, you get love.

To the work energisers, I love you.

To the work de-energisers...look in the mirror, and not out of the window...

To the boss that bullied me. Thank you for the inspiration.

Real Relationships

I had heard about Steve on the football circuit but first came across him when he did some work for the AFC Wimbledon Academy over a zoom in March 2020. I was instantly engaged and intrigued by his persona and knew I would want to work with him more. When I got asked to be manager of AFC Wimbledon in 2021, he was my first phone call. I needed him by my side when the team was in dire need of results, and in the relegation zone in League 1.

After three hours of doing laps of Dulwich Park in south London and pretty much out the goodness of his heart and without major financial gain he agreed to help try and turn around a seemingly impossible situation. Just over three months later, of helping me open people's minds, build deeper attachments and confront stereotypical thinking we survived relegation. Steve created a massive change in the team's behaviour and performance that could only really be appreciated by those who experienced it first-hand. When Steve speaks, people listen.

As a pair we mostly laughed, we sometimes argued passionately with one another as we created a remarkable authenticity amongst a group of people in a highly pressurised situation. He supported me when needed and tweaked my conscience when required. However, on a deeper level he created a process where players and staff were totally aligned. He is brilliant.

Mark Robinson
Chelsea Football Cub
Under 23 Manager

This foreword is how much Steve Sallis means to me. It has been a crazy week. I got up at 6am to write this and been thinking of words that will do his work justice. Until you see him speak then you'll understand me better. The change he creates, makes ripples daily through the work environment. His constant obsession with improvement is unique. He's on it, and how he creates a positive connection & communication with players is the best in the world. He creates an energy and spirit that lifts the player group when they are down and lifts them further when they are up.

I'm immensely proud of the difference Steve makes to my life and the lives of our Northampton Town players and staff during our promotion season in 2023. The positive impact he makes is aspirational and inspirational all in one. Steve just gets it!

Steve is able to find the blind spots within your environment whether it's managers to player, player to player, staff to player, manager to board level, players to fans, or manager to fans. For me Steve is the work game changer that helps you build a world class culture and environment which enables players and staff to take off their armour and be the best version of themselves.

He preaches daily that positive alignment throughout our organisation is essential, equipping the group with the soft skills and performance tools to shine. He helps everyone along the way, instilling complete clarity and objectivity to how we work. Yet he does this with great humour so the spirit, camaraderie, and consistent performance of everyone within our environment is x-factor. What a human. Love you brother.

Jon Brady
Northampton Town Football Club
Manager

HOW NOT TO BE A LEADERSHIP D*CKHEAD

CONTENTS

Chapter 1
WHICH LEADER ARE YOU? - LEADERSHIP DYNAMITE – ALL THE 'DO NOTS' OF 'HOW NOT TO LEAD'..............29

Chapter 2
THE BLAME GAME ...IT WASN'T ME... PUSHING THE BLAME CULTURE..............33

Chapter 3
WHAT IS MORE IMPORTANT? EXPERIENCES OR EXPERIENCE?..........39

Chapter 4
THE CULTURE OF FEAR AND WEARING ARMOUR..............45

Chapter 5
CONFLICT - KNOWING THE COGS...& THE TEAM BEHIND THE TEAM....55

Chapter 6
SELF-AWARENESS AND WHY WITHOUT IT YOU'RE FUCKED! OR IS IGNORANCE ACTUALLY BLISS? 73

Chapter 7
POEM...THE AVERAGE CHILD - BY MIKE BUSCEMI..............83

Chapter 8
LEADING A FAILING BUSINESS? WHAT IS THE ENERGY LIKE? AND HOW DOES SOMEONE TALK ABOUT YOU WHEN YOU ARE NOT IN THE ROOM?"..............85

Chapter 9
WORK GOSSIP AND THE GOSSIP GURUS..............89

Chapter 10
LEADERSHIP OWN GOALS AND THE 99% EFFECT 97

Chapter 11
SUPER STRENGTHS 101

Chapter 12
TOXIC TEAMS - SMELLING THE BAD EGG AND SPOTTING DICKHEADS 105

Chapter 13
LEADERSHIP INFLUENCE AND LOVE LANGUAGES..............115

Chapter 14
THE MAVERICK LEADER 121

Chapter 15
COACHING VERSUS MENTORING - WHAT IS BEST?..............131

Chapter 16
IKIGAI..............139

www.leadershipmindset.uk

Chapter 17
THE PROBLEM WITH GOVERNMENT LEADERSHIP..................................143

Chapter 18
THE WORK LIBERTY TAKERS AND THE LINE OF PRIDE - DO YOU KNOW WHERE YOUR LINE IS?..................................147

Chapter 19
LEADERSHIP SIMPLIFIED..................................153

Chapter 20
LEADERSHIP UN-SIMPLIFIED AND THE NARCISSIST 'HEAD FUCK' LEADER..................................171

Chapter 21
BUILDING TEAMS: IMPROVE THEM OR REPLACE THEM? IS RETENTION AND RECRUITMENT STILL AN ISSUE? THE POWER OF 'LEARNING CONVERSATIONS'..................................177

Chapter 22
FOLLOW THE PROCESS ... AND YOU GET PROGRESS..................................187

Chapter 23
LEADERSHIP SHORT-TERMISM..................................197

Chapter 24
LEADERSHIP LANGUAGE..................................201

Chapter 25
THE GAME CHANGER - HIGHER ORDER THINKING AND META-COGNITION..................................205

Chapter 26
THE TOP 25 MOST IMPORTANT THINGS YOU CAN SAY TO YOUR STAFF..................................209

Chapter 27
THE "PLUS ONE EFFECT", LEARNING TO SAY "NO" AND MANAGING THE MANAGER..................................213

Chapter 28
STOP INTERRUPTING! LET THEM FINISH - TEAM DYNAMICS KILLED IN AN INSTANT!..................................217

Chapter 29
INSECURE PERSON X INCOMPETENT PERSON = DANGEROUS PERSON..................................221

Chapter 30
THE PROBLEM WITH EXPERTS – ARE YOU A HEDGEHOG OR A FOX?..................................225

Chapter 31
10 TIPS FOR 'EMOTIONAL INTELLIGENCE' IN BUSINESS AND WHY IT'S NUMBER ONE FOR SUCCESS!..................................231

Chapter 32
BACK THEM OR SACK THEM?..239
Chapter 33
WHY AM I CHASING MONEY? 243
Chapter 34
SOCIAL MEDIA – THE POWER AND THE PITFALLS........................ 251
Chapter 35
EGO IS THE ENEMY...255
Chapter 36
MANAGING UPWARDS AND MIDDLE LEADERSHIP 265
Chapter 37
THE CURSE OF KNOWLEDGE... 271
Chapter 38
I'M OK, YOU'RE OK..275
Chapter 39
THE CC' BRIGADE – DON'T BE THE STITCH UP LEADER!........................281
Chapter 40
LEADING WITH LISTENING - TWO EARS, ONE MOUTH.........................283
Chapter 41
THE SOLUTIONS MINDSET AND YOUR FIRST MONTH AS THE NEW BOSS
....289
Chapter 42
SCHOOLS, LEADING YOUR CHILDREN AND MANAGING THE CHIMP. YOURS AND THEIRS!..293
Chapter 43
THE LEADERSHIP ONE LINERS..301
Chapter 44
HOW TO LEAD A ONE-TO-ONE MEETING 303
Chapter 45
LEADING ON PROFESSIONAL DEVELOPMENT TIPS...................................307
Chapter 46
WORKING FROM HOME? THE GOOD AND THE BAD.......................... 311
Chapter 47
CONCLUSION AND THE SERVANT LEADER..317

HOW NOT BE A LEADERSHIP D*CKHEAD

HOW NOT BE A LEADERSHIP D*CKHEAD

FOREWORD

I think to understand this book, you must understand its origins. The concepts that are presented in each chapter are not "floated ideas". They are a huge library of experiences.

Real life. Big wins & losses. Steel & style.

Steve has created an objectivity of how people learn. Because without learning we cannot grow and improve. With this book, think of it like being given a leadership road map. You know your destination, but not totally sure on the route to take, or how to navigate & in all honesty - enjoy the journey.

How do you feel or think when you hit that proverbial bump in the road?

This book will help you because Steve mentions it all.

- The controlling boss who has two mouths and one ear.
- The colleague who insists on grinding you and others down every day.
- The people around you who are there for a transaction & those who are there to deposit - Wisdom, knowledge, advice.

But then to understand where it originates, you have to also try to understand the person behind the carefully thought-out words of wisdom. You should be rest-assured that with every page you turn in this book, every sentence you consume & complete, you are getting closer to where you had hoped, when you first decided to give leadership a chance. That is all we want right? Just to be given a chance.

In February 2014, as a frustrated, 25-year-old, part time under 14 academy football coach, I stormed into Steve's office to vent my frustration about where my work life was at. He was one of the

HOW NOT BE A LEADERSHIP D*CKHEAD

Academy Management Team at Millwall Football Club in south London. I explained I felt that I was being held back, blocked, ignored. I felt I could add so much more value, should I be given a chance.

Steve looked at me while I was speaking and listened intently. He didn't speak, interrupt, or give any advice until I had finished. He just simply allowed me to spill my emotion. He was calm, took a long deep breath & said to me:

"Harry, firstly slow the fuck down. I have never been surer, of anything in my life that you will be at first team level in the premier league one day. You have 'X factor', there is genuinely no need to rush this life journey. Rushing isn't good. Stay cool. It is going to happen for you, regardless. You are young and you have to earn your stripes first. I love the passion, but success takes time. My advice to you is have a passion for improving and not proving. That is the only controllable."

I think that day I left Steve's office with a little bit more hope inside of me, that someone else shared the same belief I had in myself. I am not sure Steve actually knew what would happen, I think he was more certain that the person stood in-front of him, represented the thousands of young people he had seen in his time working in southeast London Schools.

I think he knew the look in my eye, I think he had seen it all before. A young person desperate for growth and success that just needed to vent how they felt. Who knows if I will prove him right? I think the main point is that he allowed me to share my dream with him & he in turn shared it too. That to me speaks volumes of the man. His ability to understand my passion & help direct me with his knowledge & wisdom.

If Steve was in one of my football teams, he would be my maverick 'number 10'. Given the free role. Because he is magic, and he cannot be fenced in with rules and guidelines. He needs to express himself and be allowed to be his true authentic self. I am well aware that if he is allowed that intellectual freedom in the workplace he will guarantee, to win you games!

Enjoy the book, I have enjoyed hearing about it over the last five years since his last book created great success.

Harry Watling
Former Glasgow Rangers First Team Coach

HOW NOT BE A LEADERSHIP D*CKHEAD

INTRODUCTION

"The number one relationship you need to have as a leader, is the relationship you have with yourself. The leaders who are bullies? Always remember, they have a crap relationship with themselves, so never forget it".

Without great self-awareness you're fucked. You have no hope to truly succeed. You will leave life on this planet with zero legacy. Self-awareness is a 'Superpower' you see! You need to be ultra-aware of:

- Knowing how you act
- Knowing how you interact
- Knowing how you react
- Knowing what you know
- Knowing what you don't know

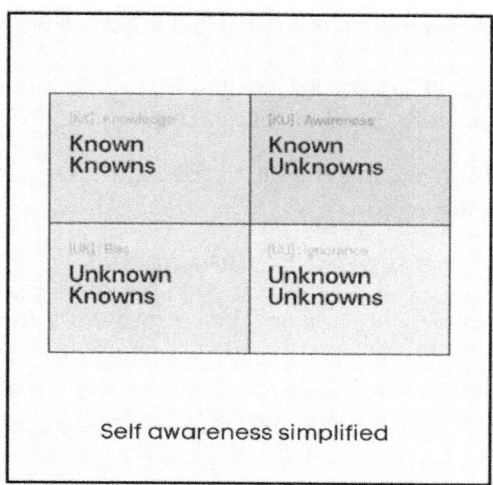

Self awareness simplified

Above, I have clearly simplified self-awareness and given you a diagram to support this type of thinking. However, I believe on a deeper level it is about developing the following with regards to self-management (the relationship you have with yourself), relationship management (the relationship you have with others), and the toolbox of empathy you give to the world.

1) Self-management should include processes like the assessment of your emotional regulation, positivity traits you have or don't have and the mental agility you apply daily. Basically, this means how adaptable you are as a human on this planet.
2) Relationship management encompasses more external processes. This may include your ability to influence others, coach or mentor people depending on the situations in front of you and your ability to deal with conflict. Finally, your ability to be a genuine team player (We not Me).

Advice: Don't be the Downgrade!

Have you ever heard of the Leadership Downgrade?

What is it? Are you one? I hope not! So let me tell you.

Everyone I know in the world, has had their favourite ever boss in their lifetime at work. So, think about this…

If you do not BEHAVE, like the best boss THEY have ever had, then you are officially everyone's:

"LEADERSHIP DOWNGRADE!"

Bloody hell. Scary right. Imagine going into work every day and being everyone's leadership downgrade. The downgrades are the dickhead leaders who treat people like shit and are generally just incompetent at their job compared to what you have previously experienced.

The staff you lead look at you as, *not at the required level*. They talk about you when you are not in the room because you are not cutting it. They can see you sinking under the pressure, being short and stubborn with people and they can smell your incompetence a mile off. You often hear the dickhead leader being spoken about in statements like…

"She's/He's just not authentic and can't talk to people properly."

Reminder:

The staff say this shit, everyday behind your back.

If you suspect this is the case, then you are reading the right book. If you are already a high achieving boss, then this book will definitely serve as a set of sound reminders for you and sharpen your current tools and hopefully add additional value to your existing tools.

People that know me well or have worked with me, know that I am a man that often provides as many questions as I do answers. Why? Because how can I have all the answers for all the strangers around the world that I know little all about? I despise the many so-called forceful social media influencers and leadership gurus that say, "You have to do it my way."

What I am not guilty about however is provoking people to get thinking.

Tip:

With this type of forceful leadership arrogance and suppressive behaviour, your staff can't feel their true authentic selves. And without being our true selves every day, we are all living a fake life, full of corporate behavioural bullshit.

Advice:

The ability to think critically is a major message in this book. An example being...

> **"The most dangerous thing in business is not having the wrong answers... but asking the wrong questions."**

Without this type of critical thinking, you are doomed as a leader. You see, two decades of inner-London school teaching enabled me to acquire more knowhow about leadership, mindset, and critical thinking tools for a more fulfilling life. The daily dysfunctional attitudes of those poverty-stricken students who would later become aspirational young people were witnessed daily, and in reality, this made me who I am today. Gang Culture, knife crime and eleven-year-olds regularly wearing stab vests under their school uniform just to stay safe from the world was the norm for me and my teaching peers. I learnt under the rigorous pressure of the flawed UK educational system that:

Simply:

- The more mindset tools you have, the more choice you have, about how to behave.
- The greater choice you have around your behaviour, the more you can positively affect the diverse nature of the workplace and beyond.
- With no behavioural tools, you are condemned to a certain lack of fulfilment and are more likely to be a workplace dickhead, coach dickhead or leadership dickhead and subsequently living a life which isn't as happy as it could be.

Have you ever met those 'eye specialist' leaders?

No, not the optician down your local high street, but the leaders that constantly tell everyone, what they do great all the time. They are the leaders that may look, but in reality, don't really see.

"I (eye) did this, and I did that. (note the sarcasm). That's it... *the eye specialist.*

However sadly, for all involved, theses eyes specialist leaders do not DO what they say they are going to do yet talk a great game. The eye specialists are the ones that just often talk about themselves:

HOW NOT BE A LEADERSHIP D*CKHEAD

Reminder:

Please reflect on the 'eye specialist leader' metaphor, because if you don't then you are officially at the start of a journey to being a leadership dickhead. The leaders that say, "Me, me, me." If you know someone like this, can you please send this book to the stupid idiot!

Reflections:

I am inspired to write this new book, as I have been thinking about it for years if I am honest. I am baffled about how many shit managers and leadership dickheads there are in our world! Whatever adjective we decide to use for these people above us in the hierarchy:

- Leader
- Manager
- Boss
- Gaffer

They are all the same in purpose, right? The sad thing is, so many of these dickhead leaders in the world of work get crap outcomes, either via the profit and loss of the business or for people's mental health and sanity either personally or professionally. The staff underneath the boss in the work 'pecking order' simply despise their daily actions. Have you yet to experience this for yourself by working for one of these dickheads? If not, I hope and pray that never happens on your life journey.

Research:

An article written by the Adecco Group in February 2022, stated that the top four reasons why people quit their job were:

1) Toxic Corporate Culture
2) Job Security and Reorganisation
3) Too much innovation (I thought it would be opposite by the way)
4) Failure to recognise human performance.

HOW NOT BE A LEADERSHIP D*CKHEAD

Note: None of the above include money, but do however include a shit working culture, and therefore shit leadership.

The above research isn't really rocket science though, is it? So, referring back to these dickhead leaders:

- Some don't listen.
- Many interrupt you all day, every day.
- Some show zero empathy to individuals they serve.
- Many simply have no duty of care for their people!
- Some oversell, and under deliver.

I mean, what the fuck! How is it possible that so many leaders get into these positions in the first place? So be mindful, dickhead leaders exist everywhere, and many are gold medallists at masking their incompetencies to their seniors.

Advice:

If you are the outstanding boss out there, I applaud you, as you already know that your job is to *serve* your staff which I assume you do with consistent love and an under-control ego. In contrast, the reality for the dickhead boss is that the staff probably SERVE you, as you sit at the top of the tree like a draconian twat, while you treat the grafters (who I call the soldiers) like shit.

Of course, we all know there isn't one defining set of leadership characteristics that create greatness for their people. Wisdom and history tell us, that effective leadership comes in many forms and the context, environment and stages of leadership styles being adapted is key.

Reminder:

As a leader you can't please everyone of course, and later in the book I will discuss many categories of leaders. For example, the *people pleaser* leaders, and I note later, that their charisma is often seen as a positive trait but remind yourself that these types of leaders can also cause havoc even if their intentions are good. The *people pleaser* leader can often avoid making the difficult decisions, which ends up upsetting the majority of their people even more. Do you know a people pleaser leader, who charms people, but mostly under delivers on most KPI's?

Advice:

Leaders get paid to lead. Many bosses often, just *manage*, and fail to lead. Are you one of those? The manager and not the leader? If so? This book will help you. The manager is in 'vision express' looking to find a vision. The Leader already has one.

Task:

As a starter activity in this book, I would like you to reflect on the SSC (Stop, Start, Continue) method.

1. What would you like to start doing to improve?
2. What would you like to stop doing?
3. What would you like to continue doing?

Start on this process to get you going. It will help you.

Leading or Managing?

I want you to read this book and think deeply about the differences between leading and managing because they are by definition alone, significantly different. I have deliberately not given you a definition for each because I want you to think about it and analyse in depth, for yourself.

Questioning Intelligence:

Early in September 1999 at the start of my teaching career, I found myself questioning the word *intelligence* on a daily basis. On one corridor, was a teacher (leader) who magically changed lives. Down the other, was a teacher who was objectively shit. However, the most significant statistics behind all of these observations were:

They BOTH had teaching degrees.

HOW NOT BE A LEADERSHIP D*CKHEAD

Which apparently meant they got through university, were both perceived as competent by their universities and were therefore qualified to add-value to the youngsters of our next generation.

As time went by, I noticed quickly that the degree of teaching quality between teachers in schools was so far apart it was nuts. Many were worlds apart in their skillset and all were getting paid the same amount in their pay cheque.

I just couldn't get my head around shocking teachers with top university degrees, who were turning up to work every day, and were getting completely terrorised. Now understand this:

i) Being shit and wanting to improve yourself is one thing, but more alarmingly there were so many teachers who lacked the self-awareness to even WANT to get better! They were just so fixed in their mindset.

"I'm cool with anyone being rubbish but being unaware that you are shit, is something I cannot accept."

More Evidence:

My fragmented relationship with the meaning of *intelligence*, started in 1988 by being placed in the 'bottom set' on my first day of secondary school, and going home to my mum confused as hell, asking her if I was thick? I was an August 22nd birthday and throughout my childhood mum always believed I was a year behind, and she was to be proved right. I believe this labelling at 11 years old, led me to being set up to fail my GCSE's five years later in 1993, but make of that what you will.

After the initial GCSE failure, a year later I went again, did some re-takes and acquired eight A-C grades. Suddenly I was seen by UK society differently, and now labelled 'brainy'. But really is that the truth? So, have a think about this…

A year earlier, as is the negative judgment in UK society I was labelled as thick, and a year later I am seen as brainy. The actual reason for my new-found 'brainy-ness' was that I was just a year older, wiser and more complete. Please note, not necessarily more academically intelligent, but just a year more mature in my outlook after reflecting from my failure the previous year.

Facts:

Imagine how many people are walking around the UK and beyond, thinking they are stupid because of this place called a *school* which seems to think labelling children is effective or even fair and an accurate assessment of measuring modern day intelligence.

I am here to tell you, that you are NOT thick! No one is thick or stupid. Everyone has the ability to improve and learn, given the correct environment. We are all equal, and we all have *super strengths* which contribute to the world we live in. There is only one of you. No one on the planet can replicate and copy the one example of you. Think about that? It makes you entirely unique to this planet. It is beautiful. You are beautiful.

Beyond the School Gates:

After some crappy A' level results in 1996, I somehow got into Greenwich University, based in south London, and this was the first time in my life I fell in love with learning at nineteen years old. This light bulb moment had taken fifteen years for me to experience (4 years old to 19). Years and years of average educational experiences and average teachers who to be honest, failed me and did nothing to make me actually feel alive and excited about learning anything. (Mrs Lewis, Mr Hickman, and Ms Hill you are not included in this averageness).

This next part of the journey was firstly to leave home from the seaside city of Brighton and go to the big smoke (London) and train to become a Physical Education teacher. This qualification and experience was the life game-changer for me, for both my personal character development and upskilling my calibre as an educationalist. I met likeminded people who were all generally working-class trainee teachers wanting to inspire London school children for the right reasons.

HOW NOT BE A LEADERSHIP D*CKHEAD

I qualified three years later in July 1999 with a teaching degree, and my best university friends in tow. As always thanks to my brothers Mallin, Wilky, Wheelo, Terry, Sully, Bally and the Shadow. We are proud to say we have a WhatsApp group called the 'Dickheads'. Clearly, we don't take ourselves too seriously put it that way. I think humour is a major quality many workplace leaders miss. You have to laugh at yourself and to not take yourself too seriously in life. We certainly don't.

From there, I had a really tough and anxiety-led year as a new teacher in 1999, in a failing into aspiring south London school. I am forever grateful to the wonderful Physical Education department that keep me genuinely sane and well. I have said this many times, but there was not one weak link in that department at Crown Woods Secondary school in Eltham, south London. So, Rambo Reidy, Fieldy and Powelly, Blayney, Fran, Taff thank you.

I was able to witness eleven high quality PE teachers in front of my eyes, every minute of every day. I still don't think the general population would exactly know what an inner-city schoolteacher does every day. While in many jobs Monday mornings at work consist of having a cuppa, putting on the laptop by 9:15am and catching up with colleagues over their weekends' leisure activities, I however, was (in my final year teaching, in 2014) having major grief and dramas with thirty, year 11 girls at 8:35am, trying to get them to enter a Science class, that they were damn right refusing to go into. This cohort of school refusers were yelling at me saying "Sallis please teach us, our teacher is shit," and they were not going in the class! How's that for a Monday morning! Proper grief let me tell you! And I can't even teach Science!

After these amazing, yet crazy daily experiences I never looked back really, and I was promoted several times in the next two decades in the education sector. First to a behaviour specialist, then middle leader, up to a senior leader, and finally onto vice-principal of several large Inner London Secondary schools. At this stage I was about to go and study for my NPQH which is the National Headteachers Qualification, but then something dramatic

www.leadershipmindset.uk

changed my life forever. One day in October 2013, my life turned on its head.

The Legacy:

An ex-pupil texted me about a job in professional football. His name was Chris Eather. I had met Chris in September 2000, when he was 11 years old. I was on 'walky talky' duty which basically was the most fun job in the world. It essentially meant chasing kids who were not in lessons down school corridors and getting paid for it. These teenage kids running away from me, were fundamentally bunking off lessons. From the first moment I met Chris I got a vibe he was sound like most kids, however whilst on corridor duty I got called to a classroom to deal with an incident where Chris was basically giving the Science teacher the "F bomb." She had sent him out of the classroom, and he was in a state of anger. I attempted to calm him down, which I was pretty good at to be fair. (40,000 kids can vouch for me.) But on this occasion, he ignored everything I said and went on to tell the same teacher to "Fuck off," in the same lesson for the next three weeks!

To be fair to Chris, he did eventually listen to my wisdom over our time together, and we are now great friends, as I am with his amazing family. He now runs a thriving sports business called 'All-Kids-Can' based in south London helping children with special educational needs via sport. It doesn't get better for a success story than that really does it? I suppose I am sharing this story because if I hadn't made the time for Chris (and his many peers for all those years as their teacher), he wouldn't have "wanted" to text his old teacher all those years later, to change my life.

Selflessness:

I didn't think when I spent all those hours helping him and other school kids that they would help me 20 years later did I? I just did it. Nick Seboa, another ex-pupil is my construction man, Danny Pierson my painter and Harry Baker from a different south London school is my electrician. I am honoured to share these stories.

I love my one liner quotes and I will share many in this book. But one I stand by is:

> *"Children won't let you care about them, until they know that you care."*

My point is however, are adults any different? Of course not.

Football:

So, Chris's text in 2013 led to a career change, and in January 2014, I joined a professional football club, Millwall FC, in an attempt to create a new legacy for myself. At this stage in my life, I had met another game-changing human being, in a man called Doctor Bob Burstow. He turned out to be the man that gave me access to a toolbox of knowledge, which was to basically change my life. I met him during my first day of my master's degree, at Kings College London. I swear to God, I was easily the most 'common as muck' sounding man that had ever entered that building, with it being the 'traditional academic' University. My pals often call me 'mockney Steve' which is a term for a fake cockney for those in the know. However, I regard myself to be extremely lucky to have met Bob, and for him to become my mentor. He believed in me from the start.

(I was now 34 years of age, and I would say, already an achiever. My current success had come through sheer hard work at this stage with a touch of charisma sprinkled in. This was probably stolen from my parents I suppose. My mum and dad were a cool 80's couple. They were stylish and loved a party and a night out, and me and my older brother Iain were often surrounded by their great, energetic and positive friends and these people were the ultimate role models for me really. So, thanks Ted, Sue, Pete, Phil, Mary and Donno.

One great memory I must share is from when I was about 10, and my dad took us out to Hove Squash and Rackets club for a night out. Dad has always liked a drink on a Friday...but this time he had his kids with him! There was a night club in Brighton at the time called the Kings club which Dad went to occasionally, except this time me and Iain were with him for the next chapter of the night out!

In this club there was a room upstairs for the kids with a pool table and sofas for the owners' grandkids. Crazy when you think about it. Dad left the club about 4am, and next to the club was a famous Brighton venue called the "All Night Café". Dad woke me and Iain up from the sofa on the top floor of the nightclub in the silly hours and we went onto chapter three of the night out, and to the café for its famous 'Gutbuster' fry up. I vividly remember all the market stalls setting up for the day and in particular Dad's lifelong mate Randell Griffiths a greengrocer, yelling to my drunk dad with his kids in tow, "Helloooo Tommy son, good night was it?" Madness if you think about it!

Anyway, back to Doctor Bob and his influence on me. He made me feel as if I was now armed to change the face of self-awareness and human behaviour forever. The world of business, education and sport needs it. I am now a business founder, and author. My previous book *Educating Football* has been extremely popular and a platform for me to challenge intelligence in a major way. Even as a young child I always questioned intelligence, and its correlation to success in life, and I plead with you to do the same.

Note: Bristol University had twelve suicides in 2019. This type of social neglect has to stop, and we need to ensure the education of our children defines what intelligence and success actually is. We need to enhance a new level of social awareness around this. EQ over IQ

The Beginnings:

As previously mentioned, my working journey began in a failing inner London school in 1999 based in Eltham in the south-east of the city. Southeast London is traditionally one of the poorer parts of the capital where the industry of teaching quickly finds you out, especially if you're shit at it.

HOW NOT BE A LEADERSHIP D*CKHEAD

If you're a teacher dickhead you basically get mullered by the lively students all day, every day. And I mean quickly. The kids and parents are so incredibly *socially savvy* that they will destroy a feeble and underperforming teacher in seconds. Now, underperforming comes in many different forms of course, so I will make this easy for you.

1) Imagine your worst ever teacher/leader? And imagine them existing in every school in the world, (because they pretty much do).
2) Now imagine your best ever teacher/leader and how they impacted you, changed your life, made you grow, gave you the confidence and the self-efficacy to succeed.

You could be reading this and thinking teacher/leader quality and the perception of their effectiveness is subjective (opinion), and based on personal opinion? But from my lens, great teachers are great teachers, and great leaders are great leaders. In a school 80% of kids are not wrong let me tell you. I appreciate there can be a varied opinion about leadership effectiveness of course but reflect on this... Does anyone recall Boris Johnson's reign and see it as moral and ethical, or even effective? If they do, they are either blind or ignorant.

Reminder:

"Wrong is wrong if everyone is doing it, and right is right if no one is doing it."

I have always stuck by my guns throughout my life and very proud of my gut instincts god has given me. For that, I am proud of myself. I don't sit on fences. I speak from the head and heart. Which is why I am probably marmite; however, people don't always like hearing the truth do they? I always believed if right was right, but no one is doing it, I will do it anyway. (Hence my previous book. People looked at me like I have got three heads in 2014 and seven years later I appear on the High-Performance Podcast, (200 million downloads) and suddenly I am more influential. It's all bollocks).

HOW NOT BE A LEADERSHIP D*CKHEAD

Shit Leaders have always existed, but how can we try to be objective about Leadership effectiveness? Can anyone with a sane mind ever say this lot are crap?

- Sir Alex Ferguson?
- Nelson Mandela?
- Mother Teresa?
- Martin Luther King?
- Mahatma Ghandi?

Generally, not! Great Leadership is great leadership, isn't it? Many say leadership effectiveness is black and white. What are your thoughts?

The Grey:

What I have noticed in my life is the alarming amount of people that think in a *black and white* fashion. They are clinical thinkers and not critical thinkers. They often think life and work is, either black or white, right or wrong? However great leaders know that in life and work, there are shit loads of grey areas.

Advice:

Knowing where the grey lies, is where the best leaders earn their stripes and gain success for their people. These types of leaders possess greater mental agility and mental agility leads to better relationships, enhanced staff happiness, and therefore greater profits. Please note: Not just financial profits. I mean spiritual ones. Ones where people feel the love between one another.

The Lens:

My business promotes explicitly, that we all see the world differently (the lens) and my belief is that if more people just understood this simple message, we would all have greater levels of satisfaction in our home and work lives.

For generations bad leaders have caused mayhem to people's home and work lives, by seeing the world through their own narrow *lens*. (Zooming in)

- Bad leaders affect their staff's mental health at work and further afield into people's home lives.
- Bad leaders hate on others, because in reality, they frequently hate themselves.
- Bad leaders thrive off power and their own ego, but inside they are generally cowards.
- Bad leaders can simply, wreck lives.

In contrast, great leaders help their staff. Great leaders say things like:

"What can I do to help you do your job better?"

Dickhead leaders promote themselves by implying:

"What can YOU do, to make me look better?"

As mentioned earlier, I am often bewildered, by our societal obsession with education and its often, *false correlation* to actual intelligence.

Reminder:

"Intelligence is about how YOU behave. Nothing else."

Task:

As an example of the lens, I would like you to complete the next task. It is dead easy. In the next sentence count how many letter **'F's'** you see and only take ten seconds to do so. When done, please look away and count again.

> FINISHED FILES ARE THE RESULT OF YEARS OF SCIENTIFIC STUDY COMBINED WITH THE EXPERIENCE OF YEARS

How many did you find? Have a look again.

Solution: 80% of people say three.

Why? Often, we don't correctly process the word "OF" for two reasons. First, the letter F usually makes the "f" sound, like in "fox". However, in the word "of", it makes a "v" sound. Secondly, you have probably read the word "of" so many times in your life, that you process it as one element, overlooking the second letter and sound.

HOW NOT BE A LEADERSHIP D*CKHEAD

Reminder:

Finally, please, remind yourself that your brain can tell you lies. How *you* see the world, is not how others see the world! And, if you can get a basic task like this wrong, how many other simple tasks do you get wrong every day? Remind yourself that how you see things is different to how others see things and so on. Please be mindful that cognitive bias exists everywhere, so don't be *that* leader, who is assumption focussed. Be the leader that is open minded and respectful of everyone's lens.

Task:

Now before we start with the main content of this book, I want you to action the following task, and note down what you perceive to be the most important traits, characteristics and behaviours for leadership success.

Write down which six words/behaviours/characteristics you would choose and then reflect on your answer.

1.

2.

3.

4.

5.

6.

i) Now as critical thinking task number one grade yourself 1-5 about where you are at with these words? 1 = Poor, 5 = Exceptional

ii) Now as a critical thinking exercise number two, put the above six words in order of importance, from the most to the least important. What did you come up with?

Further Questions to reflect on:
- What behaviours are going to get you, to the very top of your profession?
- How do these above behaviours align to your own specific 'super strengths' and personal characteristics as a leader?
- Have you aligned, correlated, and validated these words/behaviours with your actions and asked the people you work with whether they agree? What I mean is, would they say the same about you, as what you say about yourself? Food for thought.
- Is the topic of elite behaviours at work ever discussed? Developed? Nurtured? If not, why not?

Reminder:

1) Alignment = Clarity
2) Misalignment = Chaos

You heard it here first! There is chaos and misalignment everywhere in the world of work, so remind yourself that high performing businesses have to be highly aligned and on the same wavelength.

HOW NOT BE A LEADERSHIP D*CKHEAD

Chapter 1

WHICH LEADER ARE YOU? - LEADERSHIP DYNAMITE
ALL THE 'DO NOTS' OF HOW NOT TO LEAD.

"When the flower does not bloom, you fix the environment in which it grows, not the flower."

Alexander Den Heijer

Don't be a shit communicator
Don't focus on other people's mistakes
Don't hold grudges
Don't be toxic
Don't forget a fish rots at the head first
Don't look grumpy
Don't be an eye specialist (someone who says, I did this, and I did that)
Don't listen to gossip
Don't be a leadership loner
Don't say it is your idea when it's not
Don't ask people to do things you wouldn't do yourself
Don't be a 'know it all'
Don't have favourites
Don't ignore your staff in the corridor... because that's weird
Don't be arrogant
Don't forget people have lives beyond work
Don't assume people understand what you're talking about
Don't forget many people are wearing a mask, or armour
Don't underestimate the importance of politeness and eye contact
Don't be a sociopath
Don't be a narcissist
Don't forget words hurt
Don't start relationships with sarcasm; be sincere instead
Don't send aggressive ego-fuelled emails cc'ing everyone into them
Don't say "I" and "my" a lot

www.leadershipmindset.uk

HOW NOT BE A LEADERSHIP D*CKHEAD

Don't bury your head in the sand when the shit hits the fan
Don't take credit for things that you didn't do
Don't speak over people
Don't think you are better than your staff
Don't be a bully
Don't have an open-door policy, where the door never opens
Don't be afraid of making hard decisions
Don't try and keep everyone happy all the time
Don't think you always have to be right- being nice can be just as effective
Don't be passive aggressive
Don't think others see the world how you think they should
Don't be inconsistent with your behaviours
Don't criticise in public, and praise in private - do the opposite
Don't ignore your staffs' views
Don't appoint people then send them down the river after an error
Don't create a blame culture
Don't send emails to staff at 2am trying to look busy
Don't say 'me' all the time
Don't avoid delegating
Don't forget to look people in the eye and praise them
Don't have a flaky handshake
Don't forget you never get a second chance to make a first impression
Don't ask for spreadsheets at 8am on a Monday morning before saying hello because that's weird
Don't say you will accept someone's advice and ignore them anyway
Don't fail to know your staffs' and colleagues' names
Don't randomly insult people behind their back
Don't be unprofessional with your emails
Don't forget to smile
Don't underestimate that everybody knows more than somebody
Don't be stupid enough to think you're invincible
Don't be a micro-manager
Don't forget to serve your staff
Don't lack trust

www.leadershipmindset.uk

HOW NOT BE A LEADERSHIP D*CKHEAD

Don't forget to model the behaviours you want to see yourself
Don't' be indecisive
Don't try to control everything
Don't raise your voice back to people who raise theirs
Don't forget an expert hires an expert
Don't forget a minor setback can lead to a major comeback
Don't forget to talk TO people and not AT people
Don't employ people who always say yes to you
Don't say... can't ... problem... or... should ...

....DO say...can...will...could and

What is the solution to this problem?

HOW NOT BE A LEADERSHIP D*CKHEAD

HOW NOT BE A LEADERSHIP D*CKHEAD

Chapter 2

THE BLAME GAME ...IT WASN'T ME... PUSHING THE BLAME CULTURE

"Most people don't want to be part of the process; they just want to be part of the outcome. But the process is where you figure out who's worthy of being part of the outcome."

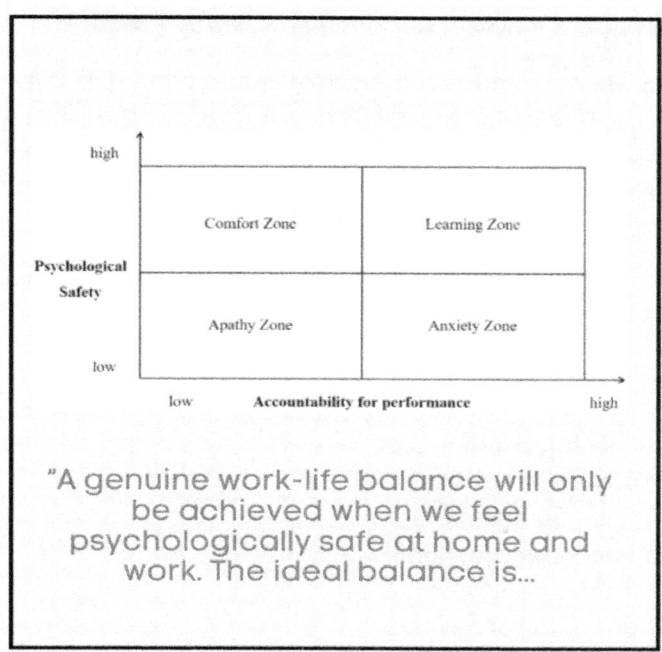

HOW NOT BE A LEADERSHIP D*CKHEAD

Remember that blame stands for:

BAD

LOSERS

ALWAYS

MAKE

EXCUSES

Reminder:

Psychological safety is the most important aspect in life for success to happen! This includes in the family, workplace, sport or friendships. We will only have a genuine work-life balance when we feel psychologically safe at home and safe at work. We've all worked with those toxic people. The ones that chuck you under the bus at any given opportunity. "It wasn't me," they say. "It was her," as they point the finger of blame, and hide from the fact that they are so engulfed in what I call *'automatic betrayal mode'*.

These twats are so quick to pass the blame, you'd think they were mimicking the regular behaviour by some of our politicians when we watch our television screens. This level of defensiveness is so instinctive from certain people, and often sadly seen as normal behaviour in many toxic work environments.

So why are many work environments so toxic?

Reminder:

Firstly, we are all different.

- Childhood differences
- Wealth or Poverty?
- One parent at home?
- Two parents at home?
- Brothers and sisters?
- House full of boys?
- House full of girls?

HOW NOT BE A LEADERSHIP D*CKHEAD

- Oldest or youngest child when growing up?
- Childhood of safety or childhood of stress?
- Only child?
- What country are you from?
- What part of that country are you from?
- What is your religion?
- What is your ethnicity?
- What is your mental health state?
- Have you had personal trauma?
- Is your physical health in a good place?
- Is your self-belief sky high or at rock bottom?
- How were your school experiences?

All of the above, can be the cause and effect of societal behaviour and causes people to:

1. Act how they act
2. Think what they think
3. Know what they know and
4. Do what they do

Advice:

Think about the above life experiences before you make pre-judgements about the people you lead and work with. There is always a reason why someone behaves like they do. Good or bad, so find out first.

The Toxic Torpedoes:

To simplify, I believe these fuckers are the highly insecure people who are often the main cause of toxicity in work and life. For starters:

- Insecure people often don't have the confidence and self-worth to admit wrongdoing.
- Insecure people will try to make you look smaller, whilst making themselves look bigger.

- Insecure people look out of the window, and not in the mirror.
- Insecure people are the masters of deflecting blame.
- Insecure people…GOSSIP

Do you know an insecure colleague, and have you ever connected the brain science as to why they are insecure and fuck people over at any, or every opportunity? This lot are the short-term thinkers. They have swallowed the stupid people's bible called "short termism". When God gave out intelligence, this short-term thinking mob obviously went missing that day.

In my previous book **Educating Football** I had a chapter called:

i) Insecure person x Incompetent person = Dangerous person – (INSEC x INCOMP)

It is obvious really isn't it! These deadly duds cause havoc at work, like a spiral of doom. Often their insecurity is extenuated because they are shit at their job, and because they are shit at their job, this makes them even more insecure!

These insecure x incompetent folk:

1) Don't have the skills to do their job properly, thus lack a level of basic competence for what they are supposedly paid for.
2) Will cover their arse with every move to hide their lack of competence. They are usually out of their depth, or/and unwilling to ask for help.
3) Perceive asking for someone else's help as weakness.

Reminder:

The wise folk amongst us know that high performing teams, see asking for help as a normal part of the high-performance process and seen as good practice. The incompetent leaders, however, see the actions of asking for help, as weak and therein lies further problems.

We have to remember this conundrum though:

    i)   Maybe they are insecure because the work culture they have entered is already toxic? Or

    ii)   Maybe they have entered the building and added to the toxicity?

Never ever forget the quote:

"People see, people do."

I have always believed that 'like hangs around with like' and the energy and behaviours we give out, are the same as we get back. A behaviour of constant moaning and complaining copies and mirrors more complaining, Anger copies anger, and optimism copies optimism. So, model the behaviour you want to see!

So, which one are you?

- A happy hoover or happy hairdryer?
- An energiser or de-energiser?

If you are not sure what the two above bullet points are exactly.

My advice... work it out!

HOW NOT BE A LEADERSHIP D*CKHEAD

Chapter 3

WHAT IS MORE IMPORTANT? EXPERIENCES OR EXPERIENCE?

"Count your age by life experiences, not years. A multitude of experiences teaches us more, than the same repeated experience."

Steve Sallis

Scenario:

I'll set the scene. There is a promotion available in your place of work. The job that everyone in the workplace would want.

Your juices get flowing, and *in your head*, this job has got your name on it; well so you think. You are not yet sure whether your closest work allies will be applying for the role, because they kept their cards close to their chest and said at the pub on the previous Friday that they were not sure. But in your head, you know that's what everyone says right, as your peers give little away. Even if they do apply, you still back yourself for this promotion ahead of them. Your brain races constantly as you think of all the possible consequences, the in-house competition, the external candidates and all the possible outcomes, including financial.

We've all been there, right? You're already thinking about having the job and salary before you have even got the damn job. The extra salary, the prestige, the growth in confidence, the boosted ego, and the extra clout you will get, as you now think about this job already being yours. You even contemplate the extra holidays, but most importantly the authority you may feel when you get the role. You have worked five years in this current job, and in *your little head* this new job has got your name on it. Well...so you think...

Two weeks after the first interview, the day comes for you to get the nod of approval. You wake up and you think you have got a great chance. You enter the office with a spring in your step; the final interview the week before went brilliantly. You wait anxiously in the lobby and eventually get the nudge from the boss's executive assistant to get the result you have worked so hard for. Excited, yet nervous you enter the office for the positive news. The CEO prepares to give you the news you have been waiting for... then you scream in desperation! "He's just got my job," and unbelievably the job isn't yours!

The Perception:

The reality of your flawed perception hurts even deeper just 24 hours later. You didn't get your rightful job and you are still fuming, betrayed, and fucked off. Livid in fact. The great esteem you held your bosses in, for so long, as 'wonderful loyal people', have turned 180 degrees and they are now viewed by yourself as complete wankers. You then find out they have given *your job* to the youngster who has zero experience. You drive home that day with your head on fire. You walk through your front door ready to cry and scream all at the same time and you yell to your partner, "No frigging experience," as you stamp your feet walking up the stairs. You scream, "They've gone and done it on the cheap. Gone for the cheap inexperienced option." (For your information: The youngster employed over you, has only been in the job three years since university).

So, you say to yourself after two sleepless nights:

- How is this so?
- Who have they *arse-licked* to get my job?
- Who do they know in hierarchy who has cheated me for this job?

The Reality:

So, be ready for my response here...

I am now officially going to stick up for the person that got your job. Yes, you heard it. The inexperienced youngster who gets your job over you and your five other more senior peers. You had the experience YES! The youngster had the EXPERIENCES!

Reminder:

The word *experience* is a dangerous headspace in the modern workplace. I am now going to explain why the word "experienced" may not always be helpful. Because after all, you might be *experienced* at being shit for many years.

- Experienced could mean you are fixed and rigid in your ways
- Experienced could mean you're a 'know it all' and never listen
- Experienced could mean you cannot be told what to do
- Experienced could mean you rarely listen to younger colleagues as you believe you know it all and they know nothing

Reasoning:
So why did the youngster get the job ahead of you? Because they were the cheap option? No no no... Agreed, they didn't have the experience you have. However, they had the "experiences".

HOW NOT BE A LEADERSHIP D*CKHEAD

Advice:

They had a set of diverse experiences in their younger life thus far, which have made them more adaptable than you to the modern world. They used words and phrases in their interview like:

- Mental Agility
- Strategy and Operation
- Evidence and Impact
- Prove and Improve

Not the same old nonsense and waffle which comes out of most people's mouths. They were highly articulate. You were not. You assumed. They didn't. You have a fixed mindset. They have a Growth Mindset.

Reminder:

- Use language wisely – this is my guidance!
- Never mistake experience for someone's 'experiences.
- Age does not always count in this situation. Age and experience can help of course, but only if more life years is correlated with genuine wisdom.

We have all met many of those old farts at work who are just negative every day; cynical and with traits that are the complete opposite of a growth mindset. You must understand that 'working experience' where situations are always the same every day, can be dangerous, compared to the diverse and wide-ranging experiences of others. Experiencing the same school, office, football club for thirty years is fine of course, if there is continuous, strategic, and organic growth in the building. Often however, we know there isn't, and the term "stuck in their ways" becomes way more common than it should.

Flash Back:

Memory 1 - I once worked at a top end boys grammar school called St Olave's in Kent, between 2003 and 2004. The staff didn't realise how good they had it. The kids were like elite behavioural machines, and all said, "Yes sir, no sir." Misbehaviour literally didn't happen. I learnt very quickly that most of these teachers, albeit nice people, would not have the skills to handle the inner-city kids, whereas, if I took the inner-city teachers into this grammar school they would cruise it with a big fat cigar in their mouths. The skills of the inner-city teaching staff were so much more diverse, varied, adaptable and effective in almost every way. They simply had to be! Inner city schools generally have kids that don't want to be there; in complete contrast, the grammar school kids generally *do* want to be there! My inner-city experiences were off the charts. We even had a full-time metropolitan police officer in the building supporting us in our work. Hopefully that says it all. PC Bob Pinkerton was a good man.

Memory 2 - Whilst working at Millwall Football Club years later, we had to borrow mini-buses from the local schools (yes you heard it), rent out school buildings for parents and player evenings, and had no proper training ground. Premier league clubs don't have that issue let me tell you, therefore the staff at these top clubs generally don't have to be as adaptable or mentally agile in my opinion. Simply at these top clubs, it is all laid out on a plate for staff and players. All very clean and all very nice, hence why I say 'too much too soon' can cause mental havoc in the game for these youngsters on the pitch. Similarly, in other industries, traders on the trading floor are earning six figure salaries in their early 20's for example and burn out is rife.

My point is we had to 'muck in' at Millwall and it was this mucking in, that made the comradery between the staff so strong and connected. We had crap facilities, yet great people. A word of advice. Facilities don't make great businesses, the people do, and the experiences of borrowing school minibuses, you simply wouldn't get at the top clubs.

HOW NOT BE A LEADERSHIP D*CKHEAD

Reminder:

What we do know about experience is in its obvious and literal interpretation, it is clearly vital for success. But take caution. Only if it is used correctly.

So, which one are you?

- Experienced and with experiences = Dream Ticket
- Inexperienced with experiences = Great but keep learning
- Experienced with limited experiences = Make sure you use this experience wisely
- Inexperienced and with limited experiences = You've got a lot of work to do

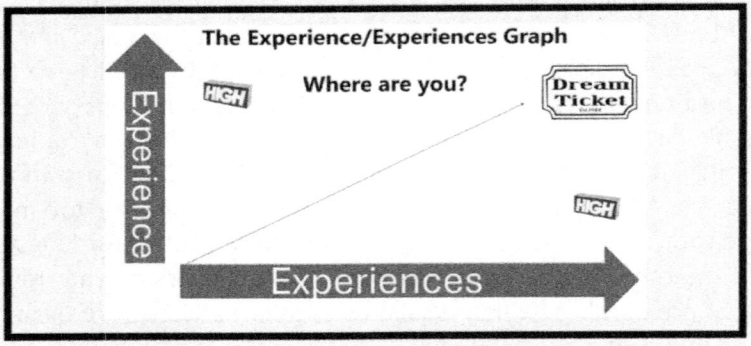

Whatever you are, keep asking questions to your peers about the problems you face. Find out if there is another way to do things? And remember,

"If you do what you've always done, you get what you've always got!"

Chapter 4

THE CULTURE OF FEAR AND WEARING ARMOUR

"To be the person who we long to be - We must again be vulnerable. We must take off the armour, put down the weapons, show up, and let ourselves be seen."

Brené Brown

What keeps you up at night? Is there a solution to sleepless nights? If you shared how you felt to work peers would it help your mindset to perform better?

The above quote is pure power from the wonderful Brene Brown and highlights the importance of EQ (emotional intelligence) in the modern workplace.

Questions to consider:

- If you are vulnerable to a person with a low level of EQ (emotional intelligence), what is the likely response?
- Have a think? Discuss this in your office as a task to complete.
- If you show vulnerability to someone with a high-level of EQ, what is their likely response to you?

The height and quality of someone's EQ pretty much defines the outcome for all concerned.

High EQ means the likelihood of you or others shedding their own emotional, physical, and metaphorical armour and therefore being 'your true authentic self' is more prone to happen.

So as mentioned in the previous chapter, someone has taken your job, the job you thought you rightfully deserved. But how do you react the next day?

1. Genuine, authentic, and pleased for them?
2. 'A fake'...genuine, authentic, and pleased for them?
3. A face like a slapped arse, looking bitter, twisted and you grunt at them on arrival?

Reminder:

E+R = O (Event + Reaction = Outcome)

1) What is your reaction to an event like this?
2) How did your reaction affect the outcome?

Emotional control is a key skill in leadership, so keep your shit together and remind yourself to *model the behaviours you want to see.*

- Did you spend all night slagging them off down the pub or when you get home to your partner, complaining that you are becoming another victim of life?
- Or... do you see the process, as a massive wake up call, and use this as a lightbulb moment in your life to liven the fuck up, and improve at work?

"Mild trauma can help us grow."

You see what I have learnt from my journey, is that we have all had trauma in many different ways. Some have had it mildly in their lives, and of course sadly some much more severe. I suppose the test is whether you choose to be glass half-full, or glass half-empty after these life tests. Do you remember a personal hero that helped mentor you through these tough moments, or are you going to be a victim for the rest of your life and tell the world that it owes you something? It is easier said than done, however when some people have had a major trauma in their life you can smell it a mile away. This trauma is visibly seen and heard externally in many adult behaviours so please remind yourself that genuine empathy is often needed.

Advice:

You could be seeing the non-promotion situation as if you *lost*. But actually, with a significant mindset change, you could say to yourself… I won.

You see,

"There is no failure, only feedback."

This was probably the 'kick up the arse' you needed to truly self-reflect, that your boxed off 'experience' simply wasn't as good as you thought it was. Options after a setback include:

- Maybe this lightbulb moment (what you also needed), has given you the fuel to sack them off (the employers of course) and leave the job with immediate effect.
- Either way the locus of control is in your hands.
- Will you blame others and be the victim and work dickhead? Or
- Will you behave with graciousness, dignity, and act like class-personified in defeat.

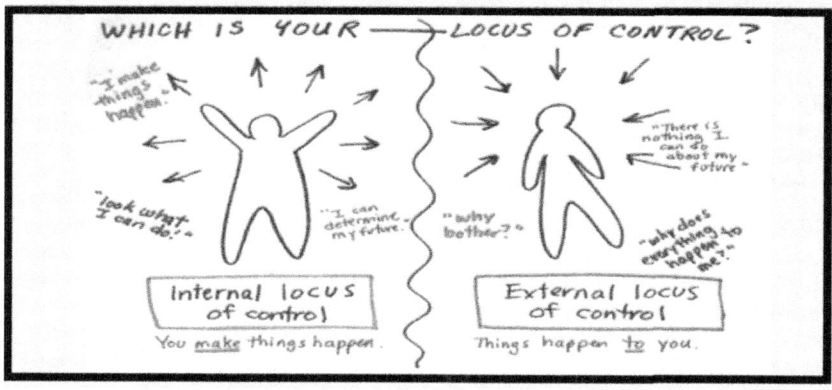

Reminder:

It wasn't just you that didn't get the job. You were one of five that were left with your tail between your legs. I have often reflected and think that modern day parents are partly to blame for this childish behaviour that flows into one's adult behaviour in later life. Many parents are forgetting about the importance of letting their children lose in life. There is a difference between losing and failing I believe.

> ***"Losing reflects the current score, however failing and bouncing back reflects our attitude."***

I truly believe that if we *normalised failure* in families from an earlier age, we would be less likely to get to the stage in life where adults act and behave like spoilt pricks, thinking that the world owes them something when they lose out on opportunities. Steve Peters the author of the game changing book The Chimp Paradox sends three major messages:

1. Life is not fair
2. The goal posts move
3. There are no guarantees

Wouldn't it be brilliant if we all knew the above three statements earlier in our lives? I share the above with all my football clients on session one, in order to give them the reality of professional sport and life before we even get going. This upskills them on the resilience needed to have a successful life. Nothing is given to you unless you get lucky, which most of us do not of course.

Advice:

Life is competitive, so get used to it early I say. Learn to lose, as well as learn to win. Life isn't all about winning. It's about loving the competition and enjoying the process.

So let us now re-visit people wearing armour. In life, everyone is wearing armour at certain stages of life.

- An 11-year-old child wears it on their first day of secondary school, because they don't want to lose face in front of their peers.
- A mum wears armour with her children after a bad day at work and puts on a *fake smile* to relax the family dynamic.
- A husband wears armour to his wife, when he says the family business is booming, but in reality, he can't see where his next job is coming from and is living his life worried sick.
- A wife wears armour to her husband after her negative hospital test results because she doesn't want to worry him.

So, do you wear armour at work or at home? If so, why?

- Do you wear armour with some people and not others?
- Is your ego a form of armour for you? If so, why is there an ego present in your behaviour?
- Does your place of work force you to wear armour due to a poisonous and toxic culture you have no control over?
- Can wearing armour ever be of benefit to you in the short, medium, or long term?
- If you are the boss at work, what are you doing to get your people to shed their armour and become their true authentic self, everyday?
- Are there genuine, honest, and frank conversations regarding armour being shed at work? If not, what are you going to do about it to help the situation?

Tip:

Just have the god damn conversation to start with. Get it out there! But of course, that takes high EQ, self-awareness, and wanting to be a cultural architect in the first place!

Task:

A simple task for any boss is to write down all of the people you work with and RAG (Red, Amber, Green) rate them for wearing armour.

1. **Greens** = they have no armour and are truly themselves every day.
2. **Ambers** = they take it off sometimes.
3. **Reds** = they wear it all day, every day.

This will at least give you a starting point for how to address the armour issues one by one, either by whole group or one at a time.

Whatever the answers to all the above questions, I wanted to bring to your attention the armour metaphor because I think it is so powerful. I often hear about great working cultures on websites and when I enter businesses, it is often the opposite, and a week later get a phone call from one of the employees of the same company saying, "Sallis, what you have heard... It's all bullshit and lies, and you need to help us please!"

In my corporate training days, I often ask people to define in a sentence the word *culture* and share their lens with the group. I often get many diverse responses, and this task further informs me in the next steps of how to help them.

Task:

What would your definition be? Mine is simple...

> **"Culture is how your weakest link feels, and what people do when no-one is looking."**

Now there's an interesting concept!

Sod all of this 'high-performance' bollocks. My definition is meaningful, simple, and inclusive. Remember that if your weakest link in the building loves their job, then the culture is supreme! End of story, no debate necessary. In contrast, if your weakest link thinks the boss is a leadership dickhead and they hate their job, then the culture isn't as good as you might think it is. Connecting to football here, how do the best managers somehow get their entire squad of 35 players motivated and loved when a third (24) of the squad are not playing any minutes at all?

Questions, answers and facts:

Only eleven players can play every week meaning twenty-four don't play. That is a lot of unhappy staff members to deal with and some footballers are not known for their high EQ let me tell you. So, what do the best football leaders do to help the players who are not in the team, yet still get them performing at maximum level when they get their one and only chance of the season. The question you need to ask yourself is how?

Coping with Rejection:

In the UK, so many kids want to grow up and be sport stars, pop stars, and social media influencers. What they don't realise (yet) is that behind the Sky Sports, YouTube, or Instagram banner, successful entrepreneurs and athletes are getting let down and rejected, week after week, and not living the life we always think they are. We often only see the glory, but not the guts that got them there! I wish successful people in the public domain would share this more.

Question:

How would you react if you were rejected by your boss week after week and not selected in the team? (Using sport as the example/metaphor here)

From the outside we don't see the resilience that the super successful people have in their mindset toolbox to get to the top and most importantly stay at the top. This is why high EQ and resilience are so important for modern day living. People who do not possess adequate EQ often sulk and then become gold medallists in what I call emotional self-harm. Fortunately, I do not mean cut themselves on the wrists type of self-harm, I mean how they behave when the shit times hit them. Often people with low

EQ haven't got the skillset, tools and emotional control to cope with rejection, so they just become jealous, sulk, shout, and blame others. They are another part of the famous 'what if brigade'. They say, *"What if I did this back then?"* You know the ones.

Advice:

Have no regrets people, and don't be part of the *'what if'* brigade please. Go and smash life. We only get one.

Sports/Business Crossovers:

As mentioned earlier in this chapter I have often wondered how Jurgen Klopp and Pep Guardiola (The Liverpool and Manchester City managers) get all of their squad players (the ones who don't get a regular game) who ONLY get 10 minutes of game time, only once a month, still CHOOSE to hug, cuddle and grasp their leaders like they are their long-lost father after a victory! It is truly incredible to watch.

In summary. These players or staff don't wear armour! Their armour is well and truly off!

Questions:

- How does a leader achieve this level of elite response and behaviour from their squad players? (Less skilled)
- Who else have they got in their backroom staff (The team behind the team) that supports this process of 'no armour' and high EQ other than just them?
- What do they ALL do Monday to Friday (Strategically) to get this positive emotional response on a match day/Saturday? (Operationally)

If you are not a sport lover just remind yourself of this.

- Athletes prepare and develop for 95% of their working week (training) and perform for only a minimal 5% (on a match day)

- The average person at work performs for 95% of their week and probably develops for 5%, if that?

There lies the difference in job roles! The pressure on many elite athletes is immense, and why I will continue to stick up for them and why the business world is fascinated by these people in sport. What job role would you prefer? The 5% performance life or 95%?

Case Studies:

Andy Bate the former Regional Director of Tarmac Ltd and one of the biggest road builders in the UK, was one of the best leaders I have ever seen in my lifetime at developing his staff. His investment in:

"The people before the product and process," was sensational!

Of course, he had one eye on:

- Performance
- Results
- Profit and loss
- KPI's (Key Performance Indicators), spreadsheets and data analysis.

At the same time however, he was *obsessed* with developing his people, so much so that they never wanted to leave, and his retention of staff was generally phenomenal. He was a very skilled leader indeed. In summary, he was focussed on **proving** his region was the best in the UK, but also determined his staff developed and **improved** more than any region in the UK. This strategic and operational balance he applied I rarely see from bosses.

The Prove/Improve debate solved right in front of my eyes!

In Andy's eyes he reinvented the term KPI. Instead of just measuring indicators of performance, he might as well have said:

- **K**eep
- **P**eople
- **I**nformed, **I**nvolved, **I**nterested, and **I**nspired!

So well done Andy.

Reminder:

High trust is the biggest common denominator for a highly successful business. Without high trust, you are fucked!

The question is. What are you doing to address it?

Chapter 5

CONFLICT - KNOWING THE COGS AND 'THE TEAM BEHIND THE TEAM'

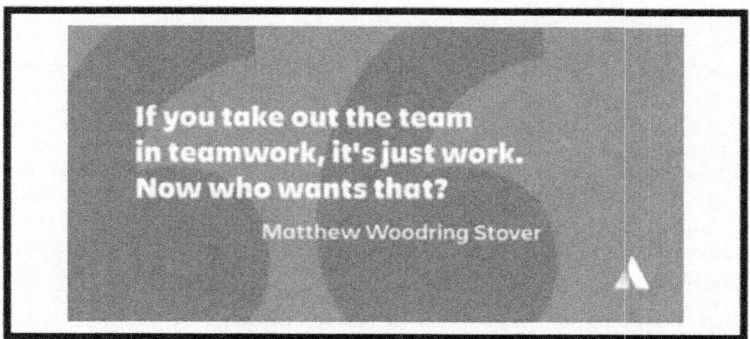

"When my boss is mad, and they take it out on me, I simply, DO LESS WORK. If they were more positive, I would do more work. But you cannot discuss your malaria problem with the mosquito."

Reminder:

"Everybody knows more than somebody."

Never forget this quote and how it applies to high performing teams - as mentioned earlier, regarding Liverpool and Manchester City Football Clubs, and the effectiveness of their *team behind the team*. The team being the players of course. And the team behind the team, the staff. All places of work have teams, but firstly I want you to think about.

Are the people in your building currently:

    1) A team of people or
    2) A group of people?

Do you see a personal difference between a team and a group?

HOW NOT BE A LEADERSHIP D*CKHEAD

Task:

Write down your ten differences between the two.

Team Characteristics	Group Characteristics

I have been fortunate enough to experience, various different types of working culture, in education, business, and the elite sport sector. I often get asked the differences between the three and if I am honest, the answer is that the same shit and same shine and sparkle happens in all of them.

Question: What is the same shit and sparkle therefore?

The god damn people of course! Yes, you heard it. The people are the problem, and the people create perfection. Often not the processes, systems, or the job itself, just the people who either possess a narrow lens on the world or who have the growth mindset.

Of course, the product you are selling or buying can be a hurdle, but the number one issue I witness is the misalignment of the bloody people in the building getting in the way of a high-performance culture. There are so many people blaming others that they have yet to realise that *they* could be the problem and should be the ones driving the positive change! I call this lot:

- The People Blockers
- The Problem Creators
- The De-Energisers
- The Happy Hoovers
- The Dickheads

HOW NOT BE A LEADERSHIP D*CKHEAD

Reminder of the 888 rule:

We get one life where a third of it we sleep, the second third we aim to have fun, and the final third we go to this place called work to find the cash to do the second one. You would think people would know how to interact with other people by the time they get to adulthood. Sadly, adolescent behaviour often occurs more frequently at work than it does in most primary schools.

I always reflect back to my times as a schoolteacher and meeting the thousands of parents, at parents evening and wondering why there were many parents out there that just didn't get how the power of education can help their own child. Many of these anti-school parents often unknowingly create a disruptive child (people see, people do) who a few years later become a dysfunctional adult. Their dysfunctional child now turned dysfunctional adult, then often turns up at work at 22 years of age (or younger) and it seems to the normal person that an alien has entered the building. Their immaturity and unprofessionalism can be seen a mile off. From my experience this is the stage where an intervention of mentoring needs to be applied.

Support Structures:

From my experiences, the education, business, and sport sectors, are all just as good and bad as each other in the people development bit. What I mean is, I have witnessed all three of these sectors developing their people in a multitude of ways. Some are doing a great job, and others simply inadequate when it comes to knowing how to add value to their people to be able to do their job better. Many industries still:

1. Send people on an online course and expect them to improve instantly. (Doesn't work)
2. Don't have any structures or personnel in place to develop from within, (peer to peer will work).
3. Hire and fire staff on impulse, like an automatic rifle, instead of giving their people the time to develop, grow and feel psychologically safe.

HOW NOT BE A LEADERSHIP D*CKHEAD

I have often thought the 'hire and fire' attitude from many leaders has probably become heavily linked and paralleled to the social media phenomenon, where instant success and gratification has leaked from the smart phone to the actual real world. Sad times may I add. Football CEO's and owners. I am looking at you here.

Actions:

High Performing teams shouldn't be that hard to create in theory. One problem is that there are so many dickheads, in so many workplaces, that the less experienced bosses can get entangled in a web of lies and deceit. So, consider these set of strategies as a solution:

1) Identify the processes needed to unite a group of potential non-dickheads in order to make them grow.

2) Have the acumen and know how to isolate the one or two dickheads and put a stop to their amateur behaviour at the earliest opportunity, for the benefit of everyone else.

Understanding & Overcoming Conflict:

Research in personality psychology has suggested that the personality trait of agreeableness, correlates with a tendency towards conflict avoidance. Because of this evidence, and my experiences I believe it correlates to the type of work colleagues who tend to:

1. Avoid conflict
2. Deny any conflict or wait until it goes away
3. Change the subject in tricky moments
4. React emotionally: Become aggressive and abusive or often dismissive
5. Find someone to else blame
6. Make any excuses necessary to not confront the issue

7. Let someone else deal with it

But why? Because simply, so many leaders and colleagues are burying their head in the sand by avoiding confrontation. I hear stories of trading floors in London being so *outcome/profit* focussed, that they forget (or choose to ignore) the *process* of uniting the people.

When managing conflict, most of us know what to do. We just don't always 'do' what we could do or, even should do. The famous rugby team the New Zealand All Blacks have a concept called 'safe conflict'. It's great. Look it up.

Below I have highlighted some pointers and scenarios that happen at work. I call them "respond or react". Give it a go and try and be the responder in your future interactions.

- They say: It will never work... You say: What do you dislike about it?
- They say: My way is better... You say: What makes that seem the best option?
- They say: It's impossible... You say: What would it take to make it possible?
- They say: I can't... You say: What difference would it make if you could?
- They say: You can't do that... You say: What would happen if we did?
- They say: That is not the best way... You say: What would be the best way for you?
- They say: It's too expensive... You say: Compared to what?

In my business model I have created a structure called the Breathe, Pause and Why (BPW). I advise all my clients to use it when experiencing conflict. It goes as follows:

HOW NOT BE A LEADERSHIP D*CKHEAD

1) Breathe and be mindful of listening first; take a breath first in order to regulate your body and mind. Breathe, keep your mouth shut and listen.
2) Pause and take a moment before you respond and actively listen to what they are saying. This pause and thinking time is paramount for a coherent reply.
3) Think about *why* this person in front of you is behaving like this? There is always a reason.

So, before you steam in with volatility, use the solutions mindset BPW method. It is not always about your 'why' in that moment. Try to think about 'their why' instead. It will help you I am certain.

Also try to think of the following:

"If you have a problem with someone, attack the problem and not the person."

A book called "Mentoring New Special Education Teachers" written by Mary Lou Duffy and James Forgan in 2005 included a wonderful poem about listening. It goes as follows:

"When I ask you to listen to me and you start giving advice you have not done what I asked.

When I ask you to listen to me, and you begin to tell me why I shouldn't feel that way, you are trampling on my feelings.

When I ask you to listen to me and you feel you have to do something to solve my problems, you have failed me, strange as that may seem.

Listen! All I ask is that you listen. Not talk or do – just hear me".

So remember:

Shut your mouth and listen!

"The problem with closed minded people, is that their mouths are always open."

Reminder:

Dealing with workplace conflict or managing difficult people is a process, and not always an event. It can take time to bond people. Great leaders find the strategy, time and patience for this. Dickhead leaders on the other hand don't have the duty of care to give a shit in the first place.

Later in the final chapter of this book I have given attention to the Betari Box. Have a look. It's pure power for conflict management and another potential solution for you to follow.

On the many corporate speaking events I speak at, my intention in my planning is that my messages are relayed with complete simplicity for the audience. I'm a big believer that when the time is right; less is more. I ask the audience with a very soft voice.

- Are you the glue at work? Or
- The fucking poo?
- "Be the GLUE"

It normally ends with laughter.

I have even created a scale called the solutions mindset poo/glue scale.

Advice:

Mirror positive behaviour and try not to mirror negative. What this means is. If you see positive behaviour from a peer/colleague, copy it, and if you see negative behaviour, don't copy it.
Simon Sinek, the renowned leadership expert from the USA talks about "The Golden Circle".

HOW NOT BE A LEADERSHIP D*CKHEAD

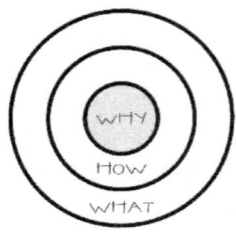

He states:

Companies know what they do, and how they do it. But he questions their 'why' for doing what they do. And that's not the money, as the money is the result. He questions people's deeper purpose for life in general.

So, what is your purpose and 'why' for life? In simple terms, why the fuck are you coming to work with no purpose? Or,

- Because you love the job? or
- Love the people? or
- Because you just want the cash and to get home as soon as possible after 5pm deadline.

Tip:

Asking your staff their *why* for doing their job is very significant. Please do not neglect the question because when you ask your people this question you will get to their very soul about some of the following:

- Why they behave like they behave.
- What their internal drivers and motivations are.
- What their life passions are.
- Why they are motivated to do one thing or try harder for one colleague, and not another.

Over my years in the workplace, you often don't need to ask people this question, as you will mostly see it on their facial expressions or in their daily behaviours anyway.

- Are they doing extra? Or in contrast
- Are they the last one in, and first one out?
- Do they act, interact, and react like they are psychologically safe and happy?
- Do they act motivated?

Now with the first two points above, trust me I am not glamourising over-working, because that is also foolish. But you hopefully get my point and will monitor this closely in your workplace.

Reminder:

Successes and failures give us clues. So do your 'clue check' so you know who is:

1) The POO, and
2) Who is the GLUE.

'The Plus 1 effect' and Workload Advice:

My advice around your working hours is to apply something I have always called the *"Plus 1" effect"*.

This means:

Do more than you have to, but then *know* when to go home. Way too many businesses glamourise long hours, but rarely measure the productivity of these extra hours. Keith Powell taught me this.

As mentioned earlier in the chapter (888), life is all about the three thirds.

- 1/3 of your life you sleep. (8 hours)
- The other third you go to work. (8 hours)
- And the other third you go to work to be able to do nice things and live a happy life. (8 hours)

Solutions to the TBT (Team behind the Team):

I often get asked by CEOs what my solutions are regarding providing a framework for adding value to the team behind the team? I would go as far to say that the dynamics and relationships between the staff in any workplace, are some of the most important relationships in life. The processes my business uses are as follows:

Step one:

- After a few months when you feel the staff need a bit of a positive injection, you should complete the 'Johari Window Task'. (follow the QR code for more details) Why?
- This is a light-hearted, yet super powerful group dynamics task which creates enhanced self-awareness which is going to be needed for high performing teams and work greatness.

Step two:

- As the boss, you may keep hearing about conflict between certain people. You may have also sensed people seem jaded, with your instincts telling you there are deficiencies in the team. This is when you educate the staff on the work of Bruce Tuckman and his 1965 Team development Model.
- His group dynamics model is simple, yet simplistic gold!
- His Forming, Storming, Norming and Performing Model is powerful, but only if used properly. To put it simply he states: "Groups form together (forming), and they try to bond, and they may even clash along the way (storming), but ultimately over time they learn about one another in such an intimate way (norming), they eventually over time create enhanced high performance for your business (performing) due to better and more *glue-like* relationships."

HOW NOT BE A LEADERSHIP D*CKHEAD

Tuckman's Model:

1) Forming Process:

   There is high dependence on the leader for guidance and direction at this first stage, however at this moment often little agreement on team objectives is set nor aligned, other than those received from the leader. In the forming stage individual roles and responsibilities are often unclear and the leader must therefore be equipped to answer lots of questions about the team's drive, objectives, goals, and relationships with each other. Be aware however, that in shit businesses, these processes can often be ignored. Tuckman suggests that team members lower down in the hierarchy should respectfully and professionally test the leader in order to get greater clarity of where the team bus is heading.

2) Storming Process

   This is the storm cloud stage where disagreement and conflict can often take place. As an example, when it comes to making group decisions. Tuckman states that team members can start to attempt to establish themselves and their position in the hierarchy and compete with other staff members, including the boss, who might receive conflict from certain tricky colleagues who would like to undermine his/her authority.

   At this stage, after the storm cloud has dispersed, the clarity of the team's purpose can improve, however statistically many concerns are still evident, and cliques can often form between certain groups of staff. Problem? This may lead to authority struggles and the big egos coming out to play. Solution? To further educate staff to maintain high EQ, focus on objectives, and avoid being distracted by negativity and emotional nonsense.

HOW NOT BE A LEADERSHIP D*CKHEAD

Compromises will be needed between the particular egos, otherwise conflict will continue to grow.

3) Norming Process

Right let us make this simple with a scenario.

You've had a disagreement at work, and you end up holding a grudge with that person for maybe 3 hours, 3 days, 3 months, or for some nutty fuckers even 3 years!

Or as an alternative, if you have high EQ, hopefully no grudges are held at all! You get it. Occasional conflict is normal

I find this the most important yet undervalued process in Tuckman's group model. I have said in many seminars across the world that the norming process, can make or break a team and a business's success. Even in families! Now let me explain in greater detail a real-life example. A former colleague of mine, named Dave Livermore (the current Millwall Assistant Manager), disagreed on many things at work We would often argue, aggressively disagree, and challenge one another's lenses. Colleagues regularly looked at the two of us like we were crazy lunatics and that we hated one another.

The truth? We are the best of friends in and out of work. You see, the conflict made us grow, made us more connected, made us understand one another at such a greater level because I always knew... Dave was telling me the TRUTH. He has a zero-bullshit persona. The same goes for my side kicks in football in Harry Watling, Jon Brady, Steve Morison and Greig Paterson at the Scottish FA. We all just say it how it is, and I think one of the beauties of the football industry is people say it how it is, so you get used to it. Of course, it takes time to be build up to that kind of professional relationship. But from my experiences it is the only way to behave. Honesty will always rule.

HOW NOT BE A LEADERSHIP D*CKHEAD

Tip:

Whenever I start a new job, I present to all staff on the below statement which I believe is leadership gold, and I would like you to reflect on. I state:

"Everything we say between 7.30am and 6.30pm at night is... Always professional and never personal."

With this *strategic language* put in place, I can safely say it is one of my ten golden nuggets to this book! The feedback I have received around this basic term 'professional not personal' from people in football clubs, schools, and businesses, regarding this sentence has proved to be a game changer for many. Tuckman confirms the 'norming' element means roles and responsibilities are now clearer and more rigorously accepted, Secondly:

- The big decisions are made by mutual agreement and aligning lenses, not just the person at the very top! 'We not Me' basically.
- Lesser decisions may be delegated to individuals or small teams within the work force and therefore commitment and unity are enhanced between the people; hopefully because democracy is at the forefront of people's minds (We not Me).
- The staff may start to gradually engage in more fun, laughter, and non-work events.
- The staff may have developed a bond over time, and generally become more glue and not the poo.
- This enhanced team-ship strategy from the leaders can enable all staff to get stuck right into high performance, as relationships are more fully embedded.

HOW NOT BE A LEADERSHIP D*CKHEAD

4) Performing Process

To make this simple. It is what is says it is. The team is high performing. But what does that actually mean in reality? My thoughts are as follows.

1) Selfless
2) Reflective
3) Driven
4) Great characters
5) Loads of calibre (technical skills)
6) Visionary and strategic
7) Operationally brilliant and get shit done
8) Open lenses on the world and emotionally connected
9) Mentally agile and open to adapt and change
10) Great listeners

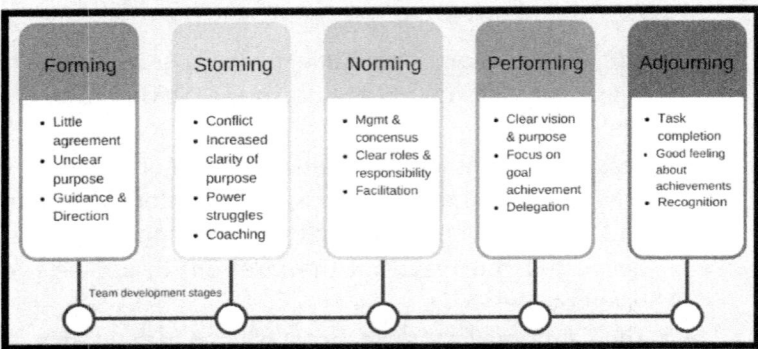

Knowing when and how to challenge:

As previously mentioned, Harry Watling is one my best allies in professional football and life and is the former assistant manager of the football superpower Glasgow Rangers in Scotland. Like Dave Livermore, Jon Brady and Steve Morison, they challenge me on absolutely anything and everything... As I do them. They say,

      i)   Why are you doing this?
      ii)   Why are you thinking that Sallis?
      iii)   No. no! You need to justify your opinion to me!

iv) How have you come to that conclusion? I don't get, tell me why?
v) What would you do here Sallis?

Reminder:

Regarding my lens around the high-performance topic, professional challenge and debate is the healthiest thing alive for any high performing environment to be exactly that. However, be mindful that challenging colleagues for challenging's sake means you can become a complete pain in the arse, and possibly seen as a disruptor in the workplace. So, remind yourself that often squad ambience is required more often than squad anarchy.

Advice:

Challenge people regularly, but also know when to shut your mouth. If you're an assistant manager (which I have been many times) another skill and a hidden art is the ability of knowing what NOT to say. In addition to this, being a great assistant is letting the boss have time to breathe. I see this as a key technique which many inadequate assistants fail to recognise and adhere to. Great team players must know when to follow.

Step three:

Have a look at the Patrick Lencioni Leadership Model. It is truly brilliant and investigates five key concepts for high performing teams. These include:

1) Trust
2) Conflict
3) Commitment
4) Accountability
5) Results

The Lencioni strategy is a no brainer for giving a structure to enhancing group dynamics at both strategic and operational level. An example of how I have applied the Lencioni model in corporate training can be seen below. I have highlighted a set of the questions for you to use and reflect on.

- What is trust from your LENS at this place of work?
- Why is trust important for our DNA here at this workplace?
- How do we gain/break trust in our work environment?
- When are the moments in the working week where trust grows/fails?
- Where in terms of our working/non-working environment can we build/break trust?

In summary, during my teaching days we used to say:

"If we feel better, we will DO better."

This type of thinking isn't really rocket science though, is it?

Step four:

The review...I swear by the saying:

"Plan...Do... Review"

Question:
So how can you measure staff moral?

Answer:
Try the Gallup 12 survey. It is power.

Finally, the following piece is stolen from leadership and high-performance expert Allistair McCaw. He says:

"Success happens when you surround yourself with the right people. Probably one of the most important decisions you can make in your life is who you choose to surround yourself with.

HOW NOT BE A LEADERSHIP D*CKHEAD

Successful people surround themselves with other successful people."

High performers understand that who you choose to spend your time with influences almost everything you think and do.

Here are my **'Special 7'**:

It includes the types of people I believe you should surround yourself with:

1. **People who are on a mission.** Connect with people who are forward thinking and those who are constantly striving for growth. These proactive people don't rest on their laurels. They regularly set goals and when achieved, they go again. (Pygmalion effect). Achievers on a mission tend to heavily avoid the idle and uninspiring lazy bastards.

2. **People who are grateful.** Fill your cup with people who practice gratitude. Grateful people are known to pay more attention to the smaller things in life. With a gratitude focussed mindset, you will place greater emphasis on the positive things. The weather, nature and kindness are the smallest yet best things to notice.

3. **People who bring out the best in you and others.** Put yourself with people who try to understand you and lift you up when things are shit (happy hairdryers). These positive souls support your dreams and goals and not shit on them. They always encourage you through the down times. They are the glue not the poo.

4. **The Energisers.** You know the ones – The cup fillers. There are two types of people when they enter a room. The first type who bring a low energy mood (happy hoovers). The second type who bring a positive energy and vibe. Hopefully you are the latter.

5. **The Doers.** This lot get shit done. It's far easier to talk about success than actually achieve it, and many people choose just to talk it, and not walk it. Talkers talk about what they will do, while

walkers have already run the race. These do-er types just get on with it and action shit! Employ them NOW!

6. **The Problem Solvers.** The one major difference between successful and unsuccessful people is that the successful and consistent high achievers are critical thinkers and optimists all in one. They come up with solutions-based approaches. They choose not to hang around the problem creators.

7. **The Truth Tellers.** An issue here is people don't always like the truth. We all like to hear the good things about ourselves. But remember in life, it's no good having too many 'yes people' around you all the time. We need people who can tell us the truth, point out our weak spots, even if it's uncomfortable. We all need people in our life who raise our standards and challenge us to become a better version of ourselves.

Remember, that you become the average of the five people you surround yourself with the most.

Choose your colleagues wisely Allistair says! I tend to agree!

Chapter 6

SELF-AWARENESS AND WHY WITHOUT IT YOU'RE FUCKED! OR IS IGNORANCE ACTUALLY BLISS?

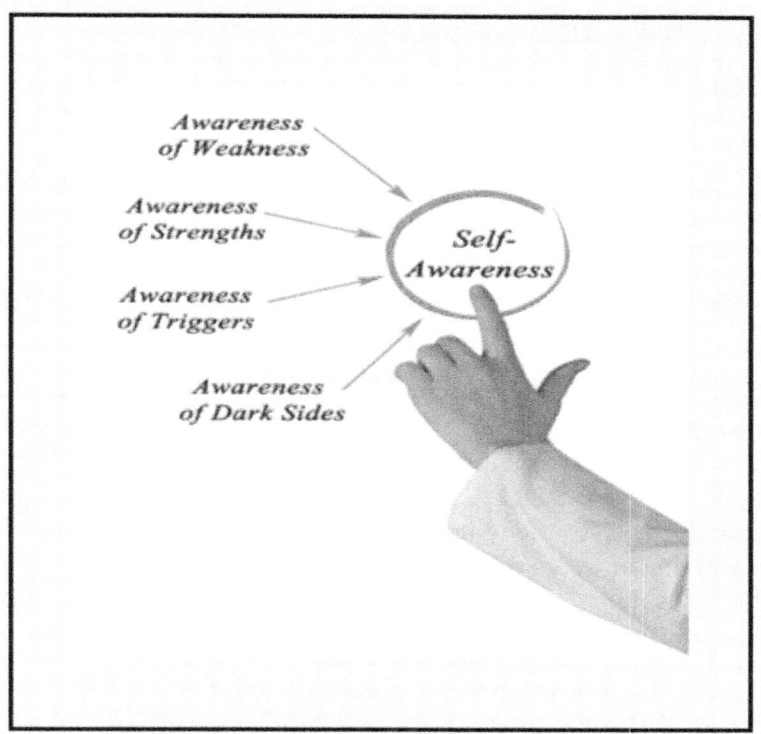

"Smart people learn from everything, and everyone, average people from their experiences, and stupid people already have the answers."

Socrates

Question: Did you know you are only six inches from success? How come you may ask? Where are those six inches you may say?

Answer: Between your ears!

Have you ever met the boss that:

- Looks... but doesn't actually see.
- Listens... but doesn't actually hear.
- Looks out of the window...instead of looking in the mirror.

You probably have, as they are everywhere.

I swear by the following saying:

"Shit leaders... see what they are looking for, and hear what they listen for."

There are many leaders in the world that show regular cognitive bias. For some, it is a daily occurrence and sadly they have zero clue that they are behaving in this ignorant and unethical manner.

Have you met leaders that regularly say what they do, but do not, DO what they say?

There are plenty of them about as well, right? The ones that talk a good game and yet do not follow up on the stuff they say they will do. I suppose this major self-awareness flaw, was the original passion for me writing my previous book *Educating Football*. I just couldn't believe the amount of people in the football and education industries that were so lacking in self-awareness. Many of them would:

- Say one thing and do another.
- Blame others at every opportunity!
- Adopt crisis management at every waking hour.
- Create havoc and panic at every problem.
- Put a problem, in the way of every solution.
- Talk over you every day.
- Not Listen.
- Have a PhD in moaning, negativity and playing the victim.

Now forget sport and education here., I have now learnt that the same trends of behaviour happen in the business world. The questions I have often posed to myself are:

1. Why do people in the workplace have major self-awareness flaws?
2. Why are companies and bosses so short sighted about self-awareness development support, nourishment, and growth?

Answer:

The facts are that these people exist in every job, so we need to address it now! In my experience of under-performance in the workplace, you can't always blame the ground staff (soldiers). Often you must point the blame at the bosses. Dickhead bosses are often so 'zoomed in' that they have not been mindful enough to 'zoom out' and see the bigger picture by playing the long game in people development. The solution is so obvious.

One simple answer = Investment in high performance education and training

Reminder:

"An expert hires an expert."

If we were all good at everything, we would have no need for each other's support in life and work.

I have been told many times by friends and family that I have made so much sacrifice during my working journey. I tell them the reality to this flawed perception that they have of me, is that it is never actually a sacrifice for me. I prefer the word *investment*. I have chosen to invest in myself since hitting adulthood. And that is exactly what businesses need to do more of:

- Invest in new knowledge, to enable themselves to grow and over time increase profit via enhancing the character and calibre levels of their people.

HOW NOT BE A LEADERSHIP D*CKHEAD

Advice:

In order, to add value to sustainable profit margins as well as human performance in a business you first, have to address the following. My advice is to do so in this order:

1) The self-awareness part

2) Assess the character of each individual, (their motivations, skills gaps, their why and finally their 'we not me' mentality)

3) How the above (number 2) affects the culture and behaviours of the overall workplace as a collective. (Glue not poo)

One such strategic approach with the self-awareness topic is the *Dunning Kruger Effect.* See diagram below.

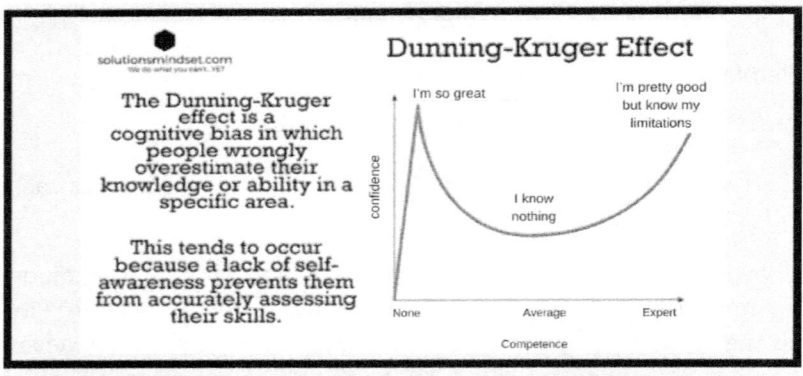

It is a brilliant, yet simplistic way of measuring someone's self-awareness around the confidence/competence scale. It's aim is to question people's confidence and competence capabilities. We have all met the *"know it alls"* at work. Those people in the office that talk a great game, but in reality, are fucking useless at their job. One name I call this lot is the 'incapable crew'. Other names are:

- The Braggers
- The Toppers
- The Blaggers
- The Serial Bullshitters
- The 'Plus Oners'.

As a real-life scenario, whilst chatting to a colleague, you might mention to the topper that you've been travelling to Australia recently, and this lot in the above list couldn't be any quicker to pipe up and respond with, "Oh I have been to Australia twice."

The second example is, you say to them, "I am going to Tenerife for a holiday next year," and this lot of 'workplace plus one'(rs) answer you back with: *"Oh really Steve, I am going to "Elevenarife."* Get it? 😊

Eventually, this lot tread on your toes so often, you're like, "Piss off will you mate. Every time I say something I have done; you say you have done it twice!".

Reminder:

Be mindful of the toppers. They exist everywhere. In summary, whatever you do or say, they have topped it!

"The toppers are the official "work dickheads."

Question:

Why are many bosses not promoting and driving a culture around the self-awareness bus enough?

Answer:

The advice I often give to businesses is to revisit it every single day. Keep re-aligning it with the work culture, KPI'S, performance management and line management. Stop talking about your product you're selling and start talking about how the people behave, in order to sell the product. This enhanced self-awareness will create a success pathway for the bloody product to sell anyway.

HOW NOT BE A LEADERSHIP D*CKHEAD

Advice:

A motivated staff cohort means more chance of profit. Add to this an ultra-high level of duty of care from the leaders, that surpasses your competitors, that makes your business become so morally and ethically sound, that every member of staff and customer talks about you positively when you are not in the room. That's what success truly is. Richard Branson said in 2014:

"Train your staff well enough so they are able to leave and treat them so well that they don't want to."

Solid guidance from a serial achiever.

Questions I get from companies I consult for are:

"Steve what should we train and educate our staff on first?"

Answer:

My number one reminder for you is to train your staff on:

"Self-Awareness"

Reminder:

Without high levels of self-awareness, your business is doomed long term.

1. Culture will become negative.
2. People will hate their job.
3. Behaviours will not be aligned, equal and inclusive for all.
4. Too many people will be playing the 'blame game'.
5. There will be lots of people treading on lots of each other's toes.

I have relayed many golden nuggets in this book and provided many opinions, however, to get away from just my opinions and personal subjectivity, I like to try and be very research-led and give people facts and research to back up my opinions. We all know people in society love an opinion on various topics, and social media has now given these folk a platform to share their bollocks on. They have their own special name also.

"The twitter/keyboard warriors"

These negative dickheads love to hide behind their phone, just like the dickhead at work does on an email. All billy big bollocks from behind the screen, but then melt in real life. Another great word to support my methods regarding these keyboard warriors is *"ultracrepidarian"*. It's a beauty of a word and means the following:

"One who gives opinions on something they know fuck all about."

So, another gentle reminder:

Don't be an ultracrepidarian!

It is an exquisite word, which will be used more and more hopefully, to describe these keyboard warriors and email odd balls.

Agnotology:

Linking ultracrepidarians to other significant and ignorant dickheads that cause havoc at work, I would also like you to draw attention to another *'x factor'* word named *"Agnotology"*. It is a game changing piece of language relating to work-based performance and culture. The meaning of agnotology is as follows:

"The study of cultural induced ignorance."

I am someone that has studied behaviour for many years but also worked with several ignorant dickheads, so when I found out it had been given an actual name I was like..." Wow yesss, this is truly brilliant!" The agnotology message is probably my favourite word of this entire of this book so share it wisely after you have read this.

Self-Awareness – The Main Event

In my business narrative, I often talk about four categories of people. These are as follows:

HOW NOT BE A LEADERSHIP D*CKHEAD

1) Unconsciously incompetent people
2) Consciously incompetent people
3) Unconsciously competent people
4) Consciously competent people

Task:

1. Can you please think about and define these four concepts above.
2. Give examples of what they mean in the workplace and how the behaviours would be seen and heard.
3. Then outline… where do YOU or your colleagues fit into the four concepts above?

Once you have achieved this, you will ultimately have the self-awareness *"master card"* banked in your brain for life. It is *gold*!

Reminder:

An academic qualification (badge of honour), the title of CEO on your office door, or a status in a hierarchy, is only valid if the person uses it properly. A good friend of mine Doctor Jacob Naish, currently working abroad at a Norwegian football club called FC Nordsjaelland, is a wise and thoughtful guy. He always says to me when we meet over a coffee:

"Sallis, intelligence, my friend, is not about having a qualification and should not be defined as such. Intelligence is about people's behaviour."

Jacob is right, of course, and to add to this way of thinking, I've come up with three areas where self-awareness can be simplified and become a vital cog in adding value to your behavioural and cultural toolbox. It is already mentioned in the introduction, yet I believe a reminder is worth it. Regular reflection is key to any high performing environment. So have a think about these:

1) How do you act with people? (both verbally and non-verbally)
2) How do you interact with people?

3) How you react to people?

Advice:

Qualifications do not help the above process, but self-awareness does. Therefore, qualifications, and a person's status or work title should mean fuck all, unless the person in question behaves like such.

A Leaders Job:

Any leader's job is primarily to support, serve and add value to the performance of their people (soldiers). A job title alone, should never be relied upon. Far too often, leaders with qualifications and in positions of authority or influence think what it says on a piece of paper, is enough to lead others. I can safely say that truly isn't the case.

As previously mentioned, I have often wondered about the UK's obsession with academic qualifications. As a 21-year-old newly qualified teacher, I made mistake after mistake, because I was young and inexperienced. I had the teaching degree of course, but what did that mean in reality? Not a lot really. I was a complete novice. A super strength I did have, was a great attitude, however.

If you think about Doctors (GPs), as an example. They are probably the most qualified you could be at anything. They spend seven years at university to acquire their qualification and some of them still turn out to be useless.

Reminder:

Doctors all have the PhD (Calibre), yet many do not have the positive persona to align with their qualification, and often when you enter the doctor's surgery you sense that 'some' basically hate their job (Character). You can feel it:

- Grumpy face
- Shit attitude and
- Arrogant persona.

Some doctors show zero empathy and when you are sat on the patient's chair with your brain racing and feeling vulnerable whilst internally pleading for their love and support, they merely dismiss you like you're just another number in their schedule.

The Flip Side:

The *game changing* doctor who makes you feel a million dollars when you walk in and out of their surgery, even though you're just as unwell, as when you walked in. These classy doctors are:

- Kind
- Sincere
- Empathetic
- Listen well and
- Actually show they give a shit about you as a human, and that is what I call...LEADERSHIP!

If any doctors are reading this, please do not underestimate your potential positive impact on your patients. (Character + Calibre).

Doctor Kenny of Eltham Medical Practice in Eltham, southeast London. If you are reading this. Thank you. You are a wonderful man and practitioner.

Plenty to reflect on in this chapter, I hope.

HOW NOT BE A LEADERSHIP D*CKHEAD

Chapter 7

POEM...THE AVERAGE CHILD - BY MIKE BUSCEMI

"All I knew, was that I never wanted to be average."

Michael Jordan

I don't cause teachers trouble;
My grades have been okay.
I listen in my classes.
I'm in school every day.

My teachers think I'm average;
My parents think so too.
I wish I didn't know that, though;
There's lots I'd like to do.

I'd like to build a rocket;
Or read a book on how.
Or start a stamp collection...
But no use trying now.

'Cause, since I found I'm average,
I'm smart enough you see
To know there's nothing special
I should expect of me.

I'm part of that majority,
That hump part of the bell,
Who spends his life unnoticed
In an average kind of hell.

The above poem is beautiful yet crucifying to read at the same time. I relate it closely to the highly inspiring colleagues I have worked with over the years who inherited below average pupils and turned them into great pupils. In direct contrast to the completely inadequate colleagues who added zero value in their roles and made the average human they served regress and actually get worse. Chapter 21 of this book is called Improve or Replace? What you will read is that many businesses are unable to improve their staff, so they simply replace.

I am going to draw your attention to two theories:

Theory 1: The Pygmalion Effect

Theory 2: The Golem Effect

I won't tell you about them for now. If you care enough, you will look them up. I am certain you will be able to relate to them both, either as a leader, parent, colleague, friend, or family member!

Reminder:

Raise the bar... One life people!

Chapter 8

LEADING A FAILING BUSINESS? WHAT IS THE ENERGY LIKE? AND HOW DOES SOMEONE TALK ABOUT YOU WHEN YOU ARE NOT IN THE ROOM?"

"You are the average of the five people; you spend the most time with."

Jim Rohn

I am not sure if you are aware of the book, "The Secret" written by Rhonda Byrne which is fundamentally based on the connections and energy between people, which she called the 'Law of Attraction'. It is in basic terms a philosophy signifying that positive thoughts bring more positive outcomes into our lives, while negative thoughts bring the same. It is constructed on the belief that our thoughts create an energy field, and that positive energy attracts success in all areas of life, including wealth, health, and our relationships. I truly believe over a lifetime:

- Like finds like
- If you give love, you get love
- If you give hate, you are more likely to get hate

Reminder:

What you give to the universe, is what you get back!

So those of you out there that are selfish twats, you might foolishly think you are winning right now, by thinking about yourself all the time, but the reality means that you are losing out on something very important, called the "long game".

Money Chasing

The amount of people I have chased for money since being in business is alarming. As a child, I would witness my dad who was a plumber for 50 years, pay people bang on time, every time for many decades. Firstly, I learnt early in my childhood that this enhanced his reputation as reliable, and secondly it avoided him getting a punch on the nose from one of the builder communities, who are generally not to be messed with. So, leaders and clients out there! Pay up quicker! Often, I get asked the question by businesses and leaders about how I can make them more effective? I have devised "The how to thrive in thirteen" and hope it will help you. These thirteen questions will certainly help get your thinking into action. After all, before you do shit, you need to think stuff through first.

1. Who are your five most influential people in the building? Both Personally and Professionally?
2. Could there be as many as ten? (Write a list of people 6-10 who give you the most positive energy)
3. How do these cultural architects add value?
4. Do your staff have/or lack optimism? (NB. Studies have shown that the trait of optimism is the most important characteristic for a business to be successful).
5. Do staff approach challenges with positivity or negativity and how do you measure it?
6. Are you placing any *trait optimism* on your business KPI's? Or are they still solely linked to data, profit and loss, outcomes, and other short-term bullshit?
7. Is EQ (Emotional intelligence) talked about as much as IQ? (If not? why not?)
8. Do you focus on the calibre of people over their character during performance management processes?
9. Do you focus on someone's current performance over their actual long-term potential? (Diagram below)
10. Does rigorous mentoring happen in your building, and how do you measure the value of it?
11. Do you know your blind spots well enough? ie. Know what you don't know? Personal and whole business)
12. What are the knowledge/skills gaps and how will you fill them?
13. Do you know when to consolidate and know when to accelerate the business?

HOW NOT BE A LEADERSHIP D*CKHEAD

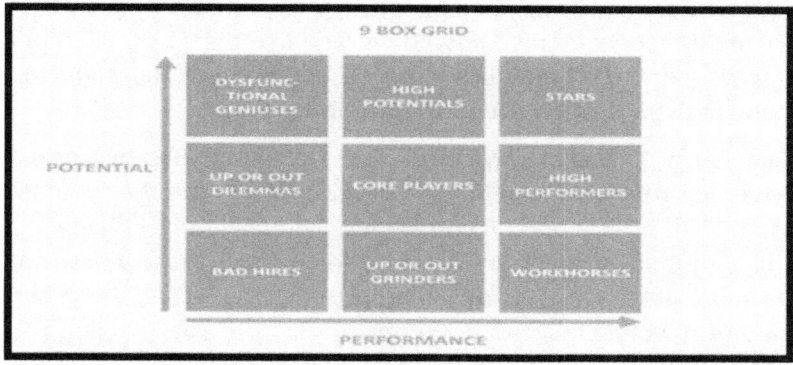

I want you to deeply consider the diagram above as seeing the long game for the people you work with. Some new colleagues can initially grossly underperform, however have the future potential to be high performers in the longer term. During my keynote speeches I show two pictures of a young athlete I have worked with. The Real Madrid and England footballer Jude Bellingham. The photos are nearly two years apart. The first is him in his England kit at under 15, pre-maturation standing about 5 feet 4 inches tall. The next photo blows people's minds with a photo of his full England men's England debut at 17 years and 136 days of age looking a massive 7.5 inches taller and an absolute powerhouse!

Seeing Potential:

24 months later he was transformed. His potential therefore... outweighing his less physically effective performances as a younger adolescent. The fabulous staff at Birmingham City Football Club played the *long game* with him. They saw his potential and created a lengthy and bespoke plan for him to truly achieve his potential.

Colleague Respect - Does your business have it?

I have always said I could never go for a drink with someone I didn't respect or value at work. It is against my working morals. I couldn't possibly spend a Friday night in the pub, with a person that has left work early nearly every day, failed to teach good lessons, worked with zero passion or had been a selfish prick. I would be living a lie if I said I respected anyone who worked like that. I simply don't respect them and essentially, I never will, because there are too many of them floating about in the world of work.

High Performance of any form, and the art of effective group dynamics, has been experienced by most of us, whether you are young, old, rich, or poor. If you are lucky enough to have been in a brilliant job in your current or past career, it will make what I say far more relatable. For those of you that have had sustained success at work it makes it easier for you to form a valid opinion on high performance based on these past experiences.

- You can easily remember your best team or group of people and why it/they inspired you.
- And you can probably remember the worst ones, and how they demotivated you.

On reflection, what constitutes good and bad job morale is highly subjective (opinion) I suppose.

But is it in reality?

Ninety-nine per cent of the schools that I have taught in, I could name the great colleagues twenty years later. I could say right now who the best and the worst teachers were in all the schools I worked in.

So, I suppose, the question to reflect on is this,

"How does someone talk about you when you are not in the room?"

The question above is related to whether you are genuinely bothered and give a shit about your life and work legacy I suppose? If you don't, I find that pretty weird. We get one life to have a positive impact on the world, so my advice is to go and do that with love and not hate. Food for thought.

Chapter 9

WORK GOSSIP AND THE GOSSIP GURUS

"Listen carefully about how a person speaks to you about another person. This is probably how they will speak about you."

Steve Sallis

Gossip is part and parcel of life. You may partake in gossip with your colleagues, your neighbours, or on social media. It is everywhere. But remind yourself of my little, made-up rhyme:

"In high performing environments gossip is seen as criminally bad... and if you hear it and you're moral... it will make you really sad."

As previously mentioned, people with low EQ often gossip more, as they have nothing else to do with their lives, so they need to find stimulation and escapism by betraying others.

Reminder:

"What Sally says about Sharon... says more about Sally, than it does Sharon."

Have you ever heard the above term? I love it. It is so true and happens regularly in many workplaces. Often these types of colleagues cannot help themselves by opening their big mouths. Their lives are often so empty, that all they can do is condemn and speak about others with a tone of judgement and jealousy.

Gossip gurus:
This fickle lot are the con artists in the workplace, fuelling and stirring up hatred with their shitty judgemental behaviour. Gossip gurus, often have insecurity running through their veins. You see, when these *gossip gurus* live in this way and attempt to wreck the

harmony of everyone's daily lives, all you need to remember is, they are just deeply bored and unhappy with themselves. That's the key message here if they try and hurt you.

- Can you even change them in the first place? And if so
- How would you go about challenging or changing the gossipers?

"Change the People or Change the People."

The above quote I heard a few years ago from a leading football leadership expert Dan Ashworth, now of Manchester United. At first it took me a few minutes to understand what it meant. He shared it with me on an online UEFA call as he was sharing his experiences and wisdom of when he entered the building at Brighton and Hove Albion football club. He explained:

1. He first needed to change mindsets of the current staff who were under-performing.
2. He then needed to identify those who were either willing or unwilling to change.
3. Finally, if the people were unwilling to change, he literally had to *change the people*. Something for you to think about, I hope. The only caveat I chose to challenge him back on, was the following:

What if the first part of the "change the people" quote, meant in reality the staff didn't need changing at all?

At the time I reflected that maybe these 'perceived underperformers' were underachieving because they previously just had been led by dickhead leaders, and simply needed a better leader to get the best out of them. What are your thoughts?

Reflections and Actions:

I often reflect on whole school meetings of over ten years ago, where mid-winter had struck. I would strategically have the word 'gossip' firmly on the tip of my tongue ready to start a Monday morning briefing.

HOW NOT BE A LEADERSHIP D*CKHEAD

As the scenario goes:

It was the middle of November when pupil behaviour often went downhill, (and so did the staff behaviour may I add). The weather was getting worse. The nights were drawing in faster and darker, and the key gossipers (gossip gurus) would gradually become worse and worse as the tiredness and fragility of the school term kicked in.

These poisonous fuckers would become more and more negative day by day, and in turn, the smallish 'staff pressure cooker' had the potential to grow into a mammoth gas chamber of what I like to call "cultural carnage".

The result:

The gossip, negativity, and pessimism could often worsen to all time high levels of 'dickhead culture'. (Important to add here that the great teachers, were always consistently positive throughout the entire academic year). The high performing teachers rarely, if ever gossiped. The teacher dickheads often went from bad to worse. From glass half empty, to basically empty. These educated adults were worse than the kids.

After years and years of these similar experiences, of sensing and smelling staff morale getting tetchy in these winter times, I would often use the following line for Monday morning briefings:

"Good morning staff, I trust you had a rested and enjoyable weekend. May I remind everyone, about the importance of staff unity and consistency in the coming weeks leading up to Christmas and poor weather. I appreciate you are all working hard but let us ALL ensure we remind ourselves to behave and conduct ourselves morally and ethically and leave the work gossip at home please. The pupils need to see us united, as do we ourselves, so thank you in advance and have a positive week ahead."

I felt this type of sensible messaging during my leadership tenure, was significant and a key element to addressing shitty staff behaviour over the longer term. Of course, we know culture can waver up and down in any business or school, so accepting that is vital, however I firmly believe it is how leaders respond in the *down times,* that really matter.

> *"Watch the pennies and the pounds will take care of themselves."*

The Down Times:

I have seen the best leaders I have worked with show their resolve, poise, composure, and mettle in the shit times and not always the glory ones. After all, it is easy to *sing when you are winning.* What I have learnt in these tougher times is:

> *"Bad Leaders care about who is right and great leaders care about what is right."*

My leadership strategy in these challenging moments and with these types of people was simply to:

1. Initially communicate with the gossipers with kindness and professionalism.
2. Over time make them feel awkward and isolated in as professional way as I could.
3. The next process was to attempt to ostracise them, bit by bit, one by one, over a period, so they knew I had their shitty behaviour in my sights, and over a term or two (13-26 weeks), they eventually had no one to gossip to.

Solution:

They would therefore be dethroned in their gossiping world and eventually feel devalued and leave the school to go and gossip somewhere else. My years of research and applied experiences often has put me one step ahead of these dickheads. Many psychological theorists that write about this topic sadly have often never *lived* any of their actual research. However, I have lived this stuff.

HOW NOT BE A LEADERSHIP D*CKHEAD

Part of my research around group dynamics has been around something called:

'Stockholm Syndrome'

How did Stockholm syndrome get its name?

Research taken from Forbes magazine says Stockholm syndrome got its name in 1973, just one year before a kidnapping of a woman named Patty Hearst. The story goes that after a failed bank robbery in Stockholm, Sweden:

"The hostages had amazingly bonded with their captors."

This response was perplexing for many sociologists post the event, as it seemed the bank employees had bonded rather closely with the robbers or, at the very least begun to trust them after nearly a week spent together in isolation. Since then, the term Stockholm syndrome is:

"Often used to describe situations where victims feel protective and have some level of affection for their abusers or captors."

Now I am not for one minute comparing this syndrome of hostage *behavioural science* to school or business culture. But what I am saying is:

1. A lot of manipulation in the workplace is common practice by certain negative cohorts.
2. Often the gossip gurus (dickheads) have the ability to *latch onto each other* for benefit of their own psychological safety. (Like finds like)
3. I have lived these situations many times where the leader of the 'gossip gang' regularly acts by cajoling others with cult-like behaviours in order for them to do the same. A bit like rotten apples in a barrel of good ones.

What I have learnt over the years is that some people cannot be changed, so my advice is they need to be *outed* for the good of everyone. Harsh but sadly true.

HOW NOT BE A LEADERSHIP D*CKHEAD

Reminder:

"No dickheads in the building."

Reflections:

As much as I as adore giving love and support to all people, there needs to be a ruthless side somewhere in the process to the equation:

Under performing x Negative dickheads = ?

You can't drop your levels for everyone, so don't feel guilty about getting rid of the dickheads.

The 33% People Process:

In most places I have worked in, I try to go off this thought process, and most of the time it has proved accurate. I section the staff into a 1/3 a 1/3 and a 1/3. To simplify this thinking, the following principles apply:

- The top third of people are always positive, consistent, and high achievers.
- The middle third could often go either way, but with proper leadership support, nurturing, and elite behaviours from the hierarchy above they can grow and improve into the top third no problem. (People see, people do)
- The bottom third I then split into two. I believe the top half of this segment can be changed, tweaked, nurtured, cajoled with rigorous and caring support, love, and mentoring. However (from my experience) the bottom half of the bottom third (bottom 6 of 6), cannot be changed. They are the poisonous fuckers and the official 'grade A' gossipers, de-energisers, happy hoovers, timewasters, problem focussed, and ultimate dickheads.

In summary, the bottom half of the bottom third often have a fixed mindset and generally put your business, school or club into minus equity! As previously mentioned, what is the solution?

GET RID OF THEM

Reminder:

The positive news though is that the other 83.3% of people can potentially 'be on the performance bus pretty quick! Woo-hoo! There is light at the end of the tunnel after all!

Advice:

In any new job I have started, I have always adopted the same strategy.
1) By about week four…Have a list of all the staff's names in front of you on a piece of paper.
2) Highlight each member Green/Amber/Red of who is the easiest to influence first (i.e. green), second (amber) and third (reds)
3) As a new leader this will give you a solid strategy. As I always say. Any strategy is better than no strategy.
4) IT WORKS!
5) Get as many people on your bus as you can, as quickly as you can. But do it strategically. One person at a time.

HOW NOT BE A LEADERSHIP D*CKHEAD

Chapter 10

LEADERSHIP OWN GOALS AND THE 99% EFFECT

"People don't leave bad companies; they leave bad bosses."

Jack Kelly

What is the 99% effect and how can it help you? It is something I created myself back in 2008, sitting in my car whilst in another London traffic jam.

Real life Scenario:
There I was sitting bumper to bumper driving my clapped out 1991 Fiat Uno. I was on the way home from a horrific day teaching feeling as frustrated as hell and venting to myself like a crazy lunatic. The frustration I felt was regarding my idiotic line manager who basically had no clue about how to lead people, let alone get the best out of me.

The story goes like this:
I was a senior teacher, and he was the deputy headteacher, and my direct line manager. He was the ultimate micro-manager, and in addition to this, he was a man who was never ever wrong.

You've met these bosses, right? We all have. They are a complete pain in the arse. I was line managing four departments in the school (which I had inherited on joining), three of which had huge issues with the retention of keeping the good staff. (Note: if good staff leave Inner-London schools it is a bloody nightmare trying to replace them).

On this day, one of the heads of departments who I line managed had turned up late for work. In my deep dive into finding out why, I'd heard from her department peers that in eight years she had never been late once!

HOW NOT BE A LEADERSHIP D*CKHEAD

99% effect = 99 days on time and one day late

The Reality:
She had just come through a divorce, had been battling some personal mental health issues, but all in all, she was a dream to manage day in day out. The biggest compliment I can give this wonderful female colleague was that I didn't have to manage her, as she managed herself with high quality behaviours every single day. She was a dream to lead.

The Perception:
On this given day my line manager (the boss) walked up to me in the corridor all flustered (as was his normal approach, being a regular crisis manager) with his ludicrous ego getting in the way, and as he often did, he began talking to me like I was about five years old.

On this occasion he stormed over to me in front of some pupils close by, saying I needed to reprimand and sanction the teacher in question with a verbal warning for lateness. My initial feelings and emotions at this exact time were:

"Why are you having this conversation with me in front of the pupils as its highly unprofessional".

My words however, in response to him were few and far between at the time, as I just let the silly twat, chat shit to me for five minutes, until he verbally boxed himself out. Whilst he was going on and on, in my head I'm thinking:

"Shut up will you! Do you realise how good this woman is at her job and you want me to sanction her for being late once in eight years? She does 99% good things every week, and you want me to pick up on the 1% she hasn't done? You can fuck right off, you draconian bellend."

HOW NOT BE A LEADERSHIP D*CKHEAD

Grin and bear it:
Anyway, what I did in the moment was pretend to my boss, that I would take the matter extremely seriously and have a word with the teacher, but in reality, that was *never* going to happen. Crisis on top of another crisis has never been my style, when dealing with these types of situations. I try and keep calm when everyone else isn't, is the behaviours I try to live by. This gives me the edge.

Negative Dominoe effect:
Effective leadership isn't always from the textbook. Far too many leaders are hugely unaware of their 'Crisis Leadership' mannerisms, and how this adds to additional crisis behaviours from others. Crisis chat adds zero value to the long game of high performing cultures. My advice therefore after mistakes from the people you lead is this.

Firstly:

1. Look at what people do...do
2. Not look at what they do not...do

It's very basic. Hence the creation of the chapter, the 99% effect. In educational behaviour training we talk about a strategy called ASI:

- **Acknowledge** (Do I acknowledge the lateness?)
- **Sanction** (Do I sanction them for their lateness?)
- **Ignore** (Do I simply ignore their lateness?)

What would you do in this situation with a colleague that is late?

Question:
I am sure you can guess what I did when my dickhead line manager asked me to sanction her?

HOW NOT BE A LEADERSHIP D*CKHEAD

Answer:
Nothing. As a great leader you don't tread on the toes of the cultural architects. If you do, that is what I call:

'School kid leadership'

And the ultimate leadership own goal.

Reminder:

Look at trends of the behaviours of your people and not merely incidents in isolation. Far too many leaders feel the need to sanction too quickly.

Sanctions are statistically proven not to change behaviour over the long term anyway. Just look at the re-offending rate from prisons.

Chapter 11

SUPER STRENGTHS

"Great Leaders are not defined by the absence of weakness, but rather by the presence of clear strengths."

John Zenger

No one good at their job should ever get imposter syndrome. If you are not familiar with the meaning it is as follows:

"A psychological occurrence in which people doubt their skills, talents, or accomplishments and have a persistent internalised fear of being exposed as frauds."

I genuinely have never felt this feeling in my professional life, and I would tell you the truth if I had. I have always backed myself at work. Why? Because school kids give you immediate feedback, good and bad. I have many *super strengths* in my toolbox which adds value to the people I serve. Training to be a teacher at 19 years of age was the making of me.

I see many businesses, schools and football clubs running blind and working in pre-historic ways. Often, I ask the CEO's or middle leaders about their identity:

- Do you know the businesses 'super strengths'?
- Do you know your own personal ones?
- Are your staff all doing what they actually excel at?
- What are every individual staff member's x-factor traits and qualities?
- Do these positive traits align with their actual job descriptions and business KPI's?

One of my biggest pieces of work in businesses, is to look at strategic and operational 'blind spots'. Too often I am seeing under performance from businesses, because for too long they have been working in ways which people are placed in roles that fits the job description, instead of turning that process on its head, and saying this obvious question to themselves:

Can I create a process (job description) for this person that aligns with their set of super strengths and creates a bespoke and tailor made (hybrid) job description?

In turn this modern leadership flexibility can then hopefully add more value to the profit of this company.

Reminder:

Many business leaders are still working in the 1980's, by placing people in square pegs for round holes. The world is evolving fast, so if you don't evolve with it, you are bang in trouble. This is why *meta-cognition* needs to get in your life!

"Knowledge changes, so you must adapt and change with it."

Mirror looking:
In failing businesses, I hear nonsense from managers like,

"Steve, this team is underperforming, and we have got some bad eggs."

Sadly, the main under-performing person is these dickhead leaders who have limited self-awareness skills and are unable to identify the obvious:

1) Why the business or sub-teams/departments are underperforming, and even fewer can say:
2) What the business can do to perform better? and even fewer say,
3) I know the solution to the problem and the problem could be me?

Findings:

HOW NOT BE A LEADERSHIP D*CKHEAD

I have found that lower performing companies have approximately 4:1 ratio with dickheads being the majority. These 80% of dickhead personas usually put problems in the way of solutions and for them, blame culture is rife. Now I completely appreciate not every business runs this way, but please hear me out on this football metaphor.

Square pegs and round holes:
Many professional football managers have been historically awful with their recruitment of players. For example, they sign a player to be a playmaker/creator/artist on the pitch, to then contradict their own decision and give them an entirely different job description and make them a builder/water carrier/soldier (metaphor).

The team ends up playing a different style of long ball, ugly football, thus setting up the skilful player (artist) to fail by asking them to do things in a completely opposite way of what they signed them for.

"Simply, this lack of self-awareness in the initial recruitment process from many leaders is setting staff up to fail time and again."

Reminder:

- Everyone is unique.
- Everyone is different.
- Everyone has different skills, qualities, super strengths and attributes to bring to the workplace.

Remember:

"Strengths lie in differences, and not similarities."

HOW NOT BE A LEADERSHIP D*CKHEAD

Real Life Scenario:
I once mentored a highly successful CEO who had a restaurant chain. He once had 85 applicants apply for a senior role. He chose a candidate for the role after a long and arduous recruitment process which consisted of four interviews over three months. At the end of the process, he came back to me as proud as punch saying, "Steve I have recruited a gem." Fast forward eight weeks and unbelievably he had sacked the new "gem" for under performance.

My response to the CEO:

"What the fuck are you doing?". You hired them, so YOU support them, that's your job. Don't hire them and sell them down the river!"

Self-awareness alert! It is similar in sport with these idiotic CEO's that hire and fire managers at a whim. They need to take a hard look at themselves before they start playing the 'blame game'. As I said earlier, look themselves in the mirror instead of looking out of the window.
So, my advice, like the 99% effect chapter above, is to look at people's super strengths and not always their deficiencies for a great business.

Remember:

"No pessimist ever discovered America. No pessimist ever flew to the moon."

Advice:

Optimism wins! Employ people that not only do the job, but also give the positive energy required for a high performing workplace. As I said previously. Happy hairdryers or happy hoovers! Go and employ some happy hairdryers! EQ beats IQ any day.

Chapter 12

TOXIC TEAMS, SMELLING THE BAD EGG AND SPOTTING D*CKHEADS

"None of us, is never as smart as ALL of u.s"

Ken Blanchard

Malcom Gladwell the famous author of several great books deserves another shout out for this genius quote.

> *"We need to accept our ignorance and say, 'I don't know' more often."*

As mentioned in the previous chapters, how many times have you thought deeply about the teams or groups of people you have played or worked with and the underperforming and disruptive people that have caused mayhem? The hard thing to identify is whether they have consciously or unconsciously behaved disruptively? Meaning, that they know:

1. They are disruptors and are deliberately/consciously doing so, or

2. They are so unconsciously rubbish that they do not know, and they chuck grenades all day, creating issues for others and completely oblivious to their actions.

Now, I admit it, I've stolen the 'no dickheads policy' from the mighty New Zealand *All Blacks* rugby team, who are well known for adopting this practice and strategy to ensure ALL players and staff don't cause any disruption. In fact, the All Blacks stole this from the Sydney Swans, who are an Australian Rules football team, which is yet another example of the importance of sharing good practice across the globe. In elite sport we often say:

"The best coaches are the best thieves."

It would be mindless to think that group cohesion in sport or business is only improved by a minority of teammates or colleagues. I truly believe any high performing team, not only shows high standards of performance on the field or in the office, but also their off-the-field behaviours are elite. High performers have discipline.

Reminder:

Success is a team sport. Remember that high performing teams are not created by fluke. Simply everyone contributes. And if they don't ALL contribute, my further questions are:

- Why is this not the case?
- Do you think some people think it is not their duty or role to improve the team morale and culture of their workplace?
- Where and when does the "we not me" process have to be truly applied and embedded?

Advice:

My huge piece of guidance is firstly to understand that a:

"Star team will always beat a team of stars."

and secondly to quickly find out who your *cultural architects* are! A definition of this from the AR recruitment article is as follows:

"Cultural architects are natural players within your business who encompass your values and drive these via their own behaviours. These cultural architects are often already in place – once identified it's then just a matter of engaging them to become more visible.

When recruiting into or around these natural players it's easy to focus on people's skills, and absolutely, these are important to building or kick starting a team.

However, it's how people behave within that culture that determines the longevity and success of the team. A team that embraces and engages within that culture and drives the right behaviours will be a team that not only communicates and delivers more efficiently in the short to medium term but will continue to do so in the long term."

So, questions you should ask yourself are:

1) Who are the people that are going to produce the goods, day in day out without you having to constantly look over their shoulder?
2) Who are the people that hold each other accountable when the boss isn't there?
3) Who are the people that show elite behaviours consistently, day in day out?
4) Who are the consistent high performers?

As previously mentioned, it is about understanding people's 'why'. Without that as the first part of the high-performance process, no one knows where anyone else's headspace is at.

Tip: I have told many businesses I support to erect pen pictures up in the office with 50-100 words of everyone's 'why'. It is easily done and creates great alignment and connections between staff. Sadly, I have noticed in my time in business that the only thing that matters is the pound note where everyone is simply obsessed with this thing called money. If that is the sole case, then sobeit, but let me tell you this, short-term thinking regarding money will eventually find you out if you want to build a successful and sustainable business. Please remember to stay people focused. Retention of the best staff is key. So invest in them and the money will come anyway.

For those of us who are involved in a team, whether in sport or work, surely everyone wants to be involved in a high performing one with a serious purpose?

Reminder:

We have one life everyone! Sadly, some work colleagues are so narcissistic that they enjoy being part of things that fail. So watch out for them.

Question:
Isn't one of the purposes of life to help others be successful and therefore to help and not hinder them?
Answer:
Sadly, for most sadists it is not, so seek them out and sack them off out of your life.
Socialisation:
Meeting and connecting with people is a big part of the human experience. Relationships, emotions, success, failure, love, respect, and camaraderie are all the feelings we want to be part of. The achievers in life have an edge over non-achievers. They get up every day with one goal and that is to improve, which is the super strength they live by. But I want you to reflect on the underperforming people on the planet...

- Have you ever thought that maybe they have potential yet are mis-managed, lack the education to do so, which often leads to their demotivation?

- Maybe under performers have yet to find their own why?

What are you?
- A lazy life floater, or a
- Work go-getter?

Demotivation:

Most of us have to work for fifty years of our lives. That's a hell of a long time to hate your job and moan about it. I'm hearing that in most office environments, staff start to 'down tools' around 3pm as people's attention spans, concentration and motivation are shot to bits.

I have advised my good friend Jonny Barrett who runs an oil brokerage firm in London to go and get a chess board in the office, a dart board; anything to keep his people fresh at work. He has done better than that and got a personal trainer employed, aiming to keep the staff fit!

Advice:

Do anything to create a marginal gain to your business environment. The traditional work setting has got to STOP. It is pre-historic and not working anymore.

Good People:

Whatever your life journey, these differing work experiences can heavily contribute to your own self-worth, and nothing, and I mean nothing, makes you feel better than helping and sharing successes with others. Achievement is a team sport. These interpersonal relationships are the key to a successful team and, therefore, a more fulfilling life. If the aspiration of team leaders and businesses was to only appoint good people (character over calibre) as the priority, then surely businesses would have a greater chance of performing better. Do you agree?

HOW NOT BE A LEADERSHIP D*CKHEAD

Using business as an example, if CEOs think that a good data analyst ('traditionally' not that important to have good people skills) doesn't have to be a good person, then they are wrong. I regard these types of businesses as lacking an ethical and moral compass, because what gives anyone the right to be a workplace de-energiser?

The question above is posed because some businesses sadly accept that it is OK to be disruptive, if the person in question happens to raise the profit margins, yet still acts like a prick every day. My view? I don't think it is acceptable, and you shouldn't either. The football managers Sean Dyche, Gareth Southgate, Pep Guardiola wouldn't sign a dickhead, and neither would Newcastle United's, Eddie Howe. This is what sport can teach business and why so many businesses use sport metaphors for their own growth.

Task:
Write 10 traits/characteristics/behaviours of a workplace dickhead:

1)
2)
3)
4)
5)
6)
7)
8)
9)
10)

Now, in case you disagree and challenge my thinking about this theory by saying that it is only the results and profits that matter, I would like to add, that I can understand your point of view regarding the cash debate, but in the *long-term*:

1. Group dynamics will never improve when there are dickheads in the building.
2. If group dynamics are poor, then the team, regardless of what level they are working or playing at, is destined to underperform in the medium and long-term.

So, in the first instance, the self-awareness required to *not* be a disruptive influence is important. As mentioned in my previous book, David Brent the character from the television show, *The Office*, demonstrated behaviour that showed he was lacking self-awareness in a big way.

Below, I have highlighted some of the common personality traits of work dickheads:

The constant jokers: They are ones who pick the wrong moments to indulge in banter, normally, first thing on a Monday morning. Basically, they are the types who laugh at their own jokes. Sarcasm is their middle name. They can often be effective in groups but lack the social and emotional intelligence to build truly unique relationships, thus group dynamics and personal relationships are negatively affected.

The blockers: These people make life difficult for everyone by being 100 percent problem focused. They often do things by the book or are masters at constantly creating problems to people's solutions by saying, "I am not sure we can do that…"

The naturally negative people (De-energisers): I call them the 'Happy Hoovers.' These people are elite at sucking up happiness from others. They see the glass as half-empty and lack the resilience or self-awareness to understand how they drag people down with every comment and word they say. These people are not who you would want in the trenches with you if life got tough. In a sporting context, these types of teammates are the work colleagues often who use blame as their only way out. They have a 'can't do' mentality. As an ex-colleague of mine used to say when he met these types of people, "Bore off, mate."

The social loafers (Ship sinkers): In crisis, these people tend to sit back and watch the ship sinking, while washing their hands of any blame. The bigger the group size, the more easily they disappear into the background. It's a bit like the TV show *The Apprentice* I suppose, where in the first show of each series, Sir Alan normally saves the losing captain for having the balls to head the team up in the first place. Now, Alan Sugar is people savvy and often despises the *silent assassins* who sit back and allow failure to happen. He doesn't accept a flaky approach to group dynamics. This is known in psychology terms as the Ringelmann effect. I call these people 'passive dickheads'. They are often quietly harmful and will finger point behind other people's backs at any opportunity.

The "I'm never wrong" dickheads: These people never say sorry, or admit to any wrongdoing, and they therefore find it hard to build truly great relationships. These are the types of performers or colleagues who deflect when they are in the wrong. They normally deceive people about their skills when in reality they are average performers, and boast when they actually exceed expectations, but they will never admit the opposite. They say words like "I" and "me". As mentioned earlier this lot are 'eye specialists', as they're the people who say, "I did this, and I did that."

So, whether you are reading this as a leader or merely as a member of a group, please promote and contribute to a 'No Dickhead Policy' in your workplace or team!

As the All Blacks are famous for saying,

"Better people make better All Blacks."

They say:

"Never be too big to do the small things that need to be done."

HOW NOT BE A LEADERSHIP D*CKHEAD

But forget about the All Blacks here. *Better* people make a *better* life.

Reminder:

Two quotes have always stood by me that keep me sane with interactions with the dickheads are:

1. You cannot reason with an unreasonable person.
2. You cannot say the right thing to the wrong person.

Final reminder, is that if you are ever in doubt with people in your building, just apply the famous FIFO method:

"Fit in or Fuck off!"

HOW NOT BE A LEADERSHIP D*CKHEAD

HOW NOT BE A LEADERSHIP D*CKHEAD

Chapter 13

LEADERSHIP INFLUENCE & LOVE LANGUAGES

"Leaders tell because they want something done... But the person listening, has got to 'want' to do it... when you tell."

Dale Carnegie

The above quote is very profound and from one of my favourite ever books. 'How to win friends and influence people'. I have been on many podcasts talking about the differences between management and leadership, and I go as far to say this.

"You can use all the adjectives you want for the boss, but often we miss the number one USP and role of a leader, and that is the word influence."

Influence is the most underused word in the field of leadership. The actual meaning of influence is as follows:

"The capacity to have an effect on the character, development, or behaviour of someone or something, or the effect itself."

My key learning regarding this is the word BEHAVIOUR! A person who can affect someone's behaviour is a genius. There are many connotations of the definition above, so the questions that you could ask yourself are:

- How well do YOU affect someone's character/ behaviour?
- How well do YOU develop others?
- Do YOU have a genuine impact on the behaviours of the people you serve?
- Have YOU got the intellectual capacity/knowhow/ calibre/character to help people in the first place?

If you can't do the above, then the solution is obvious! Get someone into your business that can!

HOW NOT BE A LEADERSHIP D*CKHEAD

Reminder:
"An expert hires an expert."

The best bosses do this. They are very clear and self-aware, and they know, what they don't know. I often hear business leaders bemoan about not having the time to build their business, performance manage their staff, inspire their staff, upskill their staff, retain their good staff and many more important processes.

Advice:

Zoom out. Press the pause button. Often managers say, "Someone should do something about that." Leaders would say, "I am that somebody. I will sort it everyone," or "I can't do it personally so I will get someone that can."

Think strategically:
Try and think strategically. Because without a strategy and long-term planning you are fundamentally doomed. Have one eye on the now, and the other eye on the future. Have one finger on proving you are good, and the other on improving yourself and your staff. It is definitely a technique I have had to learn.

Many businesses are too obsessed with targets, data and KPIs yet fail to press the pause button in order to actually monitor those targets and assess their genuine effectiveness. I still see businesses that operate without regular meeting cycles, have no agendas and regular planned meetings are not even evidenced with minutes.

These are classic signs leading to leadership *own goals* and therefore affecting high performance. Poor structures guarantee to saturate accountability when accountability is everything in high performing environments. So key questions to focus on at the end of every strategic meeting are:

- Who is doing what?
- When are they going to do it by?

- And how will we monitor the effectiveness of this action/decision?

Reminder:

Influence x Strategy x Accountability = High Performance

My strategies around influencing the person:

- Know their children's names
- Know their partner's name
- Know their parents' names
- Know their favourite sport
- Know their favourite team
- Know what their hobbies are
- Know their "why" for working in your industry
- Know their birthday
- Know where they live
- Know what motivates them
- Know to be kind, authentic and caring

SIMPLY DO ANYTHING TO GET THAT MARGINAL GAIN AND GET THEM MOTIVATED. IT'S BASIC SHIT.

As I wrote earlier,

"Children won't let you care about them until they know that you care."

Are adults any different? I will let you decide.

Love languages and the effects on leadership:

Are you aware of the five love languages? These have been written in many books over many decades about what people need, want, and require in loving relationships. Gary Chapman the author of the book with the same name describes the languages as follows:

1. Words of affirmation
2. Quality time
3. Physical touch
4. Acts of service
5. Receiving gifts

Now this book is clearly about leading people and not love, however I think they are highly correlated in terms of human motivation.

- Some staff like words, and you telling them they are great.
- Others will need your time and presence being in the moment.
- Some will appreciate you touching them on the shoulder and saying thank you (others won't).

There are many bosses out there that struggle with words and lack the *emotional literacy* for greatness but will positively action everything you ask of them instead. These could include paying for you to go on a course, or changing your job title, or giving you a pay rise. And finally, some people just appreciate you purchasing a bottle of wine for them at the Christmas dinner.

I was once very grateful to listen to Ange Postecoglu the Tottenham Hotspur football manager speak at a UEFA Pro licence event I was also speaking at. He relayed to us that he didn't like 'small chat' with his players which blew me away with shock. I had assumed (wrongly) that he would be very close to his players with words of affirmation or quality time. But it was very evident Ange's love language to his players was acts of service. He just delivers his love with:
1. Great sessions on the grass.
2. He is the most prepared for games.

3. He teaches them stuff that they didn't know before.

That's how Ange shows his love! Which way do you show yours? What do your staff want? Have you even asked?

Reflections:
Some bosses are miles off it with this sort of soft skills stuff. So, if you can do it, say it and show it, you're already getting an advantage over your competitors.

If you don't do it, and predecessors *have* done it, remember you're going to be the **DOWNGRADE** leader.

> **"Influencing people, is all about applying brilliant basics. Everyone wants to feel *important*. Do not forget it."**

HOW NOT BE A LEADERSHIP D*CKHEAD

Chapter 14

THE MAVERICK LEADER

"I personally believe mavericks are people who write their own rulebook. They are the ones who act first and talk later. They are fiercely independent thinkers who know how to fight the lizard brain. I don't believe many are born, rather they are products of an environment, or their experiences."

Ziad K Abdelnour

We have all known a maverick, whether they are colleague, teacher, family member or boss. If you are not sure of the meaning of the word, the definition is this:

"An unorthodox or independent-minded person."

I love this description, because if you had asked me to define it before I did my research, I would have struggled. What are your thoughts on mavericks?

- Are they innovators before their time? or
- Simply too emotional, and off-the-cuff for your liking?

There is saying I love that goes, "Surround yourself with people who get it." I like this quote and believe it to be helpful.

- So, do you surround yourself with maverick people? or
- People with more consistent behavioural traits?
- Do you think you can have too many mavericks in one place of work or home?

Task:

Ask your team at work what ratios you would all go for if you had to choose between:

A team of safe hands or a team of mavericks?

HOW NOT BE A LEADERSHIP D*CKHEAD

As a child, I was brought up around many maverick adults. They have been highly present in my life. Having a maverick in your extended family can be hard to handle sometimes, however when it comes to the various people you work with what are your thoughts?

- Are mavericks a help?
- Or hinderance?

I have always believed that professional and personal relationship boundaries in the workplace are a fine line, so it's key to ensure that mavericks don't turn professional goals into personal battles. I ask you to reflect on:

- Have you seen a leadership maverick cause havoc and drain the energy levels of everyone in the office?
- Would you say mavericks are generally energisers or de-energisers to the group dynamic?

That's for you to decide.

If we look at leadership mavericks throughout modern history, we can assess whether we think their leadership style was effective. In my sport, football, the highly successful football manager, Brian Clough in the 1980's, has been lauded for his quirky management style, and he gained much success from it by achieving being back-to-back European champions with a team full of underachievers in their previous roles at clubs. The Frenchman Arsene Wenger, entered British football thirty years ago with his teacher-like mannerisms, was certainly different. He could be viewed as an *educated maverick* and he was certainly unorthodox, but in a good way.

Boris Johnson came into UK mainstream first as London Mayor and then UK Prime Minister, telling everyone in the media he would make our country great again. I believe he is a maverick, but his tenure clearly being ineffective. Johnson is a narcissist for sure. In the end Boris has made himself look pretty stupid with his lies and deceit. His reign of course, was followed by the calamity of the 45 days of Lizz Truss as prime minister, and the metaphor of a lettuce having a longer life span than her reign springs to mind. Say no more. Her failed reign like many others in the business and football world I believe is heavily linked to the 'Peter Principle'. So what is it?

The 'Peter Principle':

Regarding the above story about previous UK Prime Ministers, the 'Peter Principle' theory was in full flow. It is brilliant and was first advocated in a 1969 book called the same name. The authors Laurence J. Peter and Raymond Hull discussed in depth *'Why Things Always Go Wrong'* for so many leaders.

The principle is a concept where it mirrors the many people who gravitate through the work hierarchy year after year with various promotions, that eventually lead to a:

"Level of particular incompetence."

It states that employees are often promoted based on their success in their previous jobs. They then eventually reach a level at which they are no longer competent, as the skills and calibre in one role, do not essentially translate to another (the promotion). It gives examples that often the best soldiers at ground level are not always the best candidates for many leadership positions. The principle has also been the foundation of endless scrutiny.

Question:
- What are your thoughts on promotions in the workplace being based on candidates' current level of performance, and not necessarily on their actual potential at the next level as a *leader*?

When the Peter Principle is applied, the conversations that occur at the staff Christmas party often sound like this:

Sally says to Billy:

"How the fuck has the boss got that job Billy?"

Billy Replies:

"God knows Sally, he couldn't run a piss up in a brewery that fella. He is blagging it. He has got no clue, no vision and can't speak to people properly."

Have you been part a conversation like this this before? Of course you have! People getting jobs they should not get, and everyone in the office wondering how the heck they got the job in the first place.

So, moving back to mavericks:

- What traits do these successful maverick men and women possess that so many others do not?
- How have some leadership mavericks created sustained success?
- Furthermore, are men or women more likely to be leadership mavericks?

Reminder:

In the corporate training I deliver, I try to emphasise that the main ability and quality of these mavericks is that they often *think differently* (critical thinking), compared to their peers. My experiences in the corporate and sporting world are vast, and often I witness these mavericks thinking outside the box. Often however, the maverick leader doesn't have a bloody box – they threw it away years ago! As mentioned earlier this is why *critical thinking* is paramount in the modern-day workplace, and I urge you again to use meta-cognition to form the basis of how you work.

HOW NOT BE A LEADERSHIP D*CKHEAD

I believe that *manager mavericks,* often have more creative and agile minds compared to many of their rivals and peers. A problem can be that mavericks are inconsistent and miss the vital component of applying consistency and brilliant basics to their work. The contrast in leadership styles was the reason behind my business being created. I say to people I support this:

"I am not trying to change you; I am trying to understand you. The most important thing, is to be the best version of you, not me!"

My time teaching in schools through the latter years was basically living in an *exam factory culture* where maverick behaviour was seen as disruptive.

The scene is as follows:

- Robots dressed as kids, waiting in a line for their turn to fail or succeed.
- Teachers moving down corridors like the walking dead, unable or unwilling to change the current educational narrative, that many firmly believe is institutionally wrong.

Almost everything in the education sector is stuck in a time warp. Is your business stuck in its ways? If so, what are the bosses doing to change the narrative of the future?

Bringing theory to life:

I have years of positive evidence and impact statistics to support my ability to help people's thinking about their personal and work lives. I have supported adults and children for nearly thirty years to understand themselves better, both personally and professionally. This coaching support, helps my clients acquire greater personal perspective, meaning they have more fulfilling lives. However, to do my job well, I am aware that:

"I have to think *differently.*"

Consider what I am saying here. Doing things differently only happens if you THINK more creatively in the first place. Let me introduce you to the word that changed my life, meta-cognition. It has two meanings:

1) Thinking about Thinking
2) Knowing about Knowing

For the maverick leader, to become conventional with their behaviour, would be almost impossible. Their idea of being conventional, is actually being unconventional on a daily basis. Sometimes mavericks are difficult to predict.

"I will acknowledge however that it is a lot easier to be a maverick leader, when you have had success, and a proven track record to back it up, whether that be in sport or business."

If you looked at all the highly successful managers, who portray maverick traits and got them to explain their behaviours, you would possibly see them explaining it in a *tacit* way. Tacit is a powerful word and means:

"The stuff that we do that we cannot explain."

The opposite of tacit is explicit. They are both very helpful concepts in the elite sport and leadership world we live in, and I advise you to use them wisely.

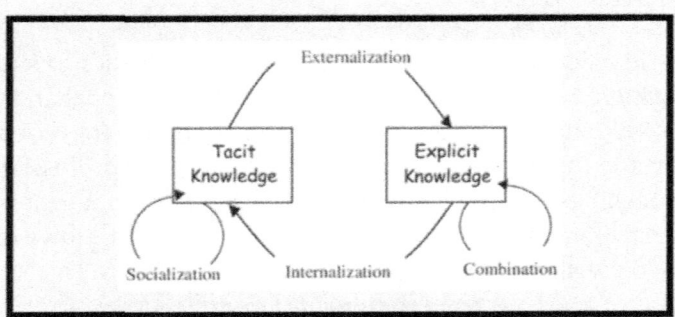

Mis-managed:
Many maverick people I have encountered in the past have been often mis-managed because they didn't conform to the norms of the tight, rigid rules and regulations set by leaders. They would gain praise and plaudits from kids, parents and peers, and would often even achieve great exam results for their classes, or world class footballers in their clubs, but often the senior managers simply couldn't handle their abstract personalities which didn't conform with their own lens on the world.

Advice:
My opinion about managing these people is that you must let them breathe. You can't merely want compliance. Compliance stifles creativity.

> *"It is not always the maverick who needs to adapt, but those in charge of them."*

Sometimes the mavericks I knew were pushed out, due to their non-conformist behaviours, when instead I felt they should have been embraced by bosses for their creativity and unique ability to achieve greatness.

What is the correct way to approach mavericks when tricky situations occur?

I'm not always sure there is a correct and clinical answer apart from the obvious awareness that they exist, however what I do know is that mavericks can be game changers if you have got the right ones. The two best teaching mavericks I have ever witnessed were Pete Nicholls, a mathematician, and Steffan Ball, a PE teacher and now Headteacher. I worked with Pete in three schools, so I have a genuine ability to judge his persona. I was with Steffan in two, but we also lived together in shitty rented house after university. Bally is probably the maddest, funniest bloke I have ever met, and now he is deservedly a headteacher and the most dedicated father of four beautiful children.

Why were they both so effective?

Pete did everything against the norm, but he was also a bloody good bloke. He was a solid, fun, and reliable colleague. He constantly challenged people's thinking and the leadership strategy if he thought they could do better. In hindsight, he was more of a maverick in the classroom with the students than he was with staff. He achieved great Maths results with his classes year after year. The kids in all year groups from 11-18 loved him. It was therefore a win-win situation for everyone.

Flaws:

He was sometimes hard work to manage in terms of following the brilliant basics of the school rules, as his pupils could be the worst dressed in terms of uniform, which completely contradicted the school's ethos. At one stage as his line manager, I spent a lot of my time covering his arse with this sort of stuff, but that's what loyalty is. It was no issue to me.

> **"I've learnt over the years that strong leaders earn loyalty, and weak leaders demand it".**

In our second school together, I had to convince the senior staff to ignore that part of Pete's maverick repertoire. The Headteacher at the time was a fucking megalomaniac nutter (control freak who never admits they are wrong) and that didn't help either of us. Pete would say to me privately over a beer that if he is challenged by these controlling leaders too often, he will fuck them off and be gone and go and work somewhere else, and I didn't blame him. He needed leadership flexibility, as did I.

Charisma and Character:

Steffan, a fellow PE teacher and now Headteacher, easily got some of the best outcomes for pupils that I ever witnessed during my time in education. He had a completely alternative approach and oozed charisma.

How did he achieve excellence?

Trust me, you would not put it into a book about traditional teaching and learning. He was the most random yet brilliant character, and he was also the best. It's also important to remember that we were in south London schools. The kids were huge characters themselves, so in my humble opinion they needed characters teaching them with the skills and techniques to handle them. I have always used the phrase 'lively' for how the pupils behaved in inner cities, so make of that what you will.

MTM – Managing the Maverick:

I will now give you a simple methodology for managing a maverick, which I have previously mentioned. Simply remind yourself of what they do well and NOT what they don't do well. Remember the aforementioned '99% effect chapter'.

Do you:

- **A**cknowledge their poor behaviours?
- **S**anction their poor behaviours?
- **I**gnore their poor behaviours?

This type of mindset towards leading a maverick is key, otherwise I advise you not to have them in the building or your team in the first place, or else they will drive you insane. I suppose this is similar to managing the flair player in sport. They are often unconventional and fail to conform to the norms.

Can you afford to have someone that is a little bit different but has the 'X factor'?

Whether you are a manager, coach, leader, or aspiring leader I will let you reflect on your own actions. But my advice to you is this. You cannot have enough of them, but only if they are willing to conform! These maverick people are innovators of our planet and can achieve excellence.

Reminder:

But just not how YOU would want it done!

HOW NOT BE A LEADERSHIP D*CKHEAD

Chapter 15

COACHING VERSUS MENTORING. WHAT IS BEST?

"The best teachers are those who tell you where to look, but don't tell you what to see."

Alexandra K. Trenfor

I often get asked this question:

"Steve how do you help people achieve greatness? Do you coach or mentor them? What are your techniques? What is the secret?"

My Answer:
There ain't no secret. I started this teaching lark in 1996. I've got it wrong, more times than I have got it right. I have studied, planned, failed, succeeded, applied, reflected, applied, reflected, and studied. It has been my life. Sometimes I just smell and sense it, and sometimes I use science to affect the learning of others. I navigate these processes via my head, my heart, or my gut. What does my gut often tell me? This is probably my best sign, to help someone instead of what any piece of technology can teach me. It's called Experience!

Labels:
To be honest I hate labels; they piss me off. Research from Dr Linda Garand in 2010 stated:

"Health care professionals use diagnostic labels to classify individuals for both treatment and research purposes. Despite their clear benefits, diagnostic labels also serve as cues that activate stigma and stereotypes."

Many businesses ask me what psychometric testing I use. normally reply with:

> "No, I don't use it often or believe in it, I just help people get better in their chosen field without labels. Whether that is coach, mentor, lead, listen, observe, create, analyse, assess, tell, want, demand, advise, apply, lead or manage a situation."

The list goes on as to how I have achieved success with all walks of society. I use every trick in the book to add value to the people I support. School teaching was the environment that made me like this, and it is easily the most underrated job on the planet for being skilful with helping people. You help people all day, every day, whether that be teacher, parent or pupil. And remember the pupils that I served generally didn't want to be there!

The help and support varied greatly from academic, personal, psychological, spiritual, emotional, or professional, but to the uninformed layman on the street it's just called teaching right! I really need to get this across to you. Seriously, what a fucking mental job it was. Someone said to me recently in a majorly uninformed manner. "Steve, have you got any mentoring qualifications?" I said,

> "Are you having a laugh? I've got 25 years, 300,000 teenagers, 10,000 teachers, 2000 footballers in the bank, and all knocking on my door asking for help. Except I am called a teacher, not a counsellor or therapist."

Last year, another cheeky so and so said to me:

> "Steve how do you go from teaching to keynote speaking, that's a bit random isn't it?"

I replied:

> "Very easy, I have been doing keynote speeches for 6 hours a day for 25 years. Except they are called, lessons and school assemblies."

HOW NOT BE A LEADERSHIP D*CKHEAD

I mean, fucking hell please! Get yourself into any inner-city school, then you will understand me a lot better. On social media people have asked how I am coping with my instant success? I replied,

> *"Instant success? Blimey. I have committed to serving others since 1996, got two degrees, written two books, worked in professional football at academy and first team level for over ten years, with some of the world's best athletes, helped Britain's poorest communities, been on Netflix twice, got thousands of failures behind me and grafted my arse off for over 25 years you cheeky bastard."*

Rant over people. Anyway, my point is, just help your people get better. Whatever your method is called. Just help them. Sod the label for you and them. Do whatever it takes, with whatever method you choose. When I go into football clubs' people always ask your job title is as if it's means something. My answer:

> *"Head of saying sensible things."*

As I said in my previous book:

> *"There are educated people who are not intelligent, and intelligent people who are not educated."*

Which one are you?
So please be mindful of the above. Be that educated AND intelligent person. In reference back to coaching and mentoring differences, I will give you some nuggets below:

Coaching (Ask)	Mentoring (Tell)
Ask instead of tell	Know a lot about subject
Enhance awareness	Advise and guide
Know nothing	Share Experience

In summary, and to simplify for you:

"A coach has some great questions for your answers; a mentor has some great answers for your questions."

An analogy about riding a bike hopefully helps to define and cement the differences between many of the techniques I use:

- A therapist will probably explore what is stopping you ride the bike
- A counsellor will probably listen to your anxieties about riding the bike
- A mentor will probably share advice from the experience of riding bikes
- A consultant will probably direct you on how to ride the bike
- A coach will probably ask you how you ride the bike

Tips for Mentoring:

Back in the day in schools, we used to use *Scaling* as a versatile tool for teachers to help pupils but also coaching the teachers in a one-to-one scenario. It is a brilliant technique for less able students with low literacy levels who may struggle with effective language to explain how they feel and why they feel it. However, it is also really effective for high performing adults. Scaling can be used in many different contexts. It can involve asking a deceptively simple question:

"Imagine a scale running from 1-10, where 10 represents reaching your goal or perfection and 0 is the opposite. Where are you right now?"

Reminder:

    i)   Try to use scaling when attempting to develop your people.

ii) The next most effective tool I use in a coaching conversation, is to encourage the coachee to describe their preferred 'future self'.
iii) The third is to ask them what they would do differently if they had that opportunity again.

I often get told by new and inexperienced mentors that they struggle to get going with 121's. So below is a structure I have used many times for you to get going. I hope it helps you.

Coaching questions you can ask linked to gaining a growth mindset:

⇒ What made you think hard today?
⇒ How will you challenge yourself today?
⇒ What can you learn from this experience or mistake?
⇒ What would you do differently next time to make things work better?
⇒ What else do you want to learn?
⇒ What strategy can you try?
⇒ Who can you ask for honest feedback?
⇒ Did you work as hard as you could have?
⇒ If it was too easy, how can you make it more challenging?
⇒ Did you hold yourself to high expectations or did you accept "good enough"?
⇒ Did you ask for help if you needed it?
⇒ What can you do to manage distractions?
⇒ Have you reviewed your work or logic for errors or flaws?
⇒ Are you proud of the end result?
⇒ Why or why not?
⇒ What's the next challenge to tackle?

Applied Theory:

In the 1960s, human psychology was further developed, and one of the key figures in the field was Abraham Maslow, renowned for his 'Hierarchy of Needs'. Another was Fritz Perlz, the founder of Gestalt Therapy. The latter therapy focuses on a person's present life, rather than delving heavily into the feelings of their past experiences. The discoveries made by these psychologists were that they started to look at what was *right* with people, rather than what was wrong, thus concentrating on their future *potential* rather than their current problems. (Football managers take note).

Reminder:

Any alternative therapy can be helpful for people. My advice is to always remind clients of what they can do, and not what they cannot do! Maybe use the above techniques and also apply my '99% effect' to your people!

Working Backwards:
This is a very important facet of my coaching and mentoring techniques. Very simply it means you have to work backwards, and not forwards. However, please note, it is all about your timelines and how long you have to develop someone. Many shit mentors get this process majorly wrong. So, things to reflect on:

1. If you have six months with someone you can coach, because you have the time for their many failures and reflections in between sessions.
2. If you have six weeks with someone who is really struggling, you mostly have to mentor. Why? You do not have the time. As an example, If I have a trainee teacher for six weeks and they are having a nightmare with their classes, I can probably sort out their personal traumas and techniques pretty quick, so why wouldn't I? I am certainly not going to let them fail and have a terrible isolated experience. I tell them, help them, and guide them to

success as quick as I can in order to get their confidence up.
3. If I have over six months with a mentee, I would choose to operate with lots of coaching techniques and be calm about embracing failure with them. I would let them suffer more (strategically), and hopefully over time and with regular and accurate reflection, they should come up with the answers and solutions for themselves. Reflection is the ultimate winner after all, but only if you have the time!

Either way, my advice is to be ultra-flexible with your approach to people development. Whoever tells you there is one way, is talking complete bollocks. There are many techniques for people to be successful. Don't be fixed with your approach and remind yourself:

- 4+4
- 5+3
- 6+2
- 7+1

Point made. There are many ways to get to eight and be correct. Often only the ego gets in the way of compromise.

Final Summary:
In my previous book, I had a chapter called *The Singer, Not The Song, where* I am trying to emphasise a metaphor that it is the *teachers* persona who brings the lesson plan to life (the singer) and not what is on the lesson plan that matters (the song)!

All the planning in the world, won't help a teacher/mentor/coach/therapist with a shit personality! The same applies to anything people related. Bring your knowledge to life and build pictures with words.

Remember:

Knowledge is nothing without applying wisdom. I often say to many coaches around the world:

"Wouldn't it be great if everyone at work just said sensible things every day?"

So be one of those sensible leaders and avoid chatting bollocks. The diagram below sums it up perfectly.

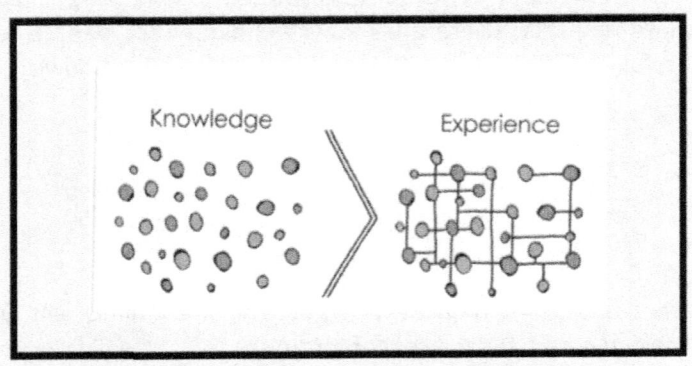

Chapter 16

IKIGAI

"I believe our ikigai is different for all of us, but one thing we have in common is that we are always searching for the meaning and purpose of our life."

Steve Sallis

How many people do you know in the world that are highly educated or have a list of qualifications longer than their arm and fucking HATE their job?

How very weird that the education system has created this, and how wrong it is.

"Everyone should love their job."

Throughout the UK I have asked over 300,000 teenagers during my school mindset project which is called "My Future Self", what they aspire to and want to achieve in their lives?

Some of these 16-year-olds are really clear, and know where their north star is, (well done parents), however most youngsters, have no clue whatsoever. Now you could say this is entirely normal. I say it's criminal. On some social media outlets, people have argued that I am stupid for asking teenagers these important questions so early in their life. Personally, I think they are stupid, that they think I am stupid. Let me tell you why:

Problem:
In the last five years I have mentored over 500 people in their twenties and thirties that have absolutely no purpose to their life. They have had over four careers and have hated every job they have had in their life and are just living a life without growth and genuine fulfilment.

HOW NOT BE A LEADERSHIP D*CKHEAD

Solution:
Start having the **My Future Self** conversation earlier.

Tasks:
1. As a start ask your child to write a list of jobs they definitely DON'T want to do.
2. Get them to identify their 'Super Strengths' much earlier in their lives. Don't REACT. Don't WAIT. (What are they 10/10 at and can it get them paid?)
3. Aim to build a dream early. An aspirational dream but also realistic to their capabilities.
4. But most of all, tell them to go and get a job in the future that they would LOVE to do.

So, this is where the greatest word alive comes in...

"IKIGAI"

It means, your life purpose. Ikigai is a Japanese concept that means your 'reason for being.' 'Iki' in Japanese means 'life,' and 'gai' describes value or worth. In summary it is what brings you joy and inspires you to get out of bed every day, instead of being all hurkle-durkle. The Venn diagram below explains it further.

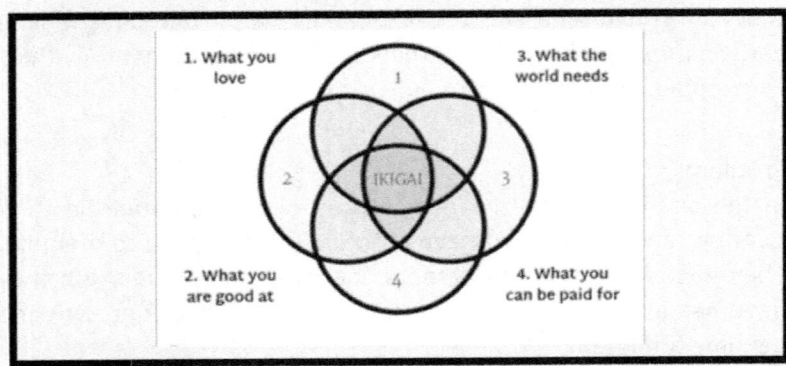

www.leadershipmindset.uk

So, start influencing your children with these four concepts regarding their future self:

1) Do something you love
2) Do something you are good at
3) Do something you can get paid for
4) Do something that the world needs

Reminder:

The world doesn't need more selfie takers on social media! I mean we all occasionally take a selfie with our mate on a night out, but regular selfie takers add no value to the world and never will. But be warned:

"The people that do it every day with no clear message; stay clear of them. They are the definition of narcissism".

Advice:

When you add value to the world, money follows. The problem with the education system is that it basically teaches you to go and work for someone else. It is completely outdated for current day life. Modern education should be teaching your children:

- Entrepreneurship
- Leadership acumen
- Character development
- Financial Skills
- Life 'know how' and much more...

Reasons:
Teachers are generally naturally academic themselves, so often have never failed at anything academic in their life. Firstly, this means the worst teachers lack the empathy for kids who are not naturally academic, and therefore the cycle of doom continues for many of the *so-called* underachievers in school and life.

HOW NOT BE A LEADERSHIP D*CKHEAD

Another huge problem is the narrow curriculum, which is positioning many kids to fail, by the so-called experts (called the *teachers,* note sarcasm) who still use labels in their schools like "bottom set". There is an obvious example of the problem. The experts are the fucking problem! Labels for children need to STOP.

Reminder:

Teach our children that we have live one life.
Stop taking it for granted.
Practice more gratitude.
Stop thinking the world owes you something.

For context, 7.7 billion people live on the planet:

- 785 million people on our planet do not have access to safe drinking water. (WHO)
- 820 million people in our world are undernourished.
- 40 million people were involved in modern slavery in 2016. (Global Slavery Index)
- 4.5 billion people don't have a toilet that properly manages human waste.
- 3 billion people do not have the internet.
- And according to CNN's Global Wage Calculator the average annual wage is £16,000 per year.
- Russia is £3,000
- Brazil is £2,500
- India is £1,300 and
- Malawi = £908 PER YEAR

Create perspective. Go and fulfil your dreams. You get one life!

But remember... **do what the world needs.**

Chapter 17

THE PROBLEM WITH GOVERNMENT LEADERSHIP

"We stigmatise mistakes. And we're now running national educational systems where mistakes are the worst thing you can make — and the result is that we are educating people out of their creative capacities."

Sir Ken Robinson

The reason it is important to challenge leadership at any level, in any genre is because the lack of unfairness in the world is growing. Not for one minute am I suggesting anarchy is the way to change unethical leadership, however currently the government bureaucrats, and many who are part of the hierarchy, genuinely wouldn't know what leadership was if it hit them on the head with a spanner.

As an example, since July 2019, the UK has been through seven education secretaries in Damian Hinds, Gavin Williamson, Nadhim Zahawi, Michelle Donelan, James Cleverly, Kit Malthouse and Gillian Keegan. It's another example of the circus, and more evidence of the complete shambles from senior people we are supposed to be able to trust. This lot create policies that affect our futures.

The second reason we have to challenge hierarchies in society is because theoretical understanding, which can lead to their outdated behaviour, is often proven to be flawed. And that's my point. Are they consciously shit? Or unconsciously? Many things can affect someone's thinking, doing, or knowing.

- Cognitive Bias
- Ignorance or
- Cognitive Dissonance

HOW NOT BE A LEADERSHIP D*CKHEAD

Renowned author Mattew Syed's book called 'Bounce' discusses the 10,000 hours theory. His outstanding book explores the examination of high performance from across the globe and draws upon the stories of sports stars, artists, musicians with the most up-to-date science; his sole aim is to uncover the major factors that lead to world class success. Most importantly he examines the many hours these world class performers have practised in their lifetime. He shares why:

- The most successful figure skaters have fallen over the most.
- A father turned his three daughters into the best chess players the world has ever seen, and how.
- Matthew's own street in Reading, England produced more top table tennis players, than the rest of Britain put together. (From one street!)

Question:

So, reflecting on the evidence above. How the heck can our politicians possibly become experts in any of their chosen fields with so little time applied to be world class at it? The evidence for this is that politician's flit from post to post, possibly every two years. They can go from health secretary to home secretary to education secretary, all in the space of three years. Fucking madness, right?

This is the equivalent to me saying, "I am now an architect." The outcome? My buildings would fall down. Why? Because I would be shit at it! Dunning Kruger Effect here we come! Like most of you reading this we have been doing our job for years, and this lot create legislation whilst in post for only a matter of months. Total madness and a very flawed approach.

Reminder:

Our country is governed by so-called experts that are nowhere near the 10,000 hours of practice in their chosen fields.

HOW NOT BE A LEADERSHIP D*CKHEAD

More evidence:

Do you remember the covid years, of 2020 and the daily television updates at 5pm, where Boris Johnson and his pals would present the covid data and statistics back to the nation. On the PowerPoint they delivered from, they couldn't even find a fucking *clicker* between them, and the presenter kept saying "next slide please" on live tv. Honestly this is another clue that shows incompetence. This *'next slide please'* fiasco went on for the entire two years, and not one of them addressed it or saw it as unprofessional! Leadership dickheads the lot of them.

Summary:

For the summary of this chapter, I have left you with some newspaper headlines regarding three narcissists: Boris Johnson, Donald Trump and Dominic Cummings.

1. "Boris Johnson's 50 worst lies, gaffes and scandals" – Daily Mirror, 9th July 2022
2. "Johnson's Lies Worked for Years, Until They Didn't" – New York Times, 7th July 2022
3. "43 times Boris Johnson lied, mocked and even broke the law" – Liverpool July 2022, Echo
4. "Twin peaks of madness: Trump's narcissism and Johnson's intoxicated rule-bending" The National - 13th September 2020
5. "Career psychopath' Dominic Cummings could make millions as a consultant or by penning a tell-all book after his tumultuous spell as PM's top aide comes to an end" – Daily Mail 13th November 2020

In chapter 19, I discuss in detail narcissism and its connection with Leadership.

HOW NOT BE A LEADERSHIP D*CKHEAD

Advice:

Please be mindful in your workplace and watch out for these serial liars. David Cameron the former British Prime minister once called Dominic Cummings "a career psychopath" saying:

> ***"He is desperate to be seen as successful and terrified of blending into the mass of Oxbridge graduates."***

That's a big quote from one peer to another of the same political party.

Reminder:

Be successful for the right reasons. Create a good legacy for whatever you choose to do. We get one life so do the right thing. The media fraud Piers Morgan recently blocked me from Twitter. Why? Because when people like me call him out for being a narcissist, he does what all good narcs do, and block people.

You see, some people who are in the limelight of the media are the masters at manipulation:

- Morgan and others they will say something that the entire planet will agree on to get people on their side.
- Then they will say ten more things which are antagonistic, hateful and cause controversy, and division all for more clicks, likes and attention. It's a personality disorder.

Chapter 18

THE WORK LIBERTY TAKERS AND THE LINE OF PRIDE.
DO YOU KNOW WHERE YOUR LINE IS?

"Don't judge someone, until you have walked a mile in their shoes."

Mary Lathrap

1. Do you know those people at work and in life, that get shat on and trodden all over more than others?
2. Or know a boss that takes persistent liberties with their staff, and treats them like a puppet on a string?
3. Have you ever been trodden all over by a boss before?

Reminder:

Trust your gut when things are not right, you will feel it.

This is why I created the term called *"the line of pride"*. Let me explain it. Everyone has their personal line where they will eventually say to themselves during mistreatment,

"The boss is now taking the piss out of me."

So, I ask you, 'Where is your line of pride?'

Reminder:

If you're working under this type of boss, I suppose you have two options:

1) Take and accept the daily shit they give you, or
2) Try and carry the confidence, knowing life is too short, to say to the boss, "Fuck YOU. I am better than this. I'm gone."

I won't lie, I have worked under a few bullies in my career, and it is extremely hard to walk away from the job you love, but the boss you hate. The job you love often just has too much satisfaction for you to completely quit. However sometimes, it can get too much and eventually these *dickhead leaders* can cause you chronic stress. It's a conundrum because the job that you adore, makes it hard to walk away.

I appreciate many life circumstances can dictate someone's personal or professional *line of pride*, but I believe there is something sadly in the DNA of the persistently 'down-trodden' colleague that means they are the ones that accept getting mistreated day after day. Often you may have looked at these colleagues, and think they have no minerals and guts to stick up for themselves during mistreatment when the bully boss is behaving like a dictator. It is a tough life dilemma for many because in fairness to the victim, many of these 'bully bosses' are hard to fight against and manipulate as if there was an Olympic gold medal available in skulduggery. They often display the following behaviours:

- They try to control you.
- They are manipulative and Machiavellian in their behaviours.
- They often keep people at arms-length and exactly where they want them. Their behaviours are often passive aggressive.
- They use and abuse people, for as long as they can get away with it.

Reminder:

Sooner or later, you have to fight back. Simply, you have to know where *your line of pride* is.

So, I repeat, where is your line?

- Are you zero bullshit, about being treated ethically and morally? Or conversely
- Do you accept that having a 'dictator boss' is part and parcel of the modern workplace? And therefore,

- Do you think certain things are "just the way they are" and you have to bite your lip to the boss, and put up with their bullshit behaviour like our grandparent's generation X and generation Jones did?

I created the *Line of Pride* (LOP) *term,* because I believe it is a regular occurrence in modern society. Too often these bully bosses get to suppress and hinder people's confidence so often and so deeply, that often our line of pride gets moved and shifted backwards towards the:

"Acceptance of taking loads of shit line."

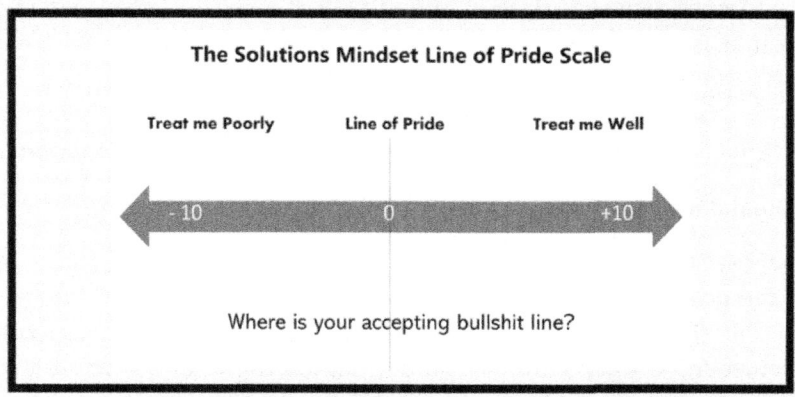

Scenario:

Day after day the boss's negative behaviour chips away at you, an email here, a negative comment there, and in the end, you gradually lose your confidence to do anything about the poor treatment.

Your 'LOP' moves from its original bassline of a good and ethical place and being quite high, suddenly to an all-time low. The bullying boss's behaviour hits you so hard, it majorly affects your health and your gut instinct and belief system start to fail you and your confidence drains to stick up for yourself.

Most people's LOP, is aligned with the moral and ethical code society tries to live by.

Many of us know the difference between:

- Right and Wrong
- Hard work and Lazy
- Kind and Unkind

But certain bosses grind you down so much, they make you lose your ability and instinct to stick up for yourself, when this constant and persistent mistreatment occurs. You become so drained, tired and confidence diffused, you don't know when the next negative email is going to give you the latest panic attack.

Solution:

"Ensure you don't let anyone move your LOP. It cannot happen".

Real life story:

I have worked in a place where the boss turns up in the car park, and grown men literally shit themselves on his arrival. Complete panic sets in, because no one knows what mood he is going to be in when he walks through the door. It led to the entire workforce who worked under him, all wearing armour (Chapter 4).

- Not one person was their true authentic self, when he was in the room.
- Not one person respected his presence.
- Just ALL GROWN-UP ALPHA MALE MEN IN FEAR.

Everyone would complain about him, call him a prick behind his back, a weirdo and whatever else, but no one would do anything about it. Some people did walk out and leave their job, because they knew where their own line of pride was, but it was alarming to see how many people put up with the bullying tactics, and their line of pride was also therefore shifted to:

"Just accepting that being bullied was the norm for everyone."

Advice:

Don't put up with these wankers. Back yourself and challenge them, or alternatively walk away and go and work elsewhere. You deserve better. Simply... Have your line of pride and stick to it!

HOW NOT BE A LEADERSHIP D*CKHEAD

HOW NOT BE A LEADERSHIP D*CKHEAD

Chapter 19

LEADERSHIP SIMPLIFIED

"A person who feels appreciated will always do more than what is expected."

Amy Rees Anderson

My brother who is an Executive Headteacher in Asia, once said to me three things:

1) To be a good leader, you have to be able to take your people on a journey.

2) If you want a good job done, ask a busy person.

3) Most of the time 20% of the people, do 80% of the work.

What are your thoughts? Is this accurate from your lens?

What are your thoughts on particular leadership styles?

- What is it to you?
- What should it look like in your eyes?
- How does it feel to you and others when you are being led poorly or well?
- What does it look like and feel like to lead a group of people for yourself?

In order to simplify the leadership topic, I believe leaders work in two ways:

- Through love, or
- Through fear

A third, a third, and a third method:

I have lived leadership, having led people in schools and football clubs for many years. One school I worked in, there were over 200 teaching staff and 2,600 pupils. Trust me, that is a lot of personalities to manage. In the past, I have line-managed eighteen people at one time. Of these eighteen:

- Approximately six were exceptional practitioners,
- Six were bang average, and
- Six were simply inadequate.

As mentioned before, I would say those ratios are probably the norm in most industries:

- What are your ratios and experiences of effective staff in your field of work?
- Do they differ to mine?

The best of these six staff, I didn't need to lead at all, as they led themselves with classy behaviours. The middle six needed regular monitoring, but once monitored effectively were successful in their roles. The bottom six were often hard work to manage and required rigorous monitoring, support, life coaching, counselling (whatever we decide to call it) and still could not perform more consistently and effectively.

Like most underperforming people, I will admit that it was a drain on my time and resources, but we must remember it was still my duty of care to support these people whether they were high achievers or not. I suppose in the corporate world these under performers would not be carried like the education system often allows, but on reflection, I suppose my super strength is that I had to develop the underperformers because, I had no choice. You cannot just hire and fire teachers in the education system in the same way as the corporate environment. (I will mention *the improve or replace method* in later chapters).

HOW NOT BE A LEADERSHIP D*CKHEAD

Advice:

You only need line management protocols for shit people.

My best Headteacher Paul Petty used to say to me:

"Sallis you only need line management for incompetent people. For good staff? just let them be."

I have been thinking about a leadership definition for this chapter for a while and have summarised it as this. I see effective leadership as:

"The genuine and authentic ability to influence people."

Now, of course there are many variables, styles and subjectivity when it comes to the topic of leadership. Situations and context are key of course, but my questions below are worth reflecting on and hopefully will help you consider your actions and behaviours in your own applied work:

- How to lead in a certain way. (Are you KPI driven? People driven? More strategic or more operational?)

- Why do you lead in a certain way? (What is your why for making leadership decisions? Do you micro-manage or let people feel free?)

- When to lead in a certain way (Do you change your leadership style for the various people you lead and situations that occur?

- Who to lead in a certain way (Are you differentiating your leadership style to suit different people? Do you know their specific needs and what gets them motivated?)

- What to lead in a certain way. (What are your Short/Medium/Long term targets, and how well do you make decisions to measure them and set interventions off the targets?) How well do you plan, do and then review?

Understanding Data:

A good teacher friend Mikey Williams once said this to me about his school.

"Sallis, we are so "data rich and system poor" in our school it is frightening. We have all this data for data's sake, and someone has forgotten, we are actually dealing with the lives of children. It's a people business."

So, regarding the data conundrum what are my thoughts?

In elite sport it is undoubtably important to use data. With data we are able to validate what our eyes see, into a fact, and not an opinion, with far greater clarity and rigour. As an example, in football.

1. Distance covered by each player to the nearest metre.
2. Sprint Distance covered to the nearest 0.01 of a second.
3. Possession statistics
4. Chances that are created on international statistical algorithms. Known as xG

Advice:

It is majorly important to not always take data literally. People that know me well in the work arena, know I live by the following:

"Not everything, that counts can be counted, and not everything that can be counted counts."

The reason the above quote is dynamite is because we need to use the data we collect:

1. To *inform our learning* and
2. Not always measure it.

So many people take data literally! The questions should be, what is the data telling us? And not always used as measuring KPIs in isolation.

HOW NOT BE A LEADERSHIP D*CKHEAD

Reminder:

Unless artificial intelligence takes over the world it is important to remember we are still in the people business. We will always need analytics of course, yet my advice is to be mindful of being data rich and systematically poor. The methods above are a highly simplified structure to get you thinking strategically about the how, the why, the when, the who and the what; with a little *data usage* sprinkled in you have the dream ticket to high performance.

I will attempt to give you my version of effective leadership, and what I believe it should look like. In my lifetime, I have worked under more bad leaders than good ones. The eleven headteachers I worked for, over the two decades were varied in ability and capability. Two were truly exceptional; five were average and the rest were useless:

Further questions:

- Have you really thought deeply about what qualities a good leader needs?
- Does leadership in sport differ from leadership in business or education?
- Does, and should, a leader's style change, at the differing levels of work hierarchy? (middle to senior leadership etc)
- What is the more important quality in a leader: autocracy or democracy?
- Or is it a mix of both? If so... Where, when, and why do you use both styles?

The diagram on page 157 poses some great questions regarding one's ability in the first place to execute the role they are hired for. In reality, I would like you to think about:

1. Your capability and
2. Have you got the capacity to deliver what you are asked to do?

HOW NOT BE A LEADERSHIP D*CKHEAD

Let me apply this for you with a real-life example from my final job in education:

I was heavily stitched up the moment I walked in the door as a Senior Leader. I inherited a failing Science department which two previous colleagues had failed at before me. I was also in charge of humanities, leading on teaching and learning in the entire school, teaching Physical Education, Geography, Maths (which I had never taught before to the worst class in the school) and teaching 20 periods out of the 30 available in the week. In addition to all these responsibilities, I had to also support every break and lunch duty five days a week, which meant having no breaks myself and making my emotional cup emptier by the hour.

My ability as a leader was unquestioned at this stage of my career, and my track record proved I was clearly capable over many years. However, the issue I had was the Headteacher above me, failing to give me the *capacity (ie; time and support)* to support my people with long lasting sustainable changes.

(NB: Another problem with many businesses is making changes that are rarely sustainable. Many make quick-fix, short-term decisions, but undermine everyone else in the longer process).

At this stage in my career, I could have been seen as potentially incompetent, however I backed myself and demanded in my line management meetings with the headteacher that he should change the staffing structures otherwise I was out of there and would resign. I knew what was right and what was wrong and wasn't a yes man for anyone. I never have been. My line of pride was red hot at this stage.

I was aware that crisis management across the school was generally horrific and other leaders in the school were getting sacked left right and centre, by the so-called Super Headteacher who was in fact the ultimate blagger, and a fucking fraud. He would regularly hire people and then stitch them up. He didn't serve anyone except himself. One day he tapped me on my shoulder like he was my father and told me to go and sort out a behavioural issue in the dinner hall. The bloke was on £200,000 a year plus salary. I looked at him like, "Go fuck yourself!" I'm thinking, "Firstly, don't tap me on the shoulder you are not my dad, and secondly go and sort the issue out yourself, you're the leader!"

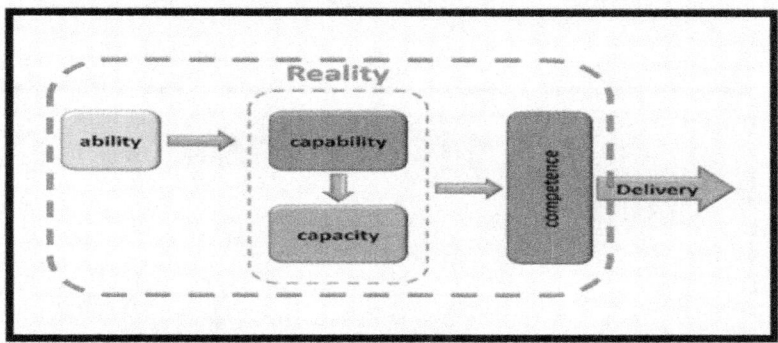

The Weak Leader Brigade:
In general, the useless overpaid headteachers I worked for included too many blaggers with horrific people skills, work shy wasters (yes, you heard it they were lazy), and serial bullshitters. Some were totally out of their depth and lacked complete authenticity. To be fair to some of them - many had solid subject knowledge around the topic of education, but just had piss poor subject knowledge around their ability to lead people.

In addition to this, a few of them lacked a personality for you to believe in them at all. They were unassertive, lacked conviction, and displayed many other traits that were just generally negative. In summary, you just couldn't believe in them as a person or a leader, which is why authenticity is the answer to excellence.

Reminder:

I believe it is paramount that aspiring great leaders need 'personality gears' in their toolbox and to ensure they are not one-paced. That does not mean behave inconsistently and be a lunatic but have the capability to shift from calm and measured to then being highly assertive and able to make decisions with conviction and ease.

- How many personality gears have you got?
- Can you move between these gears when required?

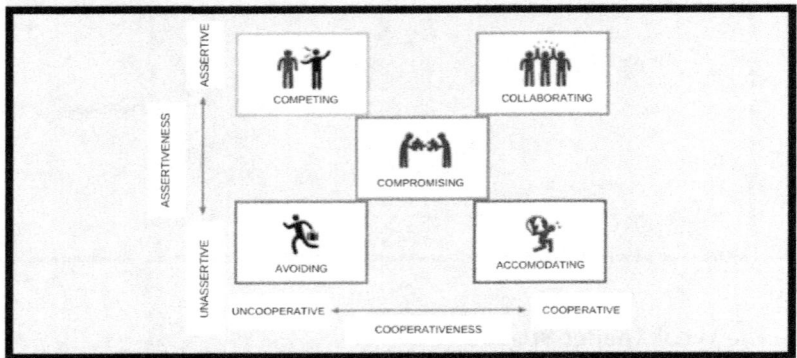

As mentioned in Chapter 15. The singer not the song...

What was missing?
But the main qualities that were missing from these weak leaders was their absence of a clear vision, strategic inability, and the lack of passion to take people on a journey with them. Other shitty traits these leaders would portray were that they would regularly say:

- "Me" instead of "WE".
- "My school" and "I" instead of "our school, and us".

I used to sit and listen to these headteachers and think:

"It ain't your school mate. It is OUR school."

These small examples are yet again a strong sign that a leader is internally focused. Success and failure give us clues and my goodness this lot were geniuses at that. They were unconscious about their dialect, and this lack of self-awareness generally stinks the room out in most places.

Leaders need many qualities, of course; they need to be approachable, positive, emotionally consistent, generous, and humble. Linking to humble leaders my dad used to say,

"Act like you cannot afford bread, until they find out you own the bakery."

Leaders also need to display high levels of integrity. But in very simple terms, I believe leaders need three main qualities:

- A clear vision and strategy that they follow through.
- High levels of subject knowledge in their relevant field.
- People skills.

Why do I say this so simplistically?
It has to be simplistic and brilliant basics have to be applied. Life is complex enough. Another reminder that "less, is often more". And the best leaders know when to press the less is more button and just get the job done. Too many leaders suffer from paralysis by analysis, and this overthinking causes a lack of execution with regards to their decision making.

The naturally unlikeable yet highly effective leader:

Have you worked for a boss who:

1. Had unbelievably good subject knowledge and knows *everything about everything and* gets great results in your place of work…
2. However, they are *unlikeable* as a person?

These types of bosses are often so knowledgeable, you cannot help but at least respect them for this quality, however they consistently show poor people skills. Many of these leaders lack effective and consistent emotional control and are experts at cutting you down with their sharp tongue in team meetings, whilst adopting a draconian and autocratic manner in their day-to-day interactions.

HOW NOT BE A LEADERSHIP D*CKHEAD

The problem for us lot lower down below in the hierarchy is that these dickheads get the company good results year after year. The executive team above this type of leader are not bothered about the rest of the people in the building. All they care about is their end of year bonuses.

In summary, this type of leader isn't likely to be on your Christmas card list and won't ever be placed in your *legacy leader* category either, but they can be effective.

"Forgive me, I did not mean to jest about your dictatorial leadership style."

The Charismatic Boss:

Then there are the charisma-style bosses:

1. They are super savvy at employing a good team around them
2. Often lead by being the masters of delegation
3. Great at the use of a highly democratic approach to their people.
4. Lead with aspiration and praise
5. Yet they may have little subject knowledge
6. But they get away with this professional technical flaw in their toolbox because they keep their staff motivated.

This, in turn, keeps business flowing, as staff members feel consistently valued by the leader's charm and personal touch.

162

www.leadershipmindset.uk

HOW NOT BE A LEADERSHIP D*CKHEAD

The contrast of this leadership style however, is often over the long-term, people can get pissed off with these types of bosses for not always getting shit done, as their loose, relaxed and laissez-faire leadership style means they often lack an effective and consistent approach to actioning things.

After all, we all hate a boss who is consistently inconsistent. They say they'll get it done and never do, however are so bloody friendly and genuine it is hard to get properly annoyed with them.

Now, clearly, I have been very basic in my evaluation of these two types of leaders, but to put it simply, combining the two examples together as a combination into one, are the key ingredients to creating an A-grade leader. When hinged together, these two would create an explicitly strong leader who would possess:

- A diverse, relevant, and super strong subject knowledge
- Enable staff to have intellectual freedom
- Lead with charm, charisma, authenticity and
- Most importantly have a clear direction of where the bus is heading and help drive it to its destination.

Reminder:

Now, regarding charisma, I am not talking about a David Brent-type 'charm'. (Remember the annoying character from the TV show *The Office?*) I mean sincere, authentic, and emotionally intelligent leadership that when needed, engages the hearts and minds of the workplace. These leaders possess positive traits, such as being in control under pressure, kindness, a caring nature and being both inspirational and aspirational, plus many other facets of what great leaders implement with regularity.

Additionally, please note:

"These managers are also good decision makers and are not afraid to upset people on occasions."

HOW NOT BE A LEADERSHIP D*CKHEAD

Advice:

You cannot always be a 'people pleaser' in leadership. A major rule in leadership is that you cannot keep all people happy, all of the time, and that is something, great working cultures understand. All levels of hierarchy must respect each other's position in the business, and everyone's respective lens on the world.

Reminder:

Please remind yourself that often great cultures are very aware of the need for certain people to be good at *following,* rather than always having too many leaders with egos getting in the way. Yes, you heard it, you don't need too many people challenging the system. Leaders need good followers in their team and cannot succeed if they have a load of disruptors in the building. It is too much hard work and kills the rhythmic flow. In schools we had a term called critical friends. These are the people that tell you the truth, but in a way that does not affect your relationship over the long term. Healthy disrespect basically.

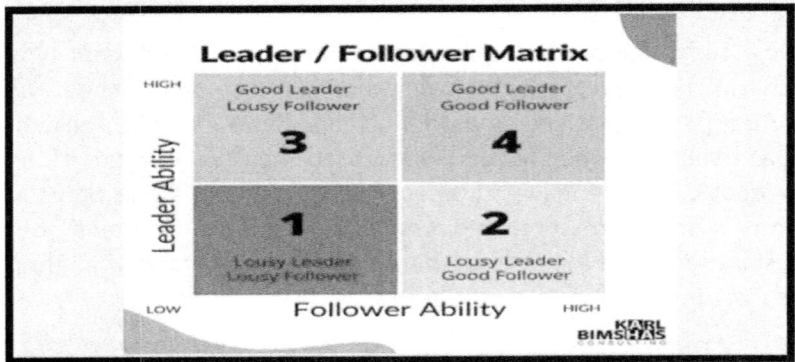

Sporting Leadership:

Looking at the assessment of leadership and managers in the football industry, as mentioned in chapter four, the German Jurgen Klopp stands out for me. I would play for him more than any of his contemporaries. In my opinion, his interesting and diverse background and journey, aligned with his unbelievably high levels of emotional intelligence shine through in the media, compared to other managers such as Conte and Mourinho who cannot handle the Gen Z's. Let me emphasise that a manager's media persona isn't necessarily their training ground one, but taking this topic on face value is important.

Forget about results and success for a moment, because we could argue about successful leaders in sport for years to come. In sport, I firmly believe it is dangerous to always see success as the ability to win trophies – it is obvious by observing Klopp's professional and personal agenda that his 'why' is much greater than just winning matches.

- I truly believe he wants to help the city of Liverpool reconnect and achieve together.
- He wants to build a club, and he wants to do it with honesty, dignity, and pride.

In interviews, he regularly smiles and portrays the soft skills that many of his peers do not. He talks openly to the media (in another language than his own) and regularly uses humour and humility. On the other hand, over the last few years in particular, Conte has often been defensive in personality (this was written before his Tottenham exit). And, when questioned, 90 per cent of the time he will claim it is someone else's problem. Even the average sports fan can see straight through fake leadership.

I believe the Portuguese maverick Jose Mourinho is also a closed, defensive character, and majorly missed the millennial and gen z boat generation. When he first came to the premiership in 2004, he was a breath of fresh air by claiming, with his unbelievable arrogance, that he was the 'special one'.

Quick Fix Leaders:

Like some quick fixes in business these types of leaders are well known to only be around clubs for a short period. They are in and out, get quick results and then fuck off. This style often has instant impact, but it holds no long-term strategy for the progress of the business. Mourinho, has been highly successful, but we could get into a debate over whether he's about to be 'found out' concerning his leadership style.

Has he understood generations millennial or 'z'? I personally don't think so.

Adapting:

Are you adapting to meet the needs of our changing society? Remember that to be an effective leader, you have to manage two ways.

1. Up towards the board and
2. Down towards your team and staff.

You may have the board above you, putting demands on you to succeed, while the staff below require your help and guidance. It's a seriously tough job being a middle leader at times. My advice is to use the Mckinsey 7'S Framework as a structure for you.

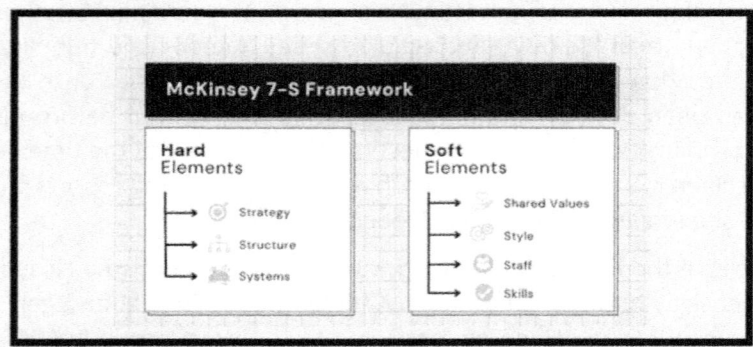

In the above strategy, Mckinsey talks about strong/hard skills and soft skills. The model was developed in the 1970s by two consultants at McKinsey PLC - Tom Peters and Robert Waterman. They identified the seven elements above that they believe an organisation needs for it to be high performing. I have often used it in my training to be able to support my clients.

Political Spectrum:

I wish we could see more dignity at the top level in modern politics. The level of conduct and behaviour in the house of commons is shocking. Jeering and heckling one another is seen as normal practice.

Advice:

It is not normal nor appropriate to undermine someone. But this lot of current politicians are so institutionalised by themselves that they all keep behaving like this because it has been the same for decades. I acknowledge that many senior politicians are more knowledgeable about their subject than I will ever be, I just wish they would respect society and each other a little more.

It's a really tough job, which the average armchair twitter warrior doesn't always appreciate. Including me! But I do not think they help themselves at times. Another example of looking in the mirror and not out of the window will help their reputation.

Measuring Success:

What's interesting in the sporting arena is that there are many world-class leaders who have all been highly successful in the past. Amazingly however, if any they fail to win the league they are working in, they will probably be perceived as failures by their own supporters, board members and beyond! This is what I call false judgment and where post-truth is highly evident.

> ***"Leadership is all about adding value to what you have and nothing else."***

Which leaders ensure their teams make the most progress with the resources available and the capacity given to them?
In rugby, Graham Henry and Clive Woodward are legends of the sport who added value to what they inherited.

John Wooden the basketball coaching guru of the 1970's, was quoted as saying:

"I think that in any group activity – whether it be business, sports or family – there has to be leadership that adds value, or it won't be successful."

The educationalist William Arthur Wood once stated that:

"Leadership is based on inspiration, not domination, on co-operation, not intimidation."

So, what about the leaders who rule through fear?

- The ones who have one default behavioural setting, which is to intimidate people.
- The ones who regularly belittle and supress the thoughts and feelings of others.
- The ones who are passive aggressive.

I regard them as narcissistic leaders who are often passive aggressive in their approach. They can act friendly one day and cold the next. This type of leader generally wants control and compliance over people. They struggle to delegate and when they do, complain about your work. Often, they hide their aggression behind emails. Please note these types of people are often emotionally in personal turmoil.

Advice:

You must not hate these leaders, however, but instead feel sorry for them. They are more than likely afraid and living life with fear instead of hope. They are naturally negative instead of positive, and although they won't show they are scared, they are certainly feeling it inside. Whenever they grind you down with these behaviours, just remember that better is around the corner and that they are intrinsically lonely people. These leaders have very few authentic relationships in the workplace and beyond.

HOW NOT BE A LEADERSHIP D*CKHEAD

HOW NOT BE A LEADERSHIP D*CKHEAD

Chapter 20

LEADERSHIP UN-SIMPLIFIED AND THE NARCISSIST 'HEAD FUCK' LEADER

"Since narcissists deep down feel themselves to be faultless, it is inevitable that when they are in conflict with the world, they will invariably perceive the conflict as the world's fault."

M. Scott Peck

I have been wanting to write this chapter for years to be honest, as I have encountered so many narcissistic leaders on my journey. I felt I needed to bring their shitty behaviour to the masses, and help support people in need, and enhance your ability to identify them as quickly as possible. Do you know one? Are they wayward? Unhelpful? Messing with your head?

I learnt many years ago:

"You can't reason, with an unreasonable person."

The narcissist leader is regularly unreasonable, and they show consistent and dysfunctional behaviours to deceive, intimidate, manipulate, coerce, or unfairly punish others to get what they want for themselves.

HOW NOT BE A LEADERSHIP D*CKHEAD

A definition of a narcissist is as follows:

"A person who has an excessive interest in, or admiration of, themselves."

The Story:

In Greek mythology, a young hunter called Narcissus, was cursed by the goddess of revenge, Nemesis, and he became so obsessed with his own reflection in a pool of water, to the point where he ends up drowning in it.

Today, millions of people around the world are similarly obsessed with their own electronic reflection and ego, by taking daily "selfie" images and posting them to Facebook, Twitter, and Instagram. Jean Twenge and W. Keith Campbell, authors of *The Narcissism Epidemic* (2009) state:

"The United States is suffering from an epidemic of narcissism, and the rise in narcissism is accelerating."

With Leadership in mind, a definition of a *narcissistic leader* is as follows:

"Narcissistic leadership is a leadership style in which the leader is only interested in him/herself. Their priority is themselves – at the expense of their people/group members. This leader exhibits the characteristics of a narcissist: arrogance, dominance and hostility."

Advice:

Narc leaders need to get identified and removed from the workplace asap. They are scumbags. If you spot one, be brave and challenge them, and if you cannot find the energy to do so, please walk away. They will mess with your heart and soul if you allow it. I have been there.

Corporate Narcissism:

Author Alan Downs, who wrote the great book, 'Beyond the Looking Glass' mentions corporate narcissism occurs more often, when a narcissist gets to the role of the chief executive officer (CEO) or other leadership roles within a senior management team. Furthermore, he states they are likely to gather a crew of co-dependents around them, in order to support their shitty narcissistic behaviour. As I have previously mentioned in this book. 'Like finds like'.

Alarmingly, further research from Mary Abbajay, says:

> *"It takes up to 22 months to emotionally and psychologically recover from the trauma of a psycho, crazy, bully, tyrannical, screaming, egomaniac boss."*

These narcissists can often obsess about company allegiance to your face, but in reality, are only really committed to number one...themselves. Strategic decision making is normally initiated on the narcissist leader's own interests, rather than the interests of the business as a whole. The result:

> *"A certain kind of charismatic leader can run a successful company on meticulously unwholesome principles."*

This is often where many grey areas occur because, many of these narcissistic leaders can still get good results yet mistreat colleague after colleague in the process. Their line managers (the board members) often, just see the enhanced profit as the only important and measurable KPI that matters. This obsession with narrow ended KPIs, is why the narcissist leaders often get away with their unethical behaviour time and again. So, beware. Often, they can perform falsely well.

Here are my "Negative Nine" of the narcissistic leader.

1. Desire to be admired
Narcissistic leaders have a great longing to be admired, and they usually tend to have a number of star-struck followers as well. Narcissists have a gift of attracting followers, and they do so with their highly developed verbal skills and articulate ways. Narc leaders are usually very skilful speakers, charming to the people they need to be with, and can deliver moving speeches. There is no shortage of charisma in many narcissistic leaders.

2. Unable to take criticism
Narcissists are deep down extremely sensitive, and this makes them particularly sensitive to any sort of criticism and feedback which hits their ego hard. They are unable to take criticism constructively, and their normal reaction is to attack people in return. They cannot tolerate being challenged and non-conformists get booted out. The narc leader is often abrasive with those who dare voice a negative opinion against the processes of the workplace. Complete control is the focus for the narc leader.

3. Inability to listen or don't want to listen
Narc leaders are horrific listeners, so don't go talking to them about a problem as they won't want to listen. Their disinterest in listening presumably develops as a defence to keep them from acknowledging any sort of criticism. Narc leaders also believe that hierarchy's rule, and people beneath them in hierarchy do not have much to contribute. Additionally, when there is a problem for them, they are the kings and queens of burying their head in the sand, and when their head comes out of the sand, they blame someone else.

4. Dysfunctional Relationships
Leaders with narcissistic disorder will not hesitate to devalue or humiliate others with no sense of remorse. They simply have no filter about giving a shit. They are ruthless and often emotionally void. They can often be ice cold in their actions.

5. Inconsistency
When narc leaders turn destructive, you must run for the hills. These people have no values about who they trample on. They are fickle and change direction often. They are easily bored and will snap at the nearest victim.

6. Kingdom building
Some narc leaders want to take over the world and create an empire. Beware however, as they will crush anyone and everyone in the process. They want to leave behind a huge legacy, and therefore actively seek to expand their influence, hire more 'yes men', or increase their reach and authority within the business. A narc entrepreneur will often keep creating one company after another.

7. Lack of empathy
While they themselves crave for empathy and understanding from others, narcissists themselves are not the most empathetic people. Some of the most charismatic and successful narcissists are not known for empathy. Reminder that a lack of empathy can be seen as actually a strength in times of chaos, but narc leaders couldn't give two fucks about the feelings, emotions, and welfare of their workforce.

8. Competitive
And narc leader is ruthlessly competitive. They are relentless in their pursuit of success. They take games seriously and see them as a test of their strength and survival skills. Since many narcissists have little moral conscience, they are quite capable of doing whatever it takes to win and stab people in the back on that journey.

9. They are shit mentors
Since they lack any sort of empathy it is very difficult for a narcissistic leader to actually mentor somebody properly or be mentored themselves. If they do mentor, they instruct rather than

coach and try to make their protégés out to be smaller versions of themselves.

Please remember my final point about these leaders is that they have most likely been hurt at some time in their life.

Because it is important to remember that:

"Hurt people...Hurt people..."

Chapter 21

BUILDING TEAMS:
IMPROVE THEM OR REPLACE THEM? IS RETENTION AND RECRUITMENT STILL AN ISSUE? THE POWER OF 'LEARNING CONVERSATIONS'

"If bad, is 5X stronger than good, eliminating bad does a lot of good. Bad eggs may not appreciate how they drain and diminish others."

Steve Sallis

A Senior Manager Ryan Orton, and a client of the brilliant recruitment company called Orbis who I support regularly, recently texted me and said thank you for all the help in getting them back to better levels of work-based performance. What did I really do, however? It goes as simply as this:

- He contacted me.
- We had a learning conversation.
- I asked how he felt, and why he felt it.
- I gave him some possible solutions.
- Asked him and others to fill out my Solutionsmindset.com leadership matrix and reflect on it for a week and then come back to me.

Solution:
He felt better about the direction they were heading in, and thus became more confident about his gut feeling to achieve a consistent high performing business.

My stance with the company was primarily a questions-based approach, or for more business-minded people, I used *coaching and meta-cognition* to help them lead with a larger toolbox of processes, so they had the opportunity to solve their problems without my help.

HOW NOT BE A LEADERSHIP D*CKHEAD

Reminder:

I often have the answers to the professional and personal development issues with my clients, but *choose* not to always give them, as I believe with my help over a period of time, they can find the solutions themselves. After that's the art of educating right?

Most importantly however, I tell clients to go and talk to their peers first and foremost, to agree on a set of interventions, so they are able to find solutions to the problems they encounter.

Let me give you a scenario:

A person you line-manage has been having a bad run of performance at work. A week ago, year ago or a month ago, they were 9/10 every week and everyone was singing their praises and saying how effective their work performance had been.

So, what do you do?

If you apply this above scenario to any business or high-performance environment, it is clear that any individual or business has good and bad days. Therefore, questions around these scenarios could be:

1. Did these people turn into bad work colleagues overnight?
2. Does a period of poor performance = a bad colleague who you want out the door straight away?
3. Does someone else's gossiping say more about themselves, than the person in need of help?
4. Have you ever made the link between bad work performance and the dickhead leader? ie: The manager being crap at their job, being the sole reason under performance from everyone else occurs.

I'll let you reflect on the below...

Remember all people on this planet are so varied and complex. It still amazes me when managers across all industries have a fixed mindset towards what they want from situations, rather than the needs of the individual they are leading or the company they work for.

Reminder:

'EVERYONE IS DIFFERENT'

In sporting terms, the art of player and team progression is the leader's ability to be adaptive to the learning needs of all players, ALL of the time. Basically, what I'm saying, is that every manager's job is fundamentally quite simple and straightforward. And that it is to:

1. Maximise the skills of every individual and
2. Get this individual's skillset to fit into the team dynamic and performance journey for all. Like piecing a jigsaw.

The hard part of leadership is tough conversations. Telling shit people who you have tried to help for several months, that they are still under performing and placing them on capability procedure. That is never an easy process.

Reminder:

I must remind you that the horrible process of telling your under-performing staff the truth, is what bosses get paid for. A higher salary means more responsibility and potentially more crap to deal with. So beware: You must be brave enough to have difficult conversations even if you don't want to. It's an art. My advice. Use the shit sandwich technique.

Constructive/Positive/Constructive

Many leaders struggle to have difficult conversations and many just tend to shy away from them by burying their head in the sand and hope the confrontation goes away. We all know however, it never does. It just makes the problems worse. So, front it, and don't fake it.

Assessing staff quality:

As I mentioned before, many people probably haven't heard the term 'assessment for learning' (AFL). To put it simply, this is probably the most significant key driver for institutional improvement in UK schools, (along with lots of the great teachers of course). When I started work at my first failing school, AFL was what the entire people improvement process was built around. This included strategies for the staff and the students.

So, what is it? Let me explain.

It is based around how various assessment methods improve the performance of the people in the building. In simple terms:

1. How you measure and know where you are at
2. Awareness of what you need to do to improve, and the further interventions from that.

AFL methods are as follows:

- **Self-assessment** – Knowledge of one's own strengths and areas for development.
- **Manager/coach assessment** - Teachers/Coaches/Bosses knowledge of pupils/players/staff strengths and areas for development.
- **Peer assessment** – Peers/teammates knowledge of your strengths and areas for development.
- **Summative assessment** - Using data, test scores, testing and KPIs to assess human performance.
- **Formative assessment** – Using learning conversations, target setting and scaffolded learning techniques to discuss with learners what they do well and how to fine-tune strategies to improve.

All of the above = THE SCIENCE OF LEARNING

What I am trying to highlight is that formative assessment strategies (to inform the learner of things they need to do to improve) is the number one component for people development. This in turn creates opportunities for 'accelerated learning', which is a topic I mentioned in my previous book. It's meaning?

HOW NOT BE A LEADERSHIP D*CKHEAD

"People simply progress quicker and learn faster!"

I mean who doesn't want that for their people in the office? Many people I have worked with closely will have heard me talk about 'learning conversations'. What I mean is, that we need to talk about learning as much as we do about performance. They are not always the same. In support of this the Department for Education are quoted as saying the following:

Pupils' progress is accelerated when they are clear about the success criteria for the intended outcomes and are able to judge the quality of their own work and know how to improve it."

So, in simple terms:

1. Know what you are good at.
2. Know where the bus is heading.
3. Know what you need to do to improve.

Reflections:

Managers in most industries often have a great level of subject knowledge, but their intervention techniques to support staff are often flawed. As an example in sporting realms, the reason elite athletes have extended periods of *bad form, under performance,* and therefore sustained professional and personal issues is generally because a lack of support and love from the staff who are supposed to be helping them. The Boss!

This professional isolation creates a sink or swim culture which any aspiring business needs to try and avoid. You may disagree and be that workplace ruthless dickhead, but I just think these types of leaders get found out eventually as they either:

1. Don't want to help people or
2. Don't know how to.

Real life Study:

I recently spoke to one COO who new in role, and mentioned, the CEO (his boss), knew loads about banking and trading floors of which he had been a part for 25 years (High Calibre), but ignored most of his staffs phone calls all fucking week, which meant that no one could talk to him about any issues they had (Low Character). Surely ignorance cannot help performance! Being an outstanding banker does not mean you can lead a team of bankers. If you cannot find the time to talk to your people and serve them = You're a fraud.

Of course, we know that poor performance is inevitable in any business at certain times. So, the question that needs to be asked is this:

Question:

Why don't more business leaders try to improve the staff instead of always replacing them?

Answer:
Because they haven't got the duty of care, moral compass or skillset to do so. Firing someone is the easier option.

My experiences in professional football around the *improve or replace* strategy and people development is completely underwhelming. Historically very few managers have the full package of tools required or the acumen to:

1. Help players improve in all areas which include tactically, technically, physically, and psychologically.
2. But most of all personally, as human beings.

Although fortunately with the new school coaches of modern times, it is changing. Most of the time, they pick (recruit) the players, and then spend the whole week moaning about them and often for the entire game/season. Moreover, if the player is underperforming, they just choose the easy option and replace them with someone else and the *replace, replace, replace* merry-go-round continues.

Recruitment merry-go-round:

HOW NOT BE A LEADERSHIP D*CKHEAD

I am seeing and hearing that this major leadership and self-awareness flaw is the norm in many industries and not just in the sporting world. It is actually quite sad, that these so-called leaders are the ones who are performing poorly, not the actual people they are supposed to serve.

Recruitment Industry Reflections:

In the UK recruitment industry, I hear the staff 'merry-go-round' is common. Managers simply replace people, instead of actually improving them. Often companies are so ruthless that they discard people for under-performance very quickly, instead of helping them as the first intervention and implementing a pit stop of support that they should apply within the business structure. Fortunately, the recruitment companies I support are not like this and are great at looking in the mirror.

Be Creative:

Consequently, I advise bosses to get creative when making their staff better, instead of doing the potentially easy and normal option of sacking people, otherwise the recruiting process starts all over again and everyone is back to square one. Maya Angelou once stated, "You can't use up creativity," so get creative!

Managing the Pressure:

Now, I am not undermining the pressure that companies are under to ensure the people in their building *deliver* what they are employed and paid for. All managers and leaders in every industry carry that burden of pressure to ensure profits improve. I get it. Results and profits keep businesses open and thriving. But remember pressure is a privilege. Keep your shit together in crisis. Panic leads to more panic. So, keep pumping the tyres of your staff.

HOW NOT BE A LEADERSHIP D*CKHEAD

Reminder:

My experiences in my career have helped me be creative and have a different mindset towards people development. An example of my adapted mindset from my time in schools is as follows:

- The kids in the school building simply cannot be replaced for under performance, compared with adults in businesses.
- In schools, you have to work your arse off as a leader in order to make the pupils achieve and improve. After a bad day, week, or term, you can't just replace the pupils and bin them off to another school. They're going to be with you for up to seven years.
- You therefore don't have the same choices as a business, which basically handpick and choose each and every one of the staff they employ, and then normally moan about them.
- In schools we put in literally hundreds of interventions of support to enable our young people to smash life and education. I have therefore noticed huge differences between education and business, and it is glaring. Education is miles ahead in this way.
- Leadership culture and behaviour from many businesses isn't as ethical as it should be, nor is it what I believe to be true and genuine leadership. Greed takes over sadly.

So, in summary, people improvement requires:

- Shit hot knowledge (technical skills) about the industry or subject you work in.
- AFL strategies that are rigorous both in a formal and informal nature throughout the working week. Supported by your quarterly performance management processes.
- Great businesses have structures that are not flaky. They have rigour.
- Remember the use of RAG ratings = Red, Amber, Green is the simplest and best way to create clarity of learning for anyone)

- The ability to impart sound knowledge to your staff so that they understand in a crystal-clear fashion:

1. What do they do well, and
2. What do they/we need to do, to be better.

Otherwise, replacing people for underperformance is the only strategy you have available to you. The main point I would like to emphasise is:

Why wouldn't you have both?

Advice:

1. Create a team "accountability" pledge to keep everyone working to high standards and motivated along the journey.
2. Then monitor these pledges with consistency and regularity. Often, I walk into football clubs that have all these impressive words on the wall which in reality mean sod all as not everyone lives by them.

Reminder:

Motivation =

Direction + Persistence + Effort + Intensity towards a GOAL.

HOW NOT BE A LEADERSHIP D*CKHEAD

Chapter 22

FOLLOW THE PROCESS ... AND YOU GET PROGRESS

"If you can't describe what you are doing as a process, then you don't know what you're doing."

W. Edwards Deming

As already mentioned in chapter 14, one of the greatest development words I know is 'tacit'. A reminder of its meaning. The stuff that you do, but you cannot always explain. Have you ever heard your child say:

"Mum, mum I can do it, but I just don't know how."

As mentioned earlier in chapter 14, the opposite of tacit, is explicit. This means:

1. You are able to articulate, how you know and what you know, in a clear and coherent way. In relation to this type of knowledge base.

Einstein once said:

"If you can't explain something simply, you don't understand it well enough."

This quote is therefore very aligned with explicit knowledge. Another meaning of explicit is as follows:

"Stated clearly and in detail, leaving no room for confusion or doubt."

When employees in businesses have access to useful and explicit knowledge from others, this undoubtably enhances the potential success of your business.

HOW NOT BE A LEADERSHIP D*CKHEAD

Reminder:

"Businesses can move much faster, when the organisation knows, what the organisation knows."

The above quote is highly significant, and I ask you to reflect on this. From my experience, knowledge held purely in the heads of one or two employees will be detrimental to the long-term success of the business. Leaders at all levels of hierarchy need to have a sound working knowledge of the business as a whole. In football terms this would be called, inter-disciplinary.

As an example, when I was a senior leader in education, I wasn't in charge of safeguarding, but I needed to have a sound understanding of its protocols. This shared and collaborative thinking is paramount and ensures others can take advantage of the 'know how' of their peers. I have often called the game of football 'movement chess', and I see business as the same.

What do I mean?
Transferable super strengths across departments in both fields is vital. As mentioned, inter disciplinary is the way to become truly high performance. 'We not Me'...

However this inclusive type of *thinking and doing*, requires one key element which I call 'mental agility'. Sadly, many businesses or humans do not possess this trait in abundance. Too many have a narrow lens.

- Do you see work as a game of chess?
- People or process first?
- Or maybe a human jigsaw - attempting to piece together a **'people centred'** process whilst at the same time trying to create a high performing environment?

The priority in sport is to, over a season (10 months), acquire the cognitive ability to 'out-think' your opponents, week in and week out. This is the same in business - trying to gain an advantage over your competitors. The comparisons between the two industries are majorly aligned.

Reminder:

For success to happen in business, you cannot think about the end point (victory/outcome) too often. You need to stay in the now and be entirely process driven. Other examples of this include:
- A process that is repeatable.
- A process that is flexible, and not rigid (mental agility).
- A process which is specific (Where is your north star?) and has an established start, middle and end points.
- A process that is measurable.

I am a big believer in the following:

"What gets measured gets done."

All of the above are examples about having *a plan and strategy* in order to know where you are going. And, as the title of this chapter suggests, a process! As another sporting example, there is nothing more frustrating than hearing team managers stating to their players,

"This is a must-win game today."

After all, that's the bloody obvious! These nonsensical and *outcome focussed* statements are ridiculous, and still happen in sport and business to this day. Alternatively, I see the reality more like this, where leaders are entirely focussed on the marginal gains and process-driven approach.

> ***"All the minor variables of an effective team performance come together (alignment), including what you do with the ball, without the ball, the teamwork and togetherness, selflessness, ruthlessness, mindset, passion, and alignment of this group of***

people. But overall, a well thought out strategy, individually and collectively, to get a desired result. 'We not Me' basically."

Modern Day Leaders:
The 'off-the-cuff' old fashioned leadership of some less able leaders in charge, needs to be a long-gone trait for the modern day 21st century. This is why the dinosaurs of the business world are starting to get found out, partially due to the growth of social media, but also the science of how we lead is out there more. The world is changing rapidly, so we older folk must change with it. The 'Millennial' generation and our societies newer and latest cohort 'Generation Z' simply won't have it, let alone generation alpha who were born in 2010!

Scary thought:
You want to hear something scary? The smart phone these young people of society carry now, is going to be the worst piece of technology they ever have! That's nuts when you think about it.

Try and think about why so many businesses fail. This can be because of an ineffective strategy and process. As previously mentioned, one of my biggest annoyances is managers who neglect to deploy a proper process regarding developing their people. In schools we call it CPD (Continuing Professional Development).

A well-known quote from Richard Branson (and which is explored further in chapter 45 and already mentioned in chapter 6), supports this ethos. He said,

"Train people well enough so they are good enough to leave, but treat them well enough, so they don't want to."

The above quote is a win-win, and something which is so blindingly obvious you would think it should happen in every company.

Often, I walk into companies and the word 'process; gets bandied about all over the place. I have noticed that most of society are still not entirely sure what the word genuinely means though.

Question:

So what is a process?

Answer:

"A plan, a strategy, of the individuals, to all contribute to their job description and execute the behaviours of 'brilliant basics' every single day."

One young football client who plays in Germany for Dortmund once said to me this, "Steve, I believe the meaning of process is:

"Failure + Fun + Development"

How good are his thoughts! Well done Jack! I am a very process-driven person and the many experiences I have encountered give me this evidence base and the confidence to be crystal clear on what is needed to add value to the new crop of athletes and businesses to achieve success. Another simpler version is below:

Process = People + Strategy + Execution = Outcome

I never use a one size fits all approach of course, but another element of my work is making it entirely bespoke to my clients' needs, which many business coaches and educators get wrong. The basics of *Core Values* will never leave my cognitive toolbox. These are as follows:

Commitment + Ownership + Responsibility = Excellence

Reminders:
- Without CORE values in your teams, you are basically doomed
- Your 'knowledge' about how high performing teams operate in an inter disciplinary way is paramount to your success.

- How the business journey looks both strategically and operationally is key in high performing environments. (You cannot run blind with this. If you don't know something, get someone in the building that does).
- In summary, if you get the *process of culture* bit wrong you are dead meat. Again, I reiterate, there needs to be a plan, a strategy, a process.

The above seems quite simple, doesn't it? Follow the process and results just come. As we all know, it is not as simple as that. Winning in sport or business is not that easy but you MUST be process driven.

Tasks to complete:
Task 1 – Brilliant Basics:
1. Write down what your team's 'brilliant basics' are.
2. Grade them (1-5) once a week, to see if people live by these basics every day.
3. Do this task on one another, which would be great for raising levels of self-awareness.

Task 2 - Time/Achievement:

1) Think about the 5 most important tasks you need to achieve?

2) Now grade them 1-10 on how happy you are with the amount of time you spend on them.

3) Now think about what you would like the rating to be. Grade 1-10 on what you wish the time was?

4) This should give you a good indication on where you are spending most of your time.

5) Is it in the area and percentages you want?

HOW NOT BE A LEADERSHIP D*CKHEAD

Key Performance Indicators:

The setting of effective and efficient KPI's is paramount for any competent business. However most importantly in addition to having KPI's, is the regular monitoring of them, otherwise your business is simply pissing in the wind. As I said earlier, "What gets measured, gets done."

Advice:

- Simply diarise and strategise monthly, weekly, quarterly when you are going to monitor the KPIs.
- Many leaders don't do this effectively. Many line managers I have had in my past who I had line management meetings with, often just forgot to address my KPIs and targets during my meetings. Talk about get out of jail.
- I would turn up, ready to share what I had actioned (or not actioned), and the meeting would just turn into a 'free for all of looseness'. I would leave the meeting and my superior wouldn't know any more about what I had done at the end of the meeting compared with what they knew at the start. A shambles basically and an example of how not to line manage. The best ones however, would hold me accountable for absolutely everything.

One boss I had was called Jeffrey Risbridger. I didn't particularly like his style, but I very much respected his attention to detail on the things that mattered. He was good at that. You could never walk into his office and blag it. He would always hold you accountable for everything you did. He would question your every decision, which I didn't like by the way.

Working Backwards:

I have often found that my three decades of successes and experiences, now enable me to work backwards. I often say to colleagues:

> ***"We have had success at this before, so we just need to work back from there."***

I genuinely believe for businesses who are yet to achieve 'sustained success' it is harder to know what direction to go in, in the first place. It is the same dilemma with regards to people development, and why I am now so clear in knowing how to the help people I serve. Often,

"I work backwards."

Why evidence leads to confidence:
- I have achieved so many successes in my career, by helping others achieve greatness for themselves.
- I have mentored some of the world's best youth athletes as clients and have seen them grow into world class adult athletes.
- I have taught 40,000 school children and seen most develop into wonderful adults.
- I have worked at four failing into aspiring, south London Schools and seen with my own eyes what human change is capable of, given the right environment and resources to be able to achieve.

So, in summary, if you lead a team:

DO NOT let your emotions decide and dictate key strategic decision making for your people. It will mostly put you in negative equity.

"The occasional rant is OK."

It's natural and it can sometimes be effective for people's work effectiveness). But normally what is required is a good, old-fashioned *hearts and minds* message, which is full of love, but also DIRECTION.

You need an A, B, C and D plan when people are involved. They are not all the same! However, if you get to plan Z you're probably bang in trouble!

In summary good processes can simply:

HOW NOT BE A LEADERSHIP D*CKHEAD

- **Help you save costs**
- **Boost productivity within your teams**
- **Enhance the customer experience**
- **Avoid constant issues with retention and recruitment**
- **INCREASE PROFIT**

And pick up the phone and call me for help if you think you need support!

Advice:

i) Use language like: 'Strategy and Operation' and 'Evidence and Impact'. This will really impress potential employers on an interview day.

Summary:
The diagram on the next page is known as the Eisenhower Matrix.

I call it:

"A posh to do list."

I have used it every Monday morning for the last 25 years. It is a brilliant marginal gain for leaders to become more strategic. I advise you to do the same. It will really help you plan your week and prioritise the important issues you need to address. BUT IN ORDER!

In simple terms:

1. Do now (Urgent and important)
2. Do it later (Important and not urgent)
3. Delegate it (Urgent and not important)
4. Eliminate it and bin in it (Not important or urgent)

www.leadershipmindset.uk

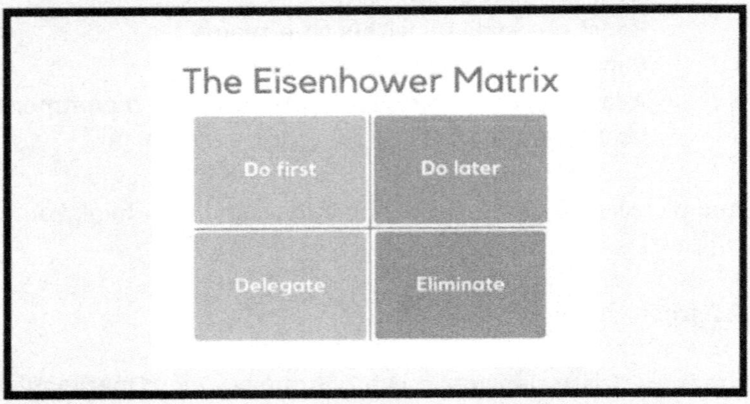
The Eisenhower Matrix
Do first
Do later
Delegate
Eliminate

I hope it helps!

Chapter 23

LEADERSHIP SHORT-TERMISM

"You can't build a long-term future, on short-term thinking."
Billy Cox

I have been lucky and flattered to be called a strategist. I take great pride in always trying to think ahead and see the *long game* in every decision I have made in business and sport, either by myself or by sharing experiences and the decision-making process with colleagues. Short-termism is a great saying, yet it is rife in business and life with many thick twats often thinking about the quick buck yet forgetting about the long game. I am still owed a few thousand pounds from several thick idiots who have bumped me for payment, so I am just going to hammer them to everyone I speak to for life! Of course, we all occasionally must adopt a short-term strategy for getting shit done, however my advice for you is most of the time you should try and work against this type of thinking.

In the above image, Barney, Fred Flintstone's best friend, has two thoughts while looking at his cow.

i) He could kill it and enjoy the benefits now, or
ii) Wait until the cow reproduces.

Eating the steak is an example of short-termism – if he eats the meat now, he will not have anything to eat in his long-term future.

Business examples of short-termism are:

- Quick financial wins with over-pricing jobs, then providing a sub-standard service, which has not thought about the customer, as the most important factor.
- Treating your staff like dogs and expecting over and above effort from them, but without paying them, what their hard work deserves.

Invisible Hours:

Remind yourself about the 'invisible hours' metaphor. Modern working doesn't require you to spend two hours a day in the car when you can spend those hours working at home. The best staff I know do thousands of invisible hours. Be mindful of this.

The above examples will eventually cause the decision maker, to *increase their level of failure* over the long term. Often some leaders are so stupid however that they do not see it in themselves They have fixed, short term mindsets.

Example:

Take the famous example of Kodak photography, a company that did not manage to strike the right balance between selling its photography products, (short term benefits) and not further investing into digital photography of the modern era (long term benefits). This would have required a high initial investment with a negative return. History tells us that after a certain point in time, the financial return of digital photography would have greatly surpassed that of the then declining photographic film business. The executive board of Kodak failed to transform Kodak's value and in 2012 the forerunners of photography, had to file for bankruptcy.

HOW NOT BE A LEADERSHIP D*CKHEAD

An ex-pupil of mine Rory McCann is now a high achieving Hotelier in the middle east. He has many experiences and several promotions under his belt at some of the world's biggest hotel chains. His view on short termism in the hotel industry is this:

> "The change in employment tenures, further encourages this short-termism. Years ago. you would likely be in a company for many years. Now if you make 3-5 years that is considered a good stint. Many staff only aim for 1-2 years and then they switch, their focus and goals. This then permeates through company culture."

The Long Game:

So be thoughtful of the long game because people will talk about you when you are not in the room!

Make sure they are talking about your legacy as a human.

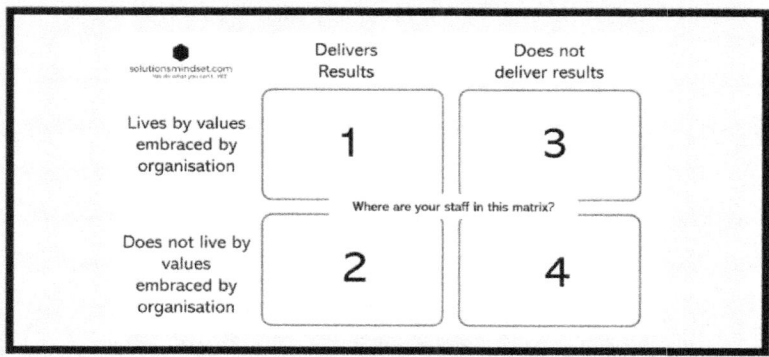

The diagram above is dynamite and from the late great Jack Welch. I have tweaked it though! I felt it would be better my way.

Take a look at Jack's version and see if you can spot the difference?

www.leadershipmindset.uk

HOW NOT BE A LEADERSHIP D*CKHEAD

Many short-term leaders want quick wins. Some people deliver results but do not conform to the company's values. They are dickheads!

I suppose the question is...

Do YOU accept people that deliver results, yet are dickheads?

You want to know my thoughts?

I don't care how good people are. If you are a dickhead, you are gone. Cultural Architects ALL THE WAY!

However, that is for you to decide!

Chapter 24

LEADERSHIP LANGUAGE

"The limits of my language, mean the limits of my world."

Ludwig Wittgenstein

Poor language can cause family arguments, divorces, misalignment with friends, confrontation between teachers and pupils and even world wars. The meaning of our words can be a complex process and those meanings, interpretations and how they are heard by others, can make or break our relationships.

Please be mindful of this. Many of the best leaders possess great language skills. The shit leaders in contrast often use say vague language like:

- "Be more aggressive in sales calls" or,
- "We need to work harder and do more hours."

Reminder:

- Limited communication skills equate to a limited chance of a successful result!
- Great leaders speak well.
- The best leaders are often the most articulate ones with an excellent vocabulary.

My advice therefore is to look at developing your speaking and listening ability, body language and vocabulary, to help improve your messages and clarity. As I say at many conferences,

"With alignment, we create clarity and with misalignment we create chaos."
And...

"If you cannot speak and act well, you cannot teach or lead well."

Great Leaders possess outstanding literacy skills: On the literacy topic I want to draw your attention to its five main elements.

1. Speaking
2. Listening
3. Reading
4. Writing and
5. Communication.

Task:

What are your literacy skills like?

- Grade yourself 1-5 on how good you are at the 5 above.
- Get your colleagues to give you feedback also.
- Is there alignment between how you see yourself and how they see you?
- Yes?...Great! If not? Why not?

Gaining the Edge:

Reflect on your body language and tone of voice regularly. *Tonality* is key to being a great influencer. Play around with your voice, loud and strong one minute and in contrast soft, quiet, and calm the next. There is no crystal ball to communication success, however great leaders know that without a clean and clear vocabulary, and a high level of self-awareness to improve it further, you are certain to not fulfil your potential. Remember that leaders that get angry are mostly angry with themselves due to their poor levels of emotional literacy. So, get good with your EQ asap! Also never forget that the most important communication skill in life is:

"Knowing when to shut up."

Advice:

As mentioned above, having a process of communication doesn't guarantee success, but what it does do, is give high performing teams a greater chance of success. It puts more odds in your favour.

History tells us that to dovetail the strategy aspect of a process driven approach, the art of great leaders is staying calm (elite behaviours) when the shit hits the fan can give the best leaders the edge. Their body language and tonality of voice, oozes class under pressure. I see these two traits as the epitome of great leadership. I suggest you do the same. And if you struggle with these techniques, pick up the phone and let me help you. The New Zealand All Blacks state:

"A vocabulary and shared set of beliefs glue a team together."

Advice:

Ensure language is understood and aligned by all staff so that everyone understands what the fuck is being said!

HOW NOT BE A LEADERSHIP D*CKHEAD

HOW NOT BE A LEADERSHIP D*CKHEAD

Chapter 25

THE GAME CHANGER - HIGHER ORDER THINKING AND META-COGNITION

"The value of a college education is not the learning of many facts, but the training of the mind to think."

Albert Einstein

Did you know:
- UBER is the world's largest taxi company and owns no cars
- Facebook is the world's most popular media company and creates no content
- Alibaba, the world's most valuable retailer, carries no stock and the
- World's largest accommodation provider Airbnb owns no property.

This little gem of research was spotted by Tom Goodwin of French media group Havas. When I read his research, I was blown away with what I was reading. It is truly remarkable and a huge clue as to how the modern work of business looks.

Question:
Why is it so important to this chapter?

Answer:
Innovation!

Reminder:

"If we do what we always do, we get what we always got."

Question: How do you know that you know something?

Task: **Write a list of ways of, how you know, that you know.**

HOW NOT BE A LEADERSHIP D*CKHEAD

To put it bluntly, the question above around knowing about knowing and the term meta-cognition *changed my life*, and if you let it, it will change yours.

Meta-cognition made me a better person, leader, teacher, coach, friend, son, brother, partner, and colleague. It has two concepts:

1) Knowing about knowing
2) Thinking about thinking

When the amazing Doctor Bob Burstow sat me in the lecture theatre at Kings College London for the start of my Master's degree in September 2010, I was blown away by the question. My head was on fire for days after. It is the question that changed my life. It is the question that made me reflect on my knowing, my knowledge, and to challenge my belief systems about what I felt to be true. It also made me challenge:

1) Why I think, like I think,
2) Do what I do, and
3) Know, what I know.

Deep reflection:
Without a deep understanding of why you think how you think, and know how you know stuff, you are doomed in life. You will end up repeating the same behaviours over and again. Einstein said:

"The definition of insanity is doing the same mistake over and again and expecting different results."

So please reflect on your thinking, doing, and knowing and why all three combined can make or break your life's successes. I have often worried how institutionalised the world is becoming with its thinking. Cognitive bias exists everywhere.
Let us use universities as an example. We know that being lectured to, is statistically the worst way to learn. They are supposed to be

the leading experts in the world for learning and development and still call their places of study:

'Lecture Theatres'''

So why don't they call them:

'Learning Theatres'''

The problem is that no one has probably thought about it, as far too many academics are 'zooming in'.

Advice:

Challenge people. However:

"Do it professionally, and not personally."

Don't be a conformist. If you think something can be bettered. Change it. If you do what you always do, you get what you always got.

Evidence:
The fantastic Amazon Prime documentary called "The Real Line of Duty" investigates the early 1990's corruption in the Metropolitan Police force. They were forced to create an undercover 'ghost' squad called CIB3 to weed out *bent and dodgy coppers* from the inside. One would assume that we should trust hierarchies and people of importance.

Police officers take an oath when they enter the profession and the public in the main, associates the police as an institution that keeps us safe from harm or when we are in trouble. This fabulous documentary challenges the mass corruption in the Metropolitan Police Force. I believe it emphasises that as people we should challenge systems from the inside and out if we feel unethical behaviour has occurred. Oh yes and for that matter remember the post office scandal!

HOW NOT BE A LEADERSHIP D*CKHEAD

An article written by Rob Whiteman in 2022 called:

"Why breaking the vicious circle of corruption is difficult but essential."

He states:
Not all of it is intentional – it could come from incompetence, from a lack of understanding regarding internal controls and processes or from promoting family members without proper accountability.

But mostly corruption is motivated by two factors:

'Need and Greed'

CMI the Anti-corruption agency state:

"Corruption is not a disease or deviation, but the historical standard. No country has achieved zero corruption, nor is any country likely to do so soon."

My thoughts on the above are for us all to keep an eye on the corruption that takes place and challenge it when necessary.

HOW NOT BE A LEADERSHIP D*CKHEAD

Chapter 26

THE TOP 25 MOST IMPORTANT THINGS YOU CAN SAY TO YOUR STAFF

"When my boss is mad, they take it out on me, and I simply do less work. If they were more positive, I would do more work, you cannot discuss your malaria problem with the mosquito."

Unknown

1. Thanks for having that unbelievable idea!
2. You know, you are really great at this. I'm so glad you are working on this project.
3. Can I help you with anything that's in your way?
4. Let me know if you run into any issues. Your success here is a big priority for me.
5. I do have a strong opinion about that, but I want to hear your thoughts. I'm sure they will inform my lens, too.

6. Listen, I trust you to do this project the way you think best. Put together a plan, please, and show it to me. Then we can confirm it, and you'll be off and running.
7. I have a favour to ask you about switching priorities. Is now a good time to talk about that?
8. Thanks again for the amazing effort you put into that project.
9. I noticed that you showed Sally how to work the report, and I appreciate it a lot.
10. What did I say in the staff meeting that set you back? Your face changed and I could see I surprised or upset you. Can you please tell me what it was?
11. I know you were disappointed that we organised the project differently from what you suggested, and I wanted to tell you that I appreciated your suggestions. I can walk you through from my lens, and the reasons I decided to schedule the project differently. I don't want you to feel that I'm ignoring your views, and I want you to keep sharing your opinions.
12. What can I do to be a stronger leader for you and help you more?
13. I wanted to tell you that I've learned a lot from you, so thanks!
14. What are you waiting for from me, that I haven't got back to you on yet?
15. It seems like there may be confusion between your role and Sarah's, and the line between your two job descriptions. Is that a topic we should talk about?
16. How are you holding up? How's your workload?
17. I wanted to tell you right away that everyone at the Managers Meeting loved your presentation - tremendous job!
18. What do you want to learn in the company that I can help you learn? Who do you want to meet on the executive team? Let me introduce you.
19. I want to support and promote your ideas, and I need your help. Can you lay out your dispute on paper so we can talk through it?
20. Listen, you are a very important person on this team. I want to make sure you get the information, support, and tools you need. Let me know if I'm not doing that.

21. Do you understand how our company makes money and how the organisation works? I want to hear your questions and answer them because the more you know, the more effective you'll be at your job, and the more great ideas you'll be able to come up with.
22. I heard that you had a tough day yesterday with the rescheduled customer meeting. I'm sorry to hear about. Do you want to talk about it?
23. How can I help you reach your goals?
24. Have I told you recently how grateful I am that you work here? Let me tell you again!
25. I do not know the answer, what do you think?

HOW NOT BE A LEADERSHIP D*CKHEAD

Chapter 27

THE 'PLUS ONE EFFECT', LEARNING TO SAY "NO" AND MANAGING THE MANAGER

"Saying no, keeps distance between you and the wrong influence."

Jim Rohn

Questions:
- When is it time to go home after a long day?
- Do you work to live, or live to work?
- Where is point of rigidity where you either, i) Battle with yourself? or ii) Battle with others to leave the office and go home?
- Are you involved in many meetings that are pointless, and generally talk about... the next meeting?
- Or are your meetings full of productivity, actions, and getting shit done?

The balance of work and life is always at the forefront of our minds. Some people work to live, and others live to work. Earlier in the book I mentioned the 'Treble 8 rule of life'

HOW NOT BE A LEADERSHIP D*CKHEAD

- You sleep for 8 hours
- You go to work for 8 hours
- And you have 8 hours a day of spare time to do what you really want with your life

Whatever your preferences, my advice is to adopt and apply the:

'Plus 1 effect' with your job.

Question:

What is the 'Plus one effect' may you ask?

Answer:

Simple. With regards to your job.

"Do more than you have to, but KNOW when to go HOME!"

I also relate this to another similar metaphor, which I describe as the **'three quarter effect'** which is based around the fitness and freshness of your staff.

Three-quarter effect:
The three-quarter effect metaphor is a reminder that your staff do not suffer from burnout. My advice is to be at ¾ of your maximum every day. Many people struggle with this approach. They are either 100% and 'all in' with their energy levels and the next day they operate at 50%.

The ¾ analogy is simply a reminder to create longevity and effectiveness to your working year. Working at 75% of your maximum will enable you to get good results but at the same time, still be consistent and remain mindful of your health and the long game. Your health is paramount.

HOW NOT BE A LEADERSHIP D*CKHEAD

Reminder:

"Your cup needs to be full, not empty, and your health is your wealth."

Many businesses now have well-being programmes for their staff, and it is paramount that leaders take care of their staff in every way; unfortunately, shit companies can be short term thinkers and not actively care. Reminders, if they are not going to take care of you, *you* need to take care of you. As the saying goes.

"If you don't make time for your wellness, you will be forced to make time for your illness."

In my work in elite sport, we have another great saying which I mentioned earlier called 'fitness and freshness'. This means:

"All the elite players are fit, but they are not always fresh."

It is a brilliant reminder for people outside the sport sector, to be kind to themselves and do things that fill their cup psychologically and physically. I have picked this analogy up and applied it to aid my business content. So here are some key questions for you to consider:

- Can you keep your staff fresh enough for them to be consistent high performers?
- What strategies can you put in place for them to be ¾ of their maximum every day?
- Is there any evidence that the number of sick days taken by staff is connected to work stress?
- Can applying 'brilliant basics' everyday be used as a model that is needed for consistent health and performance?

HOW NOT BE A LEADERSHIP D*CKHEAD

Reminder:

I believe it is highly unrealistic to expect staff to be 10/10 every day. Only idiots would have those demands.

So, think about the below and how they fit into operational actions:

- The plus one effect
- The three-quarter effect
- Fitness and freshness balance
- Brilliant basics
- And ensuring the wellness of your staff.

Chapter 28

STOP INTERRUPTING! LET THEM FINISH - TEAM DYNAMICS KILLED IN AN INSTANT!

"Let me interrupt your expertise with my confidence."

"If you interrupt someone once, you're not listening. If you're not listening, you're not engaging. If you're not engaging, you're not learning."

Steve Sallis

I used to work with two specific people. One a football coach, and the other a teacher who interrupted people all fucking the time – staff and kids included. They would drive me crazy when we used to 'team teach' together, as they were both so unaware of their behaviour. They would both portray the same ignorant behaviours.

I'd be halfway through asking the students questions in class and then they would talk straight over me, (and the students) while we were in mid-sentence. This was proper annoying, and their oblivious interrupting attitude, drove all people mad. I remember seeing the look of frustration on the pupils' faces when they did this so regularly.

- Is this what you do when you are at work? Interrupt people?

I am certain that you have worked with these people. They never let you finish your sentence, constantly interrupt, and never show any awareness about how they are behaving. They don't teach this in schools and families often, do they? Well, they should, as the corporate world loves an interrupter!

To put it simply, I've placed these people into three categories:

1. **The person who simply isn't listening to anything you say.**

Depressing, right? Why do I say it so bluntly? Because if they were listening to you, they would either:

- Let you finish.
- Acknowledge what you've said instead of you basically being white noise.
- Not interrupt you, mid-sentence time after time and day after day.

2. **The person is listening to what you say but interrupts you anyway.**

These people possibly are listening, but because they are so keen to get their point and opinion across, they let their emotions take over, and rudely interrupt or talk over you anyway. Again, this is another sign that they're probably not really listening to what you say. We have all been there, and it doesn't feel very nice to be on the receiving end of it. It can devalue a relationship in seconds, and it happens often, so be mindful of it in your place of work.

3. **The person is a loudmouth, and their personality overpowers you all.**

These people are cluelessly funny. They are the ones who believe that talking louder than everyone else in the room, makes them more worthy and correct during a debate. They can be very overpowering and emotional.

Tell them the truth:

They often have zero self-awareness and can be influential because of their strong and often charismatic personalities. However, a sharper, shrewder and more confident individual, who is willing to let them know the impact of their constant interruptions, can soon put them in their place, and my advice is you should single them out quickly in your relationship, otherwise it will go on forever.

So, in summary, if you are going to interrupt people (because we all do from time to time), simply say:

"Sorry to interrupt you in your flow Jenny, but..."

This is a simple, less clinical, softer, and more polite way of behaving, which will make you look like an expert listener.

Advice on Team Presentations:

If you have ever been part of a presenting team when coaching others at work, or presented in partnership with someone, my advice is to get to grips with the synchronicity between the two of you asap. It is vital you do this, and in contrast it is essential to understand how you can look amateur in a matter of seconds.

Jimmy Bullard and I, the ex-premier league footballer who I coached with, got to the stage where we were like an Olympic gymnastics team and everything flowed between us, but at first, I had to help him to keep his mouth shut when I was in full flow. He was initially terribly unaware and would constantly butt in.

Reminder:

Speaking over your colleague without acknowledging the interruption is a big no-no. It lacks professionalism and kills respect between the two of you, making you both look amateur in front of your audience.

My experiences of poor listeners are vast. In 2017 on return from my first England football camp, my former colleagues at Millwall Football Club asked me with genuine curiosity what it was like working in the England football set up compared to club football?

I replied in a very straightforward way:

"The knowledge about football on the grass and off the field strategy, was no better than any club in the world. What was significantly evident however, was that the England staff were the best listeners I have ever worked with in my entire life."

This experience of 'top level listening' from the England coaching staff during my time at St George's Park, the home of English football, was the best I had ever witnessed. Make of that what you will.

Advice:

"We have two ears and one mouth for a reason, and leaders that do not listen will eventually be surrounded by people, who do not speak."

As Dean Rusk the US Secretary of State once said:

"One of the best ways to persuade others is with your ears, and by listening to them."

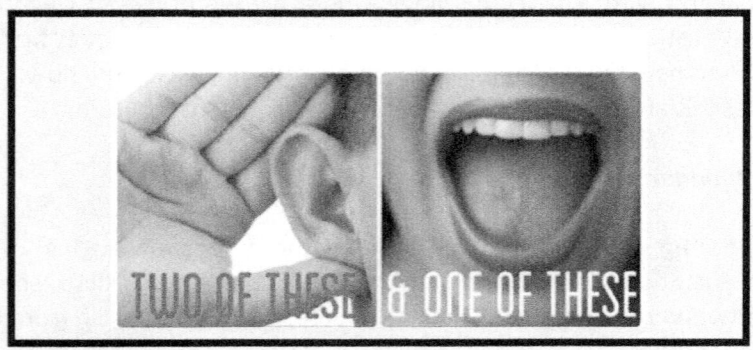

HOW NOT BE A LEADERSHIP D*CKHEAD

Chapter 29

INSECURE PERSON X INCOMPETENT PERSON = DANGEROUS PERSON

"Arrogance, ignorance, and incompetence. Not a pretty cocktail of personality traits in the best of situations. No sirree. Not a pretty cocktail in an office mate, and not a pretty cocktail in a head of state. In fact, in a leader, it's a lethal cocktail."

Graydon Carter

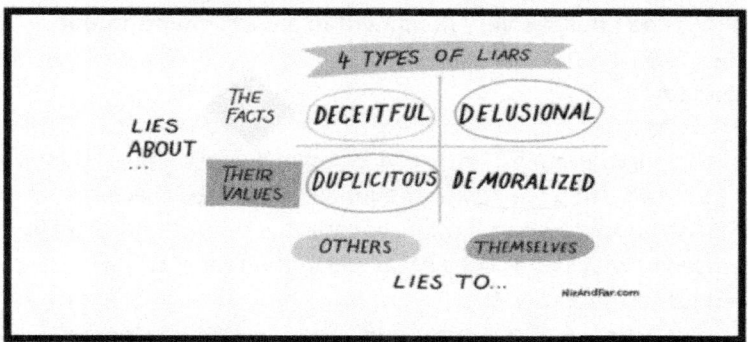

The title of this chapter... It is power! Also mentioned in chapter two.

Reminder:

These fuckers are dangerous! Let's be honest, in business and life there are dishonest and untrustworthy people. We've all met them.

- The backstabbers in the workplace.
- The types of people who have nothing better to say than negative things about you or other people.
- The people that spend their life covering their own backside by spitting out nonsense.

- The sour and negative colleagues that are out of favour with the boss and thus create poison in the camp.

Why do these types of people act in this way?

As my mum used to say,

"Unless you've got something positive to say about someone, don't say it at all."

That is worth thinking about. So, what about these people mentioned above? Let's start with the following quote:

"Confidence is silent, insecurities are loud."

Insecure people and incompetence can often go hand in hand in society, and I believe very much within a work environment.

Reminder:

From my experiences, insecure people often behave this way, because this can be linked to their incompetence. Therefore, these types of people generally feel constantly threatened. Mostly by themselves may I add. They are living in the fear state, yet some of them just don't know it.

- Secure people don't need to get involved in gossip or get jealous of others. Secure people celebrate others' successes. They simply have the personal confidence to feel good for others.
- Incompetent people often fail in work and life, which makes them become more insecure, and so the negative cycle continues, and in turn cocks up the work experiences for everyone else. These insecure people are often the grenade chucker's. They love a life drama.

To put it bluntly, these people are the ultimate twats, and the gold medallists at being the work blockers. Their consistently dangerous behaviour is worth avoiding, yet they exist in all industries. They usually have nothing else to worry about, apart from being negative about other people's lives. This lot, have the international award for "gossip gurus". They display traits such as the following.

- Blame others.
- Never admit wrongdoing.
- Lack trust in themselves and others.
- Get satisfaction from the failures of others, instead of trying to help them out.
- Have self-serving agendas.
- Display general inefficiency.
- Fail to honour commitments.

Question:

When in a workplace have you experienced the 'gossip gurus' creating problems within the dynamics of the group?

There is a saying that I learnt during my football days many years ago from inside the changing room. It goes,

"Like hangs around with like."

Workplaces are often no different. People attract each other: The good to the good, and the bad to the bad.

As mentioned in chapter eight, the law of attraction is something I believe in massively. I have talked about the unconscious incompetence (shit staff who do not know they are shit) of certain people, who are so blissfully unaware of their behaviours.

Be warned about the consciously incompetent colleagues:

- ✓ Sometimes these conniving bastards, know exactly what they are doing to upset the apple cart and experiences for all. These consciously incompetent folk are totally *aware* of their negative behaviours, and consistently and consciously chuck people under the bus at any opportunity. I am not really sure which is worse, knowing that you are not a genuinely good colleague (consciously incompetent) or, not having a clue that you are completely shit. (unconsciously incompetent)

I do know however, that these work piss-takers are worth avoiding professionally and personally, and I advise you to pick your colleagues wisely, and ensure you work alongside the conscientious, sincere and authentic folk (high EQ). I have been pretty fortunate in my career and have worked with loads of skilled and loyal people. My experiences in the workplace have been generally positive, but it hasn't always been that way. I have worked for, and worked with, the leadership narcissist and I believe:

> *"That these lunatics are pathologically incapable of understanding people behaviour. They fail to understand, respect or apply the importance of positivity and authenticity."*

Advice:

Watch out for the:

Insecure x incompetent person (x = multiplied).

Unless they have a *growth mindset* and want to improve and learn, they can be really very dangerous. Sadly, most of these people wouldn't have a clue what a growth mindset was if it hit them in the face. If they did know, they wouldn't understand how to change themselves anyway.

Reminder:

- These people are often fixed in their thoughts
- Flippant with their emotions
- Stubborn with their ways
- Moody with their persona
- Spoilt when they do not get their way
- They are unwilling to change and that's even if they know they need to change in the first place!

Which type of person are you?

Chapter 30

THE PROBLEM WITH EXPERTS!
ARE YOU A HEDGEHOG OR A FOX?

"When experts are wrong it is often because they are expert on an earlier version of the world."

Paul Graham

A psychologist at The University of Pennsylvania, Phillip Tetlock, studied so-called expert predictions in a landmark twenty-year study, (Yes! 20 fucking years of elite bullshitting from experts), which he published in his 2005 book called 'Expert Political Judgment'. He focussed particularly on:

- How good was the knowledge of the expert?
- How can we know the expert's knowledge is true, valid, and accurate?

Tetlock interviewed 284 people, who made their living "commenting or contributing with guidance on trends in business, politics and economics". He asked them to assess the odds that certain events would occur in the immediate future, both in the areas in which they specialised and in areas where they had less knowledge.

Tetlock, incredibly gathered more than 80,000 predictions. He asked these various 'experts':

1) How they reached their conclusions.
2) How they reacted when they were proved wrong.
3) How they evaluated evidence that did not support their positions of influence or knowhow.

The experts were asked to rate the probabilities of three alternative outcomes in every scenario.

1) The persistence and trend reoccurring of a particular status quo in question.
2) More chance of something happening (such as political freedom or economic growth)
3) Less chance of that situation happening.

The results were devastating. These so-called experts predicted worse than they would have done had they simply assigned equal probabilities to each of the three potential outcomes.

In other words, these experts who spent their time, and earned a living, studying their trade, produced poorer predictions than dart-throwing giraffes. Madness!

His reasons and hypothesis:

Tetlock stated, the person who develops more knowledge in a chosen field, can often develop an enhanced illusion of their talent, and become unrealistically overconfident. Tetlock discovered the more famous the forecaster, the more flamboyant the forecasts!

> *"Experts in demand were more overconfident than their colleagues who were out of the limelight."*

More Evidence:

Tetlock also found, that many of these experts never admitted they had been wrong with their predictions, and when they were compelled to admit their mistakes, they had a large assortment of classic excuses. The experts claimed:

- They had been wrong only in their timing.
- An unexpected event had intervened to make them wrong, or
- They had been wrong for the right reasons.

Classic politician behaviour isn't it! This lot were basically the master deflectors of blame and cognitive ignorance was in full flow!

Reminder:

Experts in all fields are just human at the end of the day. In many industries, so called experts are dazzled by their own brilliance and when the ego gets in the way there is a major problem. Tetlock stated,

"Experts are led astray, not by what they believe, but by how they think."

He uses the jargon from philosopher Isaiah Berlin's essay on Tolstoy "The Hedgehog and The Fox". The title is a reference, to a piece written by ancient Greek poet Archilochus, meaning:

"A fox knows many things, but a hedgehog knows one big thing."

Hedgehogs know this one big thing and have a world theory. They account for particular events within a clear framework and have impatient behaviours towards those who don't see the world how they see it. They are highly assured in their views. They are also specifically reluctant to admit their mistakes.

For 'Hedgehogs' however, a failed prediction is almost always "off, only on timing" or "very nearly right". They are opinionated and clear, which is exactly what television producers love to see on programs of course. Remember: Opinions sell.

Scenario:

We've all seen it. Two hedgehogs on different sides of a political issue, each attacking the idiotic ideas of the opponent, make for good television.

Foxes are more likely to be maverick thinkers. They don't believe that one big thing dictates history. Instead, the foxes recognise that reality is created from the interactions of many diverse concepts, including a massive amount of luck, often producing hefty and unpredictable results. It was the foxes, who scored the best in Tetlock's study, although, their performance was still poor. However, their personality types are less likely than hedgehogs to be asked to partake in television debates.

In another study by Paul Meehl, 'Intuitions vs. Formulas', Meehl reviewed the results of 20 studies that had investigated whether clinical forecasts based on the 'opinions' of qualified professionals were more precise than statistical forecasts based on an algorithm. In one study, qualified therapists interviewed a class of students for 45 minutes. They had access to their high school grades, several tests and a four-page personal statement from every student. In contrast, the statistical algorithm used only a fraction of this information. Nevertheless, the algorithm formula, was more accurate than 11 of the 14 therapists.

Meehl summarised that subjective (opinion) confidence in a judgment, is not a reasoned evaluation of the probability that this judgment is correct. Meehl recalled that:

"Confidence is a feeling, which reflects the logic of the information received, and the cognitive ease of processing it."

He reflected that it is wise to take ambiguity seriously, and declarations of high confidence mainly tell you that a person has constructed a coherent story in their mind, not necessarily that the story is TRUE.

What I have said at many conferences rings true with the above.

> ***"People see what they are looking for and generally hear what they are listening for."***

So be mindful. As mentioned in the last chapter:

> ***"Confidence is silent, insecurities are loud."***

Food for thought people! Don't be the loudmouth.

My final message around so-called experts, were the issues I have highlighted around teachers:

I suppose the issue that always confused me most about teachers was that they all had a teaching degree, and I would still see the following.

- Some lack passion for the job.
- Some genuinely dislike children's company.
- Some have never failed at anything academic in their life, so they cannot empathise with people and children who do struggle.
- Some could be good, but they are simply working in the wrong type of school, i.e. inner city teaching just doesn't suit them.
- Some younger teachers think quick promotion is their right, even without the necessary experience or expertise.
- Some older teachers are negative and possess a glass half empty mentality.
- Some modern school leaders simply cannot lead to save their life and think leading involves spending their time monitoring their staff and filling in tick boxes of what they aren't doing well, instead of focusing on a teacher's super strengths.

- Some moan like babies constantly and simply don't realise how lucky and privileged they are to teach and help our future generations excel.
- Some are simply in the wrong career and perceive their job as something that pays the bills.
- Some are unlucky at the start of their career. They may have been mentored poorly by university lecturers or school leaders. Therefore, they get into a mindset of simply 'thinking what they think' and 'knowing what they know' is right ... when they could not be more wrong! Retraining the minds of these staff is tough, to say the least.

So, I have stated the problems quite clearly and not held back, so make sure you assess these issues earlier to avoid the world phenomenon of:

"Hating your job."

So are other industries any different to mine in education?

Many people with degrees, some are good at and some really bad.

How?

Chapter 31

10 TIPS FOR 'EMOTIONAL INTELLIGENCE' IN BUSINESS AND WHY IT'S NUMBER ONE FOR SUCCESS!

"Leadership is all about emotional intelligence. Management is taught, while leadership is experienced."

Rajeev Suri

Emotional intelligence should be a widely talked about term in all workplaces, as well as in the modern world we live in, but too many businesses are still focussing heavily on IQ not EQ.

In this chapter, I will discuss why it's an overlooked but critical life skill. The word intelligence is rarely linked with emotions. We often use intelligence to define someone's academic ability (IQ) or the extent of their knowledge about a variety of subjects. A definition of emotional intelligence is:

"The ability to identify emotions in yourself and in others, and to use this ability to manage your relationships with those around you."

As mentioned in chapter 16, the British education system, and its obsession with GCSEs, A Levels, and other nationally accredited qualifications, seems to have only one way to define intelligence. I find this topic thought-provoking, because during my time in education I worked with teaching assistants who hadn't acquired formal higher-level qualifications but who were ironically more skilled than many of the traditionally *more qualified teachers* higher up the food chain. Some teachers are miles off it.

Regrettably in business, it is rare for colleagues to get through the door with just these EQ attributes alone (emotional intelligence) as IQ and university degrees still dominate the workplace setting. The corporate world is obsessed with IQ, and this is still stop dominating the recruitment process. One business I consult for called Tarmac Ltd have a "Talent Development Pathway". When I heard this, my reaction to the boss Andy Bate was,

> *"WTF Andy... Talent? What is talent? Andy, you need to call this a character development pathway! Character rules over calibre and talent any day."*

Talent:

Talent has a traditional definition, that means something is born and natural. I think everyone may have different opinions on this topic but ask any expert and they will give the same answer... NO! As I mentioned previously, talent will never be enough for success. In metaphorical terms, it may buy you a ticket for the aeroplane, but it won't help you get the round the world trip you desire. I have seen thousands of 'talented' athletes and academics who are unable to successfully navigate various aspects of their professional and personal lives because their EQ is hindering them, and IQ has been seen as the only way to succeed.

The talented lot can often end up falling short in both professional and personal facets, because of this lack of understanding regarding who they truly are. Limited self-awareness can hinder them from achieving genuine success and contentment. They struggle to be humble or kind and many see the world as owing them something because of this so-called talent; mummy and daddy have generally brainwashed them, blowing smoke up their arse for far too long.

So, with this in mind, relationships that are built between colleagues, and those who can offer help and support are a vital component to long-term success. 'We not Me'.

Reminder:

The leader/follower relationship is key, and I advise many leaders through my mentoring that sometimes you have to shut your mouth, put your ego away and learn to follow. That is what your staff are for. They are employed to TELL YOU what to do sometimes!

Questions:
- Would a team be more successful if the cultural strategy around driving emotional intelligence was applied?
- Would the group of staff enjoy greater personal bonds and unity, if higher EQ was evident and applied across the company?

Reminder:

"The signs of outstanding leadership, appear primarily among attitude and behaviour of the followers. Successful people do daily, what unsuccessful people do occasionally"

In contrast:

Can a business still thrive and achieve great performance outcomes if the team is full of lone wolfs and selfish behaviours? *I think we all know the answer.*

In my experience, institutional change (football club, business, or school), as well as higher productivity and success rates, will only be achieved if the emotional intelligence of the staff regularly contributes to enhancing morale, cohesion, and harmony, with selfless acts taking place day after day. Years of research has proven that the more this type of behaviour is displayed in your teams or work environment, the more you will ALL succeed, which again supports the term 'we not me'. The key to all this however, is keeping your unity through the bad times.

Reminder:

When to apply 'Me over We'...
You cannot drink from an empty cup. There needs to be balance between this selfless, high EQ, and the 'we not me' mentality, and ensuring you are number one' in your life. It can be a fine line,

however. There will definitely be times when it is vital to ensure you *take care* of yourself first and foremost (me over we), I believe it is paramount that you think about this. After all, if everyone was kind and selfless all day, but clueless about how to take genuine care of themselves, then the team-ship strategy would be a flawed process anyway.

Advice:

1. You have to try to recruit expert performers in the building first and foremost (high calibre).
2. Creating a dynamic, vibrant and high EQ culture should be a very close step two.

Now, think about how you could introduce this process into your leadership methodology.

The Ten Tips:

In the following section, I have devised a list of what I consider are the attributes of having high levels of emotional intelligence. Perhaps some of them already apply to you, or maybe they don't. If this is the case and you would like to be a better leader or colleague, listener, or expert in your field of work, then here's how to do it:

1. **You have self-confidence** but not arrogance. Confidence is knowing you're good. Arrogance is thinking you are better than others. You are in tune with your strengths and weaknesses, and you know how to use them effectively. Most importantly, you're not afraid to admit that you're wrong or incapable of doing something. You are comfortable with asking for someone else's help or advice and you never let your ego take over.

2. **You know your feelings**. You have a heightened sense of self-awareness and you're good at looking in the mirror, to determine

exactly how you're feeling, and more importantly, what exactly is making you feel that way.

3. **You respectfully challenge** people if you have problems with them. You don't let negative moods overwhelm you, and you never unprofessionally 'go off' at people. You know this doesn't work! Instead, if you're fucked off with someone, you portray your feelings calmly and securely and let that person know exactly what's winding you up. That way, you can solve the problem quickly, efficiently, and most importantly, calmly.

4. **You're calm under pressure.** People often look to you for calm when things go wrong because you don't crisis manage like others. You are the go-to person at work, at life, when things aren't right. You're the solution finder, not the problem creator!

5. **You are intrinsically self-motivated**, which means you are the driver behind your own desire and enthusiasm for smashing life. Because of this, you don't let small failures bother you or deter you from getting success.

6. **You try to understand the views of all.** You're able to look outside of your own lens. You understand that the perspectives of others are different to yours, and that this is OK, and often healthy. This allows you to relate to people on multiple levels and communicate in ways you know everyone will understand. You understand deeply that 'strength lies in differences and not similarities'.

7. **You listen really well** and show care when you listen. Even more so, you ensure that you attempt to understand everything people tell you, and you never interrupt (my pet hate) or try to manipulate or control the conversation. This makes people more willing to open up to you in the short, medium and long-term.

8. **You're emotionally empathetic** and accurate at reading people's feelings, and because of this you're more likely to understand how they may respond. This helps you meet people's needs better. You know when it's a good idea to speak out and when it's better to just keep your mouth shut. You serve your staff, not the other way around.

9. **You communicate well**. You articulate your thoughts in a simple way, so that people know exactly what you're talking about and what you want from them. The simplicity and clarity with which you explain yourself, means people are eager to listen to you, and follow your lead and wisdom.

10. **People around you feel calm**, and you are self-aware at making people at all levels of hierarchy feel relaxed. People feel comfortable being their true authentic self around you, and you have the ability to laugh at yourself. This is vital, as it's a key characteristic of a successful leader. Don't take yourself too seriously.

Summary:

Be aware of the IFI affect:

- Intent
- Frequency
- Impact

Scenario:
You say to your colleague:

"Did you stand on my foot accidentally?"

Be mindful of the consistent low EQ offenders:

In the office we all make mistakes at work of course, however, remember the 'IFI method' as a structure for how to judge people who lack high EQ. These persistent wrongdoers need to be addressed and challenged because they possess zero self-awareness and can drive you mad.

- **Intent** – Was this action intended to make me feel this way? Did you stand on my foot accidentally?
- **Frequency** – Is this a one off or does it always a happen? Do you always stand on my foot?
- **Impact** – How important is this action in our relationship? You stand on my fucking foot every time I see you, and this affects our relationship.

Question:
How would the above behaviours effect my overall well-being? Quite a lot I assume. It is like the dripping tap in your house. In the end, you go mad.

I hope you enjoyed these reminders and, most importantly, believe that you can get your staff to achieve these high-performance behaviours and adopt an ultra-high EQ.

After all, sustained success is a built process of regular discussions around self-awareness, and definitely not fluke or luck!

Tip:

I would get EQ put into all peoples KPIs and performance management processes.

HOW NOT BE A LEADERSHIP D*CKHEAD

www.leadershipmindset.uk

Chapter 32

BACK THEM OR SACK THEM?

"No one is broken, and no one needs fixing. In the correct environment anybody can achieve."

Steve Sallis

The dilemma:

Jim (fictional character) has been underperforming for six months now. But so has the business he works for. He has just got divorced, moved from a million-pound house into a one-bedroom flat, and his father died 18 months ago. In reality though, he is a coaster at work, a family man who 'works to live'.

He has worked for the business for 27 years. He is in his early 50's and thirteen years away from retirement. He is averagely skilled but incredibly loyal and reliable to the business. The younger staff love him, because he's a good laugh. The older staff despise him because they think he is lazy.

In Jim's case, there are obviously lots of 'grey' areas about his potential sacking— on the one hand he is loyal and a pleasant member of the workforce, however, his performance is below par.

Add to that, his recent personal challenges, mean that he deserves a degree of empathy from leaders; the decision is not always easy or black and white.

So, what do you do? Back or sack him?

Advice:

Successes and failures often give us clues. So my advice, when anyone is under performing at work, like the Jim scenario, is to look at trends of behaviours compared with *'one off'* situations and stay objective with your decision making.

Regarding Jim. What would you do?

This is another reason I hate gossipers. Gossipers could try and add fuel to the fire, creating scenarios that may or may not be true and contribute to Jim's demise. The decision should be made with facts and not opinions and without external noise. As the saying goes,

"Loose lips sink ships."

A great Swedish motto I learnt years ago is, "En svensk tiger," and this means:

"A Swede keeps silent."

Maybe we all need to remind ourselves of that occasionally! Remind yourself that before you pre-judge anyone, be sure to look at repetitive behaviours (trends). We can all have a bad day at work, so stay focussed on trends. I say it to football managers I mentor all the time.

"If we lose one game I am not bothered. If we lose two, I am still not bothered. If we lose three, then let us look at our process."

Reminder:

In my experience most under-performers are either just mis-managed or have still yet to find their own 'why'. Great leaders coax this shit out of their staff. So be that leader!

HOW NOT BE A LEADERSHIP D*CKHEAD

Quitfluencers:

The business 'HR champions' are a business-based in Gloucester, England. They are quoted as:

"A Quitfluencer is someone who quits their job, starting a domino effect; prompting others in the organisation to at least consider their own positions, with a proportion following suit and subsequently quitting also."

A report from Adecco Group suggests, that a quitting spree will influence 70% of colleagues to consider leaving and as many as 50% will follow through on the idea over the following 12 months. The report refers to this as quitting contagion and it is markedly higher in 'Generation Z' compared to data from the Baby Boomer demographic.

Emotional Contagion:

While human empathy is still being researched far and wide, what has surfaced from the analysis is people's unconscious ability to copy the feelings of each other, (people see, people do).

This leads me to some research I carried out whilst at Kings College University called the Emotional Contagion Scale. It is a fifteen-question procedure constructed to measure the probability that a person will mirror five basic emotions of others: These are:

1. Sadness
2. Fear
3. Anger
4. Happiness
5. Love

Not everyone has the same tendency to follow, or reaction to the emotions of others of course, and the system of measurement may shift dependent on the environment each person finds themselves in. But there is no doubt about it, humans can 'catch feelings'.

HOW NOT BE A LEADERSHIP D*CKHEAD

Summary:

1. Get some research done with your team on the 'quitfluencers; and apply the Emotional Contagion Scale.
2. Don't let your company talent leave at all costs!
3. And before you sack, back.

Chapter 33

WHY AM I CHASING MONEY?

"If you want to be rich, simply serve more people."

Robert Kiyosaki.

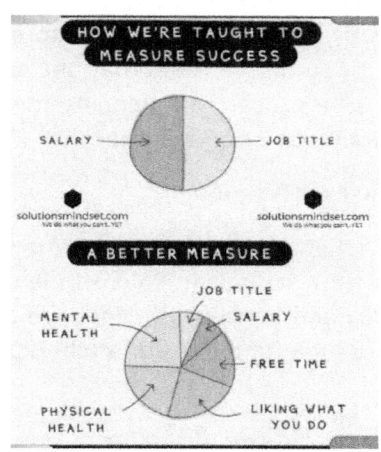

What is your relationship like with money?

Mine is brilliant, for the simple reason that when you enter an education career, you know you're not going to earn any real money. You do it entirely for the satisfaction of helping children. To some people, money means freedom to live, to others it means family security, and to many more it represents expensive holidays, self-worth, and status. To the lucky few it means little as they never have anything to worry about it.

Does money come and go?

My dad never had a lot as a kid, lived with an outside toilet, and lived in a 1950's council house. He has done well for himself nowadays having retired at 70 years old after fifty years as a plumber. He is now slowing down and golfing three times a week. If a lack of money as a child had been what defined him, his life would have been over at fourteen. Instead, he relied on his pride, courage, confidence, resilience, and intelligence to pull himself up, and start a new life from ground zero, commuting 120 miles a day from Brighton to London to do his gas and heating qualifications. "Money is fleeting, go for it" he'd always say.

I suppose if money equalled happiness, lottery winners would be the happiest people on the planet, except they are not. Research from America tells us, lottery winners are more likely to declare bankruptcy within three to five years than the average American. Studies in the UK have proven that winning the lottery does not necessarily make you happier or healthier.

So will money alone ever be enough?

Often society thinks that once you reach that "target" and financial goal, you'll feel like you've made it. Paid off the mortgage, got the big house, flash car, and no debt. Wrong. I've seen it again and again. Instead, these types of money infatuated people often want more and more.

"It's an obsession"

Often, what they have, is never enough. Money becomes a *fixation* for these types of people. The data around social science tells us that focussing on money as a goal won't complete you, because money does not have an end point. The purpose of money is that you can afford to buy clothes, food, cars, homes, education, health care, and all the other things that you may think you want or need.

Oprah Winfrey's net worth is $2.6B, and she is quoted as saying:

"I still know, I am not my income. I am not the lifestyle my income can afford me. I let money serve its purpose. But I don't live to earn money. I think that's why we have such a beautiful relationship."

So, what is your relationship with money like?

HOW NOT BE A LEADERSHIP D*CKHEAD

Task:

A task I often give clients is below. Grade yourself 1-10 on your happiness in each of the below areas:

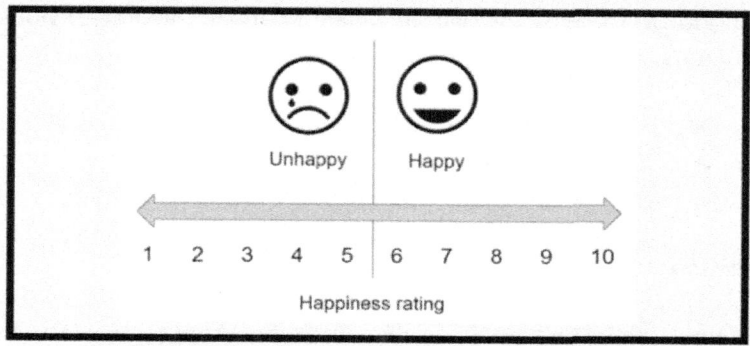

1. Fun and Recreation
2. Physical Environment
3. Business/Career
4. Finances
5. Health
6. Family and Friends
7. Romance
8. Personal Growth

From the Above:

What stands out to you?

What needs addressing?

How can you improve the scores on all the above?

What are your timelines to improve yourself?

How will you measure it?

HOW NOT BE A LEADERSHIP D*CKHEAD

Advice:

"Health is not valued, till sickness comes."

Can money change the way you feel about yourself? Often, we can look at the wealthy people we know of and become envious. You may say:

- I wish I were them.
- They must lead such amazing lives.
- Their social media is full of success and happiness.

Reminder:

Comparison is the head fuck killer, and judgement and jealousy will destroy you.

A client recently said to me,

"Steve, I look at Jenny, and see what Jenny does, and want to be where she is, and I don't realise Jenny looks at Sarah, and wants to be where Sarah is."

The comparison above is so dangerous, and my advice is to *run your own race*. Buddhism teaches us that if we focus on achieving enlightenment, and a state of inner peace and comfort, we are more likely to reach a place of inner contentment. We know that eternal happiness is something which cannot be achieved and does not even exist. Remind yourself that happiness is a feeling, which comes and goes.
So, if you think money will give you confidence, or make you feel more complete, think again. Tom Bilyeu, the co-founder of Unicorn Quest Nutrition, says:

"Despite how powerful money is, it can't change the way you feel about yourself. That's where most people go wrong. They want to be powerful; they want to be cool. They want to be admired, and most important, they want to admire themselves.

But money can't do anything to change the way you feel about yourself. Your insecurities will survive becoming wealthy. If you're not proud of who you are, money won't change that. If you don't believe in yourself, money will fail you there, too."

Purpose:

Money alone doesn't give you a sense of purpose. If you want money just for the sake of it, you won't be inspired enough to deal with the challenges you will encounter on your journey. You need a strong life vision, and a purpose for genuine contentment. According to Steve Taylor, Ph.D., author of *Out of the Darkness*,

"The need for purpose, is one the defining characteristics of human beings. Human beings crave purpose and suffer serious psychological difficulties when we don't have it. Purpose is a fundamental component of a fulfilling life."

Case Study - A Different Perspective:

Name: Chris Gankerseer
Age: 36
Profession: Sports Agent

Why am I chasing the money?

A great question and one I nearly found myself stuck on when Steve asked me to contribute to his research. Some of the things that come into my head and for different reasons, are:

- To feel valued.
- A sense of achievement.
- To have security.
- Greed.
- Status.
- Because it might be the answer to happiness.

HOW NOT BE A LEADERSHIP D*CKHEAD

Yes, I like to earn money. Yes, the ultimate dream for most of us, is to be rich. However, personal scenarios do change that objective. I recently became a father of two children: a boy and a girl. This now shapes my perspective on this question differently, but not completely.

Rewind to 2020. I worked hard in my career, so that I could own a home (once it's eventually paid off), go on nice holidays and live everyday having nice experiences - whether that was to eat at great restaurants, enjoy nights out, or maybe even treat myself to an expensive watch when I got my next bonus. All things that become the 'norm'.

Outside of these material things, I believe a lot of what I do is because of what I experienced in my environment when I was growing up; what I saw my parents do. As Steve says regularly, "People see, people do." My Dad had a successful career until he chose to retire in his early 50's. This gave me a certain outlook on what earning money might look like. Not purely about money but what else was important. He could have gone on to work for another 10 years, if not more, and lived a more lavish lifestyle for sure.

Not that we have ever discussed money or anything around this subject, but knowing the man he is, he knew what was important to him. He created a safe, secure life and future for his family and when he had done so, it was enough. He now lives a simpler, relaxed life and can enjoy the fruits of his hard work.

I guess learning to cherish what you have, do what you enjoy, maybe live a simpler life, make memories, and spend times with the ones you love are some of the things I can, and do, now value more. Yes, there is a balance to all of this, and nothing is the right answer. I guess it comes down to the time in your life, and what works for you. I live a fast-paced life in London as a sports agent, but what I do now know is that time with my family is worth more than any new material object.

So why do I now chase money? - security, a safe haven for my children, a feeling of wanting to provide the best possible experiences and environment for them just like I had. How we chase it might be an even more important question, as it throws up the conundrum - Money or Time? And that, I cannot answer.

What is your life purpose, therefore?

"Studies also tell us that chasing a passion can be more lucrative in the long run that any pound note."

When a human has a vision and a goal, the money will eventually follow. A bit like I am doing I suppose. I have never had any money being a teacher. You certainly don't go down the education route if money is your main driver. (Not with the cost of living in London anyway.) But recently I have started to earn some good money. The great thing about my relationship with money is that I have never spent lots of money because I have never really had any. Now I have money and still don't know what to do with it! All I require in life is basic shit. A good gym, and a game of golf once a week, a nice meal out here and there, and to treat my loved ones. That's all I need. It's a good place to be. I see myself as fortunate that after 25 years I have carved the life that I want, and not the life I don't want.

Your Future Self Advice:

Create the life and manifest the one that you WANT and not negatively impact the one you do NOT.

- Doing work that doesn't get you excited can be draining. In the end, you become a robot just going through the motions of working to live.
- Doing a job that you love, allows you to be creative. It fills up your cup up with energy.
- When you're passionate about your career, you actually end up working more, because it doesn't *feel* like work. By chasing your passion, you'll be more fulfilled, have better

connections with people you encounter and potentially still make as much (or more) money, than someone chasing status and income.

Don't get me wrong, money is necessary. It is not inherently bad and can be used to accomplish extraordinary things. But if you don't feel content with yourself *before* you make money, the money isn't going to make your glass full. You'll just be another unhappy human with a fat bank account scratching your head, wondering what went wrong in life and possibly blaming others.

Reminder:

Don't be the richest man or woman in the graveyard! Live in the now! Success is a lifestyle, not a destination. Chase the passion, not the money. Find something that makes you feel like you love it so much, you'd do it for free. The money will come, and when it does, you will understand what real fulfilment feels like.

Reminder:

Chapter 34

SOCIAL MEDIA – THE POWER AND THE PITFALLS

"Social media is about sociology and psychology more than technology."

Brian Solis

Social media has played havoc with our mental state, and the *comparison game*.

"Watching what the rest of world are up to - can destroy us if we let it."

The behavioural change that social media has created is in such a messed-up place that we have entered a new paradigm entirely. I am going to break it down into two narratives. The power and the pitfalls. The 'power' parts of this are:

- Staying connected with your friends and family worldwide via email, text, FaceTime
- Rapid access to information and research
- Banking and payments at our fingertips
- Online learning and content discovery (YouTube)

The 'pitfall' parts? Facebook hate, Instagram selfies, Snapchat shit, Tik Tok timewasting and finally Twitter (now called X), where the infamous keyboard warriors spout shit, and lots of nonsense comments.

The poisonous people behave in way relating to a phrase called "post truth", which was nominated word of the year in 2019.

*"**Post-truth** is defined as 'relating to or denoting circumstances in which objective FACTS are less influential in shaping public opinion, than appeals to emotion and personal belief."*

HOW NOT BE A LEADERSHIP D*CKHEAD

The reason I am sharing this, is because my corporate training is based heavily around 'The science of how we learn' and the importance of the process of creating high levels of objectivity in leadership and high-performance environments. Sadly, the nonsense of subjective media bullshit has the ability to *wrongly influence* decision making in many businesses globally.

In contrast, one positive impact of social media is that it has helped create many positive communities which add much value to the world. Conversely, you could argue that it has also enhanced dangerous and extremist behaviours and given far too many nutters a voice to influence in entirely the wrong way.

Ultracrepidarians:

Too many idiots have an opinion on things they know nothing about. These ultracrepidarians as mentioned in previous chapters are everywhere! Even in your office!

Linkedin Fraudsters:

I find the web platform Linkedin fascinating. People can make their profile look and sound a million dollars. From afar you're following these people and are often highly impressed with their 'virtual profile'... until you meet some of them in actual person, and you quickly chuckle to yourself, as you immediately learn many are blagging it massively. They range from:

1. Socially awkward
2. Great CV writers yet,
3. The reality is they have little about themselves
4. Creating an online fake mirage and
5. Having nothing about them what so ever

HOW NOT BE A LEADERSHIP D*CKHEAD

Don't miss out:

Social media should be pure power for aspiring leaders. It should add value, upskill, and energise dickhead leaders to be able to thrive very quickly. It is EASY. Just watch YouTube or read a website link. The *knowhow* required to be a great leader is now at the press of a button and available in a matter of seconds. You don't need to go on any corporate training course to be a good leader these days. You just need to go on your smart phone and get reading. This will enable you to hit the leadership jackpot in an instant.

Marketing:

We have seen social media change the narrative of how businesses are run. Gary Vaynerchuk is one of my inspirations and I advise you to follow his great work in this area of promoting your brand and business. Gary talks a lot about success being quite easy compared to the days without social media. Your potential future success can be defined by a smart phone he will say. No cold calls, no newspaper adverts...

Zoom out:

- Many modern-day people are always sending WhatsApp messages instead of picking up the actual phone. My advice if you want the leadership edge? Apply brilliant basics and make those calls.

- Texting is a perfect way to miscommunicate how you feel and misinterpret what other people mean.

HOW NOT BE A LEADERSHIP D*CKHEAD

Chapter 35

EGO IS THE ENEMY

"The first rule of leadership: put your mission above your ego. The second rule of leadership: if you don't care about your people, they won't care about your mission. The third rule of leadership: if someone has to tell you the first two rules, you're not ready to lead yet."

Adam Grant

The above quote is golden, and the title of this chapter is stolen from the wonderful book written by Ryan Holiday of the same name. He puts forward the argument that often our biggest work issues are not caused by external factors such as other people, situations, or environments. Instead, he says our problems are created internally, from our own attitudes, narrow beliefs, selfishness, and ego.

I asked in an earlier chapter the question of how you know that you know something? I reminded you that this question could change your life if you let it. It changed mine.

Reminder:

Have you ever thought... what if your 'knowing about stuff you know' is ever wrong?

To make this crystal clear.

"Don't be the ignorant twat who has narrow beliefs on the world which you think are true, but in reality, you are factually wrong!"

Yes, the blind and ignorant person in the workplace. As mentioned, the ultimate ultracrepidarian.

HOW NOT BE A LEADERSHIP D*CKHEAD

"And in this corner, still undefeated, Frank's long-held beliefs."

My Story:

In January 2014 I left teaching and joined Millwall Football Club as Head of Education and Player Welfare and also part of the Academy Management Team. When I joined, I was overwhelmed with the good practice that went on in the game I loved, and alarmed at how bad some of the bad practice was.

Problems:

- The shit processes stood out to me immediately.
- Many people across the game had fixed beliefs about what they saw as effective youth development.
- Many people didn't listen very well.
- Many people simply didn't like change.

Solutions:

- Educate the uneducated around new knowledge quickly
- Influence slowly
- Get people on my bus as quick as I could
- Educate with facts and science and not opinions

HOW NOT BE A LEADERSHIP D*CKHEAD

You see when change occurs this is what normally happens. The myriad of change normally works like this:

1) First, people ridicule you, ignore you and look at you like you have three fucking heads.
2) Then they laugh and ridicule you together.
3) Then they fight and challenge you. (Fight with you like you have three heads)
4) Then they realise you were right all along. And if you are lucky they realise they were horrendously wrong.

The day I appeared on the High-Performance Podcast which has now had 200 million downloads many people crawled out of the woodwork and texted me saying, "Wow well done Steve, it was such a great listen." Many of these texts I appreciated, others I just laughed at, as some were the people that previously had ridiculed and chosen not to listen years before.

HOW NOT BE A LEADERSHIP D*CKHEAD

Story:

It was his first day as Carlsberg CEO, the global brewery company, and Cees't Hart was given an elevator card by his personal assistant. The card was designed to lock all the other floors for the elevator, so that Cees't could go directly to his solitary office on the top floor of his new spectacular building which had a stunning view of the city, Copenhagen. These views were of course the non-monetary bonuses of his senior position, that clearly aligned with his authority and importance.

Cees't spent the first few months adjusting to his new job like most people would, and whilst completing his 'business gap audit' during those first few months, he noticed that he saw very few people on most days. You see, his elevator key card didn't allow him to stop at other floors, and only a select group of his senior team worked on the top floor with him.

His acute self-awareness ability allowed him to notice and admit that he hardly interacted with the majority of his employees and this observation led Cees't to make the decision to move from his corner office on the 20th floor, to an empty desk on a lower floor amongst the majority of the foot soldiers.

When asked about this mindset to change, Cees't explained,

"If I don't meet people, I won't get to know what they think. And if I don't have a finger on the pulse of the organisation, I can't lead effectively."

This story is an excellent example of how a leader, had the self-awareness to avoid the risk of blinkered-ness that comes with holding senior positions.

HOW NOT BE A LEADERSHIP D*CKHEAD

Ignorance:

Ignorant behaviour is a real blind spot for many senior leaders who think sitting in the ivory tower barking orders at their staff and with a door that is *never open,* is effective. I urge you to think about the office space in terms of how you create equality and harmony in your environment. Too many leaders sit alone in their office.

Reminder:

In short, the higher many leaders climb the working ladder, the more they are at risk of getting an overblown ego. And the greater their ego grows, the more they are at risk of ending up in their lonely 'bullshit bubble', and most probably losing touch with:

a) Their soldiers on ground level.

b) The company culture in general.

c) Their client base.

Let's analyse this dynamic more closely. I think it is paramount to reflect on the below and how people's behaviour changes after our promotion.

1) As we rise in the ranks, we acquire more power. And with that power, people below us in the hierarchy are more likely to want to please us by:

   - Listening more attentively
   - Agreeing with us more
   - Pretending to laugh at our shit jokes.

HOW NOT BE A LEADERSHIP D*CKHEAD

Summary:

The behaviours of others stroke the ego to a greater extent, and when the ego is stroked, it grows even further.

David Owen, a neurologist, and Jonathan Davidson, a professor of psychiatry at Duke University, call this the "hubris syndrome," which they define as a:

"Disorder of the possession of power, particularly power which has been associated with overwhelming success, held for a period of years."

Unlike most personality disorders, which appear by early adulthood, hubris syndrome develops only after power has been held for a period of time and can therefore become established at any age. Football managers are a classic case for this.

Reminder:

An unchecked ego can distort our perspective or twist our belief system and is the reason why 'yes men' and women are NOT who you need around you as a leader. Jennifer Woo, CEO and chairwoman of Asia's largest luxury retailer, The Lanne Crawford Choice Group, states:

"Managing our ego's craving for fortune, fame, and influence is the prime responsibility of any leader."

When leaders are caught in the grip of their ego's craving for more power, they lose control. The human ego makes us more susceptible to manipulation from others. It can narrow our field of vision, and often it warps our behaviour, causing us to act against our values. So, the question is, how do you manage your leadership ego?

HOW NOT BE A LEADERSHIP D*CKHEAD

Ego issues:

The human ego is like a target we carry with us, and like any target, the bigger it is, the more vulnerable and susceptible it is to being hit. In this way, an inflated ego makes it easier for others to take advantage of us. Because our ego craves positive attention, it can make us vulnerable to manipulation and the 'yes' people that surround us in the office can infect us even further.

When people know this, they can play to our ego. We then become the victim of our own need to be seen as great, and we end up being led into making decisions that may be detrimental to ourselves, our people, and our organisation.

An inflated ego also blindly corrupts our own behaviour. When we believe we're the sole architects of our success, we tend to be ruder, more selfish, and more likely to interrupt others. This is especially true in the face of setbacks and criticism. In this way, an inflated ego prevents us from learning from our mistakes and creates a defensiveness that makes it difficult to appreciate the vast array of lessons we have previously learnt from our failures.

Reminder:

"Success is a team sport!"

Finally, an inflated ego narrows our vision. The ego always looks for information that confirms what it wants to believe. Basically, a big ego makes us have a strong confirmation bias. Because of this, we lose perspective and end up in a leadership bubble where we only see and hear what we want to. As a result, we can lose touch with the people we lead, the business culture we are a part of, and ultimately our clients and sponsors.

The word epistemology basically changed my life, and its meaning is pure power. It means the study of knowledge. Epistemology looks into how knowledge moves, changes and evolves over many topics and generations, but often people get fixed into their own knowledge bubble and don't get out of it. Epistemology teaches us to be cautious with our knowledge. As the diagram below shows:

1. What we think is true and
2. What we believe to be true.

The vast array of poorly justified beliefs that we hold onto can harm us over the short and long term.

Reminder:

The diagram below shows that the tiny bit of knowledge is stuck inside our beliefs and truths. To simplify. What knowledge is for you, may not be knowledge for someone else. So be mindful.

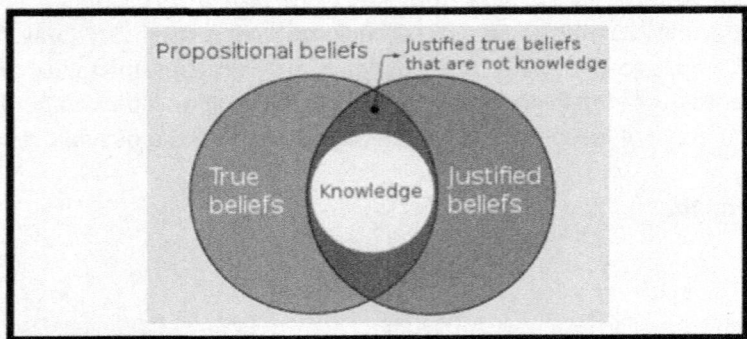

Advice:

Breaking free of an overly protective or inflated ego and avoiding this in leadership is an important and challenging component for success. It requires selflessness, shit loads of reflection, and bundles of courage. Here are a few tips that will help you zoom out:

- Consider the perks and privileges you are being offered in your role. Some of them enable you to do your job effectively. That's great of course, however some of them are simply incentives to promote your status, power and ultimately your ego. Consider which of your privileges you can let go. It could be the reserved parking spot or, like in Cees 't Hart's case, a special pass for the elevator.
- Support, develop, and work with people who won't feed your ego. Hire people with the confidence to speak up and basically people that know more than you.
- Try to educate your people on the Science of High Performance. It has many ways. One of them is to be as objective in your decision making as you can be.
- Humility and gratitude are cornerstones of selflessness. Make a habit of taking a moment at the end of each day to reflect on all the people that were part of making YOU successful on that day.
- The above helps you develop a natural sense of humility, by seeing how you are not the only cause of your success. Actively sending a weekly/monthly message of gratitude to those people is paramount.

Inflated egos often come with success. These can include:

- A bigger salary
- A nicer office
- The extra fame

Often ego can make us feel as if we've found the utopian magic wand to being the ultimate leader. But the reality is, we haven't.

Reminder:

Leadership is about the people you should be serving. If we believe we've found the universal key to leading people, we've already lost. If we let our ego determine:

HOW NOT BE A LEADERSHIP D*CKHEAD

1. What we see
2. What we hear, and
3. What we believe, we can let our previous success, potentially hinder our future accomplishments, so stay curious.

This thinking will give you an edge.

Advice:

I have always believed the below strategy will help aid the growth mindsets needed to be genuinely high performing. I have always used the "Four L's" as a process.

1. What we **liked** with our current performance
2. What we have **learnt** with our current performance
3. What we have **lacked** with our current performance
4. What we have **longed for** with our current performance

Try it!

Chapter 36

MANAGING UPWARDS AND MIDDLE LEADERSHIP

"Micromanagers who dictate and control your every move, prevent you from exercising independent thought, creative problem solving, and risk-taking – all things that lead to growth."

Mary Abbajay

In your opinion what is the hardest leadership position in business?

You might immediately say the top of the tree? I often hear that the worst part of being at the top is loneliness, so please remember that if you're on that journey to the summit.

However, I believe the hardest leadership position is right in the middle. As mentioned, being at the top can be lonely, but you still have all the support networks at your disposal. My belief is that it is a true art to be a good and effective middle leader.

My reasons:

1. You must be the good cop to all your soldiers on ground level.
2. You must keep all the people above you in the hierarchy *sweet* on many occasions.
3. You must be a master deflector and filter noise, yet at all costs be a protector to your soldiers, when the shit comes down from above you.
4. The soldiers on the ground level are your army. If you lose your army psychologically, you are fucked. If you fail to be loyal to your army, you will get found out fast.
5. You must manage upwards with leaders that do not always see the bigger picture like you do. Many senior leaders sadly forget what it was like to be a soldier getting shit on at ground zero.

6. Leaders above you lack the self-awareness to know they sometimes have to be the bad cop. (An additional problem is that you didn't hire your underperforming soldiers. They did! (This is another example of classic work politics). They hired them and then expect you to manage and lead them.

Advice:

When senior leaders asked me as a middle leader to have difficult conversations with the soldiers, I was always reluctant. Not because I was avoiding confrontation, but often because I knew it was impossible to be good and bad cop with the same people, all of the time, as their middle leader. Senior leaders can often forget they get paid 10k extra to have difficult conversations, so if they want shit done by the soldiers below me, (that I was trying to motivate) they would need to do it themselves.

Tip:

I would also tell my bosses when I felt uncomfortable being part of the imminent negatively slanted meeting, and would ask if they could do it for me, or even support me as a second option?

Why?

This would test their mettle and resolve, and you would see the despairing look on their faces of:

"Shit I'm not comfortable with that either."

This *managing upwards* technique meant I was putting the onus back on them to practice what they preached. So, I played dumb and got them to have the difficult chat instead.

Questions I often hear from my one-to-one clients are the following:

- How can I impress my boss?
- How can I manage their behaviour better?
- How do I stay aligned with them?
- What can I do to avoid unwanted surprises from them?

Managing Upwards Reminder:

The concept of managing upwards might simply suggest the thought of an incompetent manager whom you can't stand to work for. They might be:

1. Micromanaging you,
2. Giving crap and ineffective feedback, or
3. Forcing you to work longer hours because they are themselves disorganised and generally not at the required level of performance.

However, the main attribute of managing upwards isn't always about trying to "fix" the shit manager or manipulating them into doing what you want. Let me explain in more detail my thoughts regarding this technique.

Advice:

Having been an assistant many times managing upwards is about bringing out the best outcomes for you. When done effectively, managing upwards makes your job so much easier. But how do you do it effectively?
Here are my 'Elevating Eight' tips of managing the manager:

1. **Be clever…a step ahead…yet authentic**

People who are clever at managing up, take the time to get to know their boss, so show genuine interest in their manager's well-being, hobbies, family, and basically anything to get them on your bus, rather than you, on theirs.

2. **Communicate regularly**

A great way to manage up when it comes to communication, is to understand your manager's preferred communication channels. In addition to your regular line management meetings (if you have them), say,

"If you have a question, how would you like me to reach out? Email? Text? Phone? Line management meetings? Will your door be open or closed?"

By actively listening to your boss's wants and needs then you can communicate with them in a highly effective way.

3. Be emotionally in control

Are you a crisis manager panicking at every issue? Or do you remain calm and positive under pressure and cope well with problems? Can you help your boss when they're under pressure and experiencing issues themselves? This is paramount to managing up. If you are mindful and self-aware enough of your boss when they are dealing with extra stress and pressure, offer to help them run a team meeting, or take on an additional duty to reduce their workload. Keep them sweet as often as you can. Keep them in your pocket, not you in theirs.

4. Managing the manager

While you don't need to be a coach in the traditional sense for your manager, providing useful feedback is a huge nugget for successful partnerships in this relationship. When your boss asks if there are things, they can do to help you develop, give them an honest answer. Then, hold them accountable for what they have said… and if needed, get it in writing!

5. Dual wins, and find out their why?

You both want to grow, so grow together. Understanding the boss's plans for their own career development can help you manage up. If your boss has a desire for promotion, ask how you can support them achieve that goal? Remind them that if they look out for your career development, then you help them with theirs. Simple!

6. Professional not personal

Remind your boss during disagreements and when misalignment occurs that every conversation you ever have with them is always professional and never ever personal. This will help build trust during conflict. Without high trust, you're both in the shit. And remember the black, the white and the grey. There is grey everywhere at work.

7. Gap Audit and Super Strengths

If you have different super strengths than your manager, dovetail off them. Managers are not always familiar in every way of high-performance work, but perhaps you can help them excel? Take the time to give them support with new technologies and strategies that align with each of your super strengths.

8. Ensure constant alignment

Alignment = Clarity. Misalignment = Chaos.

Do you both help see the vision and strategy in crystal clear fashion? If not, let them know it makes a difference for you to be highly aligned. When your manager knows that you understand how your role contributes to the success of the process and company, they can ensure a greater focus on results.

HOW NOT BE A LEADERSHIP D*CKHEAD

HOW NOT BE A LEADERSHIP D*CKHEAD

Chapter 37

THE CURSE OF KNOWLEDGE

"It is often said a little knowledge is dangerous, but too much knowledge can often cause mayhem. The more you know, the more problems you have, to teach others what you know."

Steve Sallis

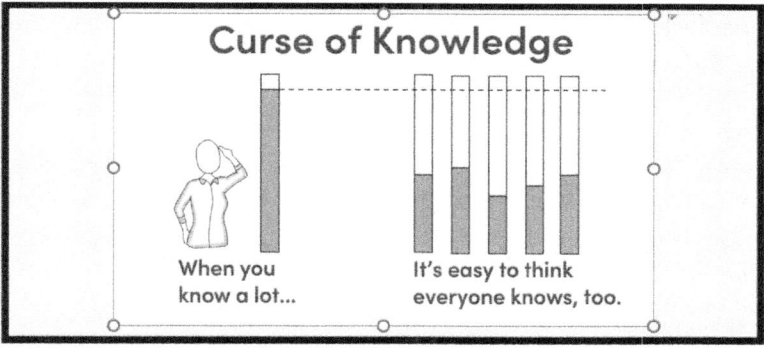

Task:

1. Think of 5 songs.
2. Then one song at a time.
3. Tap the 5 songs on a table to a friend or colleague and ask them to guess the songs...
4. Before you start give a percentage of what you expect their success rate to be after you have tapped the songs.

In 1990, a University of Stanford psychology student called Elizabeth Newton demonstrated a theory and called it the *curse of knowledge* by studying a simple game in which she gave people, one of two roles:

'Tapper' or 'Listener'

HOW NOT BE A LEADERSHIP D*CKHEAD

The tapper was asked to choose a well-known song, such as "Happy Birthday," and tap out the rhythm. The listener's job of course, was to guess the song that was being tapped. Over the course of the experiment, one hundred and twenty-five songs were 'tapped out' on the table.

Results:

Alarmingly, the listeners guessed only three of the songs correctly: which is a win rate of 2.4%. In a twist to the game, and before the listeners guessed, Newton asked the tappers to predict the probability that listeners would guess them correctly (Task 4 above). The listeners foolishly predicted 50%.

But why?

When a tapper taps, it is pretty much impossible for them to avoid hearing the tune in their head while playing along to their taps. Generally, all the listener hears is a weird randomness of noise which sounds like a morse code-sounding load of nonsense.

Summary:

The tappers were stunned by how much the listeners struggled to pick up the song.

The problem:

Once we know something, ie, the tune of a song, we find it hard to imagine not knowing it. Our knowledge has therefore been "cursed", and we can have trouble sharing that knowledge, because we can't re-create the listener's current head space of knowledge.

As mentioned before, the amount of misalignment that goes on in the business world is vast. All high performing businesses rely on highly effective communication, but many suffer from gigantic information imbalances, just like the tappers and listeners encountered.

My advice therefore to leaders, is to lessen the curse of knowledge by explaining the various work strategies we face daily and think about how they can be applied into simplified and learnable language for all.

Reminder:

This type of thinking from leaders is what inclusion and high performance really is!

"Less is often MORE!"

HOW NOT BE A LEADERSHIP D*CKHEAD

HOW NOT BE A LEADERSHIP D*CKHEAD

Chapter 38

I'M OK, YOU'RE OK

"Parents, deliberately or unaware, teach their children from birth how to behave, drink, feel and perceive. Liberation from these influences is no easy matter."

Eric Berne

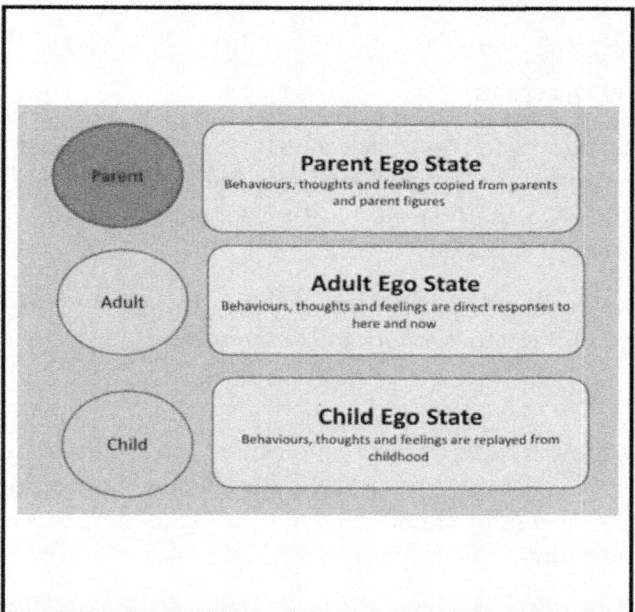

What is the above diagram?

Transactional analysis is the technique used to analyse the process of communication whilst interacting with others in the moment. It requires us to be aware of how we think, feel, and behave during conversations, interactions, and relationships with others. I will explain the following in a highly simplistic way so you can get the idea of it.

The Parent ego state:

When we are in Parent ego state we think, feel and behave as our real parents or carers did when we were children. It's like someone has pressed "play" on a recording and we play back (behave, speak, interact, feel and think) what we saw.

The Adult ego state:

The Adult ego state deals with the here and now reality. It is the processing centre and important because it is the only ego state that is not connected to the past. If I asked you how to make a cake you would probably tell me from your Adult ego state.

The Child ego state:

The Child ego state plays back thoughts, feelings and behaviours that we experienced as a child. From the excitement we feel on our birthday to the fear we have of being abandoned. This ego state is rooted in our past.

You can see straight off that out of the three ego states we could be in two of them that are rooted in the past.

Be mindful:

This can spell trouble in our relationships and is one reason why much work in TA psychotherapy is done updating the Adult ego state with new information and challenging child or parent ideas and behaviours.

Reminder:

People often mistakenly think from their Adult ego state. This work is known as "decontamination of the Adult".

I also need to mention that the description of ego states above is very, very basic. There are many different ways of thinking about the ego state model.

HOW NOT BE A LEADERSHIP D*CKHEAD

Scenario:

I will set the scene. You are in a one-to-one meeting at work. The outcomes at the end of the meeting have four possible outcomes:

- I'm not ok & you're not ok.
- I'm ok & you're not ok.
- I'm not ok & you're ok.
- I'm ok & you're ok = WINNER

In life and work we have of a list variables and conclusions from our communications with people. They range from:

- Agreements
- Disagreements
- We think and want to win arguments.
- Hate it when we lose arguments, along with many other diverse outcomes to conflict

Advice:

Please try and ensure that you leave all interactions with I am ok, you are ok. When dealing with thousands of children this was paramount. An example being, when I dished out the million detentions I did as a teacher. If the child turned up on time straight after the school bell, I would let them leave immediately and go home. They would look at me like "Is this guy for real?". I just wanted them to know that I am human, am empathetic and do want that child going home being "OK". With me and life itself.

The Genuine Team Player:

In reality, family life creates many similar scenarios to the workplace. I believe the ultimate and most genuine team player, will have rational thoughts and a unique narrative around the topic of conflict. They are more likely to say:

- If I lose, everyone loses.
- If we win, everyone wins.
- If I win and you lose, we both lose.

Sadly, not all colleagues we work with feel and act like this. So, the question is how do we acquire the skills and knowhow to put the ego in the bin and become truly 'we not me' in our behaviour? Remember:

> *"If you want to go fast go alone, if you want to go far go together."*

When I read the book, "I'm ok, you're ok", written by psychiatrist Thomas Harris in 1967, I was smiling from ear to ear at how simple he made complex theories. He discussed a concept called *transactional analysis,* which originated from a man called Eric Berne in the late 1950s.

Reminder:

Have a serious think about how you think and how you feel before behaving in a certain way.

Task:

Look at these examples and determine which of the three ego states they represent (parent, adult, child), then check your answers underneath.

1) "I can't get that task completed on time because finance never gives us the info. They're just a pain in the neck!"

2) "Listen…Get Jack to drop that client now and get on with customers who will actually give us business for a change"

3) "We've been affected so badly by COVID that I don't think we'll ever be able to get back to how things were. No company could thrive under these conditions".

4) "So, we've covered all the issues we're facing now and are clear on what challenges we must deal with first. Let's discuss who is going to take charge of the short-term issues and then come to a decision on how we ensure we don't get into this situation again. Agreed?"

5) "What resources can I provide to help you become more successful? Can I get someone to assist you on the project, or do you just need more time?"

Answers:

1) This is an example of an adapted **child ego state**. The blame is being placed on someone else, without determining what changes need to be done to accomplish the end goals. Until the person shifts to a more problem-solving and less 'blame-others' state, this will be perpetuated for a long time.

2) This aggressive stance is typical of a critical/controlling **parent state**. Sometimes it's necessary to be dogmatic and tell people what to do, but if it's the common way a manager speaks to his or her staff, you run the risk of losing collaboration and only achieving tasks through power and authority.

3) This adapted **child state** again looks at situations from the 'helpless' viewpoint. Straight after this expression, the person should start looking for solutions that are under their control, instead of playing the blame game for things they have no influence over

4) This comment shows a high degree of emotional intelligence and is looking for answers and solutions. It reflects an **adult ego state**.

5) This shows a helpful and grateful attitude to what their staff member is trying to achieve. They are also looking for solutions, so they are approaching from a **'nurturing parent' state.**

HOW NOT BE A LEADERSHIP D*CKHEAD

www.leadershipmindset.uk

Chapter 39

THE CC' BRIGADE - DON'T BE THE STITCH UP LEADER!

"I hate these people. They want to throw you under the bus just to "establish" the fact that they know, how to let your boss know, when you screw up."

Steve Sallis

Let's make this chapter one of the shortest book chapters in history.

STOP CC'ING PEOPLE INTO EMAILS BY CHUCKING THEM UNDER THE BUS AND MAKING YOURSELF LOOK GOOD.

IT IS SCUMMY BEHAVIOUR!

Reminder:

Poor cc'ing creates a culture of toxicity and causes fractions amongst the people. And my goodness does cc'ing the entire team and selling colleagues down the river... make people want to QUIT!

HOW NOT BE A LEADERSHIP D*CKHEAD

Chapter 40

LEADING WITH LISTENING - TWO EARS ONE MOUTH

"I like to listen. I have learnt a great deal from listening carefully. Most people never listen."

Ernest Hemmingway

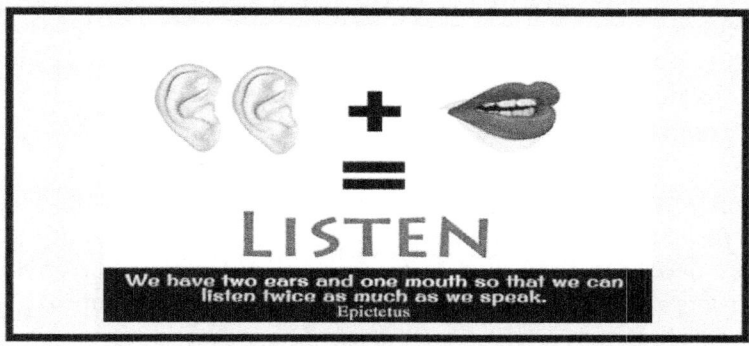

The biggest, most under-developed life skill in the world right now is in this chapter you are about to read! Listening. It's as basic as can be. It is *really* basic, but I rarely meet people these days who actually genuinely listen. You know? Like properly listen.

Do you?

I am going to draw your attention to something called 'active listening' which is something I studied throughout my educational journey over many decades. It is a technique whereby the listener genuinely listens attentively to truly understand *what* is being said and *why* it is being said. It also aids memory of what is being said.

Here are my 'Super Seven' for Active Listening

Helps you problem solve – Leaders should always be focussed on what employees have to say to them at all times. I really like the saying, (LPDR) listen, plan, do, review. Live by that if you can. It hits all areas of a high-performance leader and is a simple way to add value.

Opens your Mind - Your lens on the world and life is not always the truth remember. People don't see the world, how you do. The way you understand life from your belief system, is only one way to look at issues, therefore listening to other people's perspectives allows you to look at situations from a different lens, some of which you may not have considered before.

Deep trust is formed between peers by genuine listening skills - As you cultivate the habit of listening in a sincere way, you get more people to open up. I call this mirroring. They can mirror you, and sense that you will not be reaching random conclusions based on bullshit details and ideas. They also realise that you care enough about them to listen attentively but also consistently.

Builds patience - The ability to be a good listener takes huge levels of self-awareness and you need to develop it with consistent effort over time, as mentioned in point three above. As you gradually improve at being mindful of your listening, an automatic advantage is that you develop patience. Patience to let others express their feelings honestly without judgement and interruptions, will add huge value.

Enhances skills and understanding - Great listening skills make anyone more confident, competent, and capable, regardless of their position in the hierarchy. The more you can get clarity from meeting cycles, formal and informal conversations, means the more alignment you will get. Listening also builds your 'know how' and helps a genuine learning culture to thrive not just survive.

HOW NOT BE A LEADERSHIP D*CKHEAD

Saves time and increases profit - Effective listening not only reduces risks of misunderstanding and mistakes that could be very damaging to the business, but it also saves time and money by avoiding starting a task or a project over again. Employees therefore do not waste precious time and a specific budget can be utilised more effectively.

You become more approachable - As you present yourself as a patient listener, peers feel more confident about communicating with you. Being there for them in times of need, shows loyalty and who doesn't want to feel that?

Additionally, I would like to add-value to your awareness of:

- Introverts
- Extroverts and
- Ambiverts

and remind you to be aware of these three personality types when it comes to the listening stakes. My experiences of these three personality types are based on my personal observations during my three decades in the workplace.

Below is a very basic observational structure in the world of extroverts, introverts and ambiverts. I hope it helps you also reflect on where you potentially are? But also, how others behave, act, interact and react to life's listening skills in the game of life.

Thoughts:

I believe extroverts are great talkers and introverts are great listeners. Ambiverts are a combination of the two. Great teams need a mix of the three I believe. Statistics from the American Trends Panel suggested that 77% of people fall between introvert and extrovert. 12% were extroverted, 5% introverted and 6% did not indicate a response.

Try this if you are an Extrovert:

- Be ultra self-aware about your listening skills and try to focus on what the other person is saying and thinking before you choose to open your mouth.
- Never assume that silence means agreement, and whilst in meetings be mindful to ask others if they agree or disagree, and THEN listen for their responses.
- Understand that some quieter, more reserved peers need 'thinking time' before responding, so give them the opportunity to reply and embrace awkward silences. Not everyone is like you!
- Ensure that you are inclusive, and ALL people have the opportunity to express their thoughts, feelings and emotions, but ensure you avoid forcing peers to speak. Live and let live is a good piece of advice I have learnt.

Try this if you are an Introvert:

- Try to create the confidence to speak up in meetings and ensure you don't force others to second guess your thoughts. If you disagree with someone, respectfully say so. (Remember - Always professional never personal)

- Understand that some people do their thinking out loud. (This is me). Be mindful not to take everything as concrete (black and white), as often people might just be expressing their thoughts.
- Develop your non-verbal communication. This includes smiling, small gestures and nodding. Anything to be part of the conversation.
- Have the confidence to know that your involvement is always important, and therefore try to express your expertise even if it is not fully clean and clear.
- Understand that some louder peers prefer to have people that 'say it how it is'. Silent assassins exist so don't be perceived as one of those. Silence can be golden, however,

my advice is that people need to know what your thoughts are.

In summary:

"Listening is not simply hearing the words that are spoken. Listening is understanding why the words are spoken."

HOW NOT BE A LEADERSHIP D*CKHEAD

Chapter 41

THE SOLUTIONS MINDSET AND YOUR FIRST MONTH AS THE NEW BOSS

"You're either part of the solution, or part of the problem."

Eldridge Cleaver

This chapter will focus on the **"Tremendous Ten"** which includes some of the solutions and process driven work I have delivered in corporate training. They are the linchpin to help businesses achieve *High Performance* with their staff.

Reminder:

As mentioned a million times, it is important to note that self-awareness *has* to be the start of any development journey. Without it you're a fraudulent, and so is your business. Secondly, I would recommend genuine education and upskilling around the critical thinking process as mentioned many times in this book.

Advice:

Critical thinking is paramount and a process that modern day, high-performing environments will need for decades to come. So go and look it up and do your research.

The New Boss:

I think one of the biggest bits of advice I can give a new boss in a new leadership role is this... DO NOTHING but listen!

Errors:

The one biggest error I have witnessed from many new leadership newbies in my lifetime is the new boss trying to prove themselves too early, and making changes before they even know their role properly.

Tip:

Ensure you do a GAP audit as your number one strategy. Then, listen, listen, and listen again. Meet your people, informally, find out their names, partners' names, children's names and most importantly what their 'why' is for coming to work?

Further advice:

- Wait before you action anything.
- Be sophisticated.
- Be measured.

Note:

The Tremendous Ten (Tasks) below that initially need to be worked through can be serious or playful. Whatever you decide. Why do I say playful? Because learning does not always have to be formal and serious.

Task 1:

i) A High Performing Business/Team is inside this bubble. What eight characteristics/behaviours would you include inside this bubble which constitute high performance from your lens?

ii) Now with your 8 words take out four and keep four. The four you keep are more important than the four you lose.

iii) With the four words that are left. Put in order of importance and number them 1,2,3 and 4.

iv) Now with the top two words grade them 1-10 of where your current business is at with these.

My two High Performance words are:

1. Trust and
2. Competence.

What are yours?

Task 2:

Get each member of the team define the word *culture*.

Task 3: Time/Achievement:

- Think about the 5 most important tasks you need to achieve?
- Now grade them 1-10 on how happy you are with the amount of time you spend on them.
- Now think about what you would like the rating to be. Grade 1-10 on what you wish that timeframe was?
- This should give you a good indication on where you are spending most of your time.
- Is it in the general area and percentages you want?

Task 4:

In the education, leadership, and social science world, we often talk about four categories of people. These are as follows: Please describe what they mean and how they apply to the workplace:

1) Consciously competent people
2) Consciously incompetent people
3) Unconsciously competent people
4) Unconsciously incompetent people

HOW NOT BE A LEADERSHIP D*CKHEAD

Task 5:

What is more important in this industry for success? Experience or Experiences? Discuss this in length with your team.

Task 6:

Write down the 3 top super strengths of your colleagues (professional or personal).

Task 7:

What is the difference between a 'team' of people, and a 'group' of people? If your colleague says you're crap at your job... but says sorry the day after.... but doesn't mean it... does it count?

Task 8:

Would you rather have - A Team of "Safe Hands" or a team of "Mavericks"?

Task 9:

Write 5 traits of a know it all.
Order them 1-5 and place them in order with 1 being the most prominent characteristic of a know-it-all and 5 being the least prominent. (All points could be considered important, but this exercise promotes critical thinking).

Task 10:

Contact me for more golden nuggets to help you and your business thrive, not just survive, including the famous Leadership RAG rating; the ultimate document which with my mentoring changes lives!

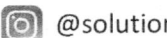	@solutionsmindset	in	Steve Sallis
	@solutionsmindset		@stevensallis
	@solutionsmindset		

www.leadershipmindset.uk

HOW NOT BE A LEADERSHIP D*CKHEAD

Chapter 42

SCHOOLS, LEADING YOUR CHILDREN AND MANAGING THE CHIMP. YOURS AND THEIRS!

"Humans try to establish the truth, and then base their beliefs on the truth."

Steve Peters

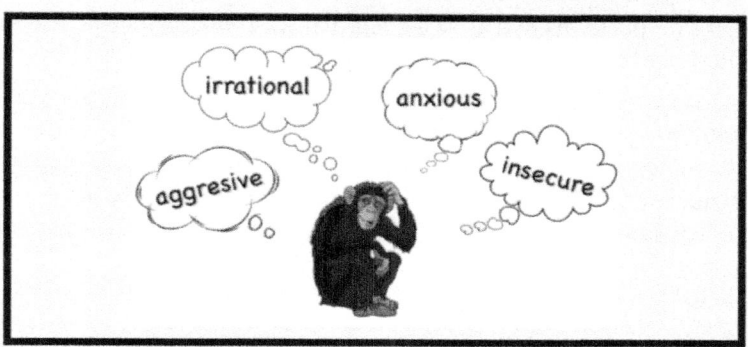

Leading as a parent:

If you are a parent, it is important to know that if you say one thing and do another your child is going to get very confused.

- Some parents say education is really important, but then let their child off homework.
- Some parents say school is crap, and then guess what? their child thinks school is crap.
- Some parents say smoking is bad for your health but then smoke themselves.
- Some parents say don't lie, but then tell lies.

No wonder so many children and adults are confused. I truly believe that poor parenting and our flawed education system is a major factor for adult under performance. We need to teach children for the modern day. A 2017 McKinsey & Company report estimates that AI and robotics could eliminate about 30 percent of the world's workforce by 2030. The World Economic Forum predicts that technology could displace 175 million jobs by 2032, but it could also create 133 million new ones.

Mental Health:
Depressingly, Bristol University has had 19 suicides since 2018. Where on earth are we at as a society if we think academic success should override one's self-esteem and mental health?

Reminder:

The number one relationship we need in life is the relationship we have with ourselves.

Question:

"Are schools exam factories?"

Thoughts:
The educational system often suits the more able students and fails the less able. I suppose the sad part is that we use the word able as someone who can pass an exam.

1. What about those wonderful children that cannot pass an exam but have super strengths in other areas?
2. What about the kids in the middle of the class academically. They could either pass or fail but are relying on the luck of a great or shit teacher to define their future?

Failure gone wrong:

Many 16-year-olds are not allowed to fail due to various pressure from inside the school. Heads of department are now getting sacked for poor results, CEOs of academy education trusts usually only have around 24 months to make an impact, or they are out of the door, and Headteachers' reputations are regularly tarnished amongst their communities, for not adding enough *rapid value*, compared to the rival school down the road, etc.

But we know in 2024 compared to the draconian 1970's that failure is really healthy for our personal development. Many modern-day flaws also take place in education. Poor school and parental leadership could mean the following for your child. Your child won't know how to:

- Learn realities of life
- Lose with dignity
- Fail in life without a catastrophic response

The questions that need to be asked more often are:

1. The teachers and parents cannot want success more than their own kids surely?
2. Why is society not embracing failure more?
3. How can we re-frame failure as healthy?

"Sadly, failure isn't an option for many Headteachers."

Additionally:

- Failure isn't an option for OFSTED (UK government advisors).
- Failure isn't an option for the government as they have to be seen as better than their rivals.

So, is there a solution?

Carol Dweck and Howard Gardner's work is definitely work looking up. I mention in my previous book about the word talent. I dislike the word.

HOW NOT BE A LEADERSHIP D*CKHEAD

Reminder:

No one is born talented. The only gift we are given is our genetics. Data tells us that successful people have just practised far more hours. The challenge is to remind ourselves to keep praising commitment and effort. So, if your child is high in commitment but low in talent in a certain sport or school subject, they need to be given a huge 'well done'.

If they are lazy and talented, then they are not talented they are just lazy. The following diagram will give you some pointers as to where your child is at and help you lead them to success.

In summary, think about these four concepts concerning your children:

- High in talent and high in commitment? (Dream ticket)
- High in talent and low in commitment? (Ask, "Why no commitment?")
- Low in talent and high in commitment? (Enjoyment is everything)
- Low in talent and low in commitment? (Why bother?)

Remember, you really need to think about context here. If your child has little skill but has practised more hours than their peers, then it's unlikely they will ever be 'x factor' at that discipline.

However, you don't want to put them off their love for the hobby, as they may well enjoy it recreationally in the future. Leading these types of less able kids too hard, is often destined for a stressed-out kid and failure.

In contrast, if the 'talented' child cannot cope with the high demands you place on them, and they end up quitting (low commitment), then at least this has happened early on, because if they cannot cope now, they are unlikely to do so as the pressure grows later in life. Context is key here of course. It isn't an exact science. Just be mindful of the pros and cons to all development models. I help parents with this regularly.

Finally, please reflect on the below diagram for your children.

Tip:

Get this printed on the kitchen wall, in the bedroom, basically everywhere! Manifest this stuff!

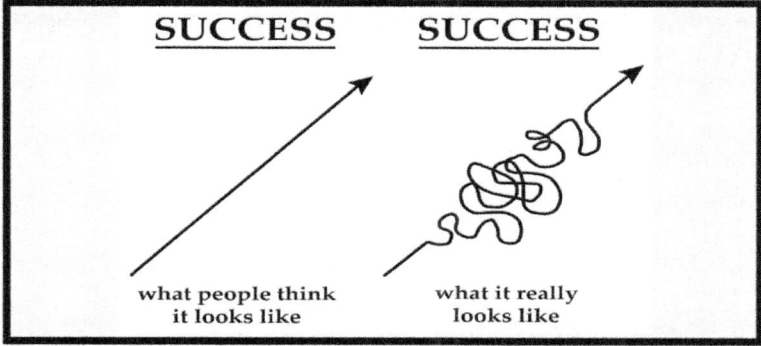

Managing the Chimp:
Having a highly tuned emotional toolbox is paramount to Leadership effectiveness. We call it 'Controlling the Chimp' and what Dr Steve Peters', author of the renowned book 'The Chimp

HOW NOT BE A LEADERSHIP D*CKHEAD

Paradox', explains in his writings, around emotional control (EC). Without sound EC:

- Consistent success when trying to develop people effectively is unlikely,
- And accelerated progress for your business becomes more unlikely.

When I was a teacher, I taught some of the craziest classes known to humanity:

1. Pupils telling me to, "Fuck off"
2. Pupils randomly walking out of my classes because I said they cannot go to toilet
3. Pupils throwing chairs across the room, and often,
4. Ignoring everything I said to them.

EC for me, was so difficult to learn in my early twenties. However, with years of failures, practice, and shit loads of self-awareness by looking in the mirror, I improved my self-regulation, class by class, week by week and year on year. Without this personal growth I would not have been able to last in this environment for very long and low EC is probably the main reason teachers lose the respect of the young people they serve.

Tip:
My one self-talk strategy was to say to myself in crisis was:

1. Breathe
2. Stay calm
3. Keep smiling and
4. Speak well and softly

This managing of my own potential chimp worked then and still does to this day. If I lost my temper, it was game over. Any teacher will tell you that teenagers love you to bite and lose your shit.
EC game plan:

HOW NOT BE A LEADERSHIP D*CKHEAD

I have always said to trainee teachers that you need an emotional game plan as well as a practical, physical, and intellectual one. This is why positivity eats pessimism for breakfast. It is key to understand that it is not always about managing your emotions.

"It is about managing your reactions to your emotions."

Reminder:

Please remember that failure is massively helpful. Learn to embrace failure as a family. After all, it is important to remember:

1. There is no failure, only feedback and
2. You never lose, you either win or learn.

Question:
Have you ever wondered why many leaders with the best plans and strategy still fail?
Answers:

1. They get unlucky
2. They are often unlikeable, and their emotional control is shite.
3. Many great leaders are just *perceived* failures from the outside world.

As much as I have just mentioned the importance of being process driven in this book, if you are a leadership dickhead and regularly upset people then it won't matter what processes and strategies you adopt because it is proven that upset people are more likely to 'down tools'.

People under the reign of dickhead leaders tend to just emotionally drift away as staff motivation regresses daily. This de-motivation is often linked to leadership behaviours like the following:

- Poor language

HOW NOT BE A LEADERSHIP D*CKHEAD

- Poor tonality
- Poor feedback
- Not making you better and
- So emotion-led, that the boss loses sight of the actual process of getting people to WANT to do things for them.

Dickhead leaders are the kings and queens of:

"Words becoming personal, and not professional."

The best leaders do the opposite, they never make it personal.

Advice:

Ensure that you are mindful of:

1. It is not just what you say, it is what the people hear!
2. It is not always what you say, it is *how* you say things.

Chapter 43

THE LEADERSHIP ONE LINERS

"A fine quotation is a diamond in the hand of a man of wit, and a pebble in the hand of a fool."

Joseph Roux

The quotes below are the ones I recite daily. If you're a parent...

Advice:

Print them for your child. If you're a boss, print them as well. I swear by them. I suggest you do the same.

- People see, people do.
- An expert hires an expert.
- Everybody knows more than somebody.
- A smooth sea never made a skilled sailor.
- You cannot reason with an unreasonable person.
- You never lose, you either win, or learn.
- Strengths lie in differences, and not similarities.
- There is no failure, only feedback.
- Not everything that counts can be counted, and not everything that can be counted, counts.
- Do whatever it takes to ensure that you know that something is true.
- Just because you taught it, doesn't mean to say they learnt it.
- If you do, what you always did, you'll get, what you have always got.
- Be the person, your dog thinks you are.
- Shit leaders, see what they look for and hear what they listen for.
- Every conversation we have is always professional and never ever personal.

- Model the behaviour you want to see.
- We not Me.
- With alignment we create clarity, and with misalignment we create chaos.
- Winners never quit; quitters never win.
- Process = People + Strategy + Execution = Outcome
- Are you the leadership downgrade?
- Be the glue and not the poo.
- You cannot say the right things to the wrong people.
- Look in the mirror and not out of the window.
- You are the author of your own life.

Reminder:

Does your motivation in work and life dwindle because you are not living a fulfilling life? Then change it!

"You are the author of your own life."

HOW NOT BE A LEADERSHIP D*CKHEAD

Chapter 44

HOW TO LEAD A ONE-TO-ONE MEETING

"If you don't go after what you want you will never have it; If you don't ask the answer is always no; If you don't step forward you are always in the same place."

Nora Roberts

In this brief, yet thorough chapter, I have given you a strategy and narrative of how you could conduct a one-to-one session with a colleague. Many people looking to enter the mentoring and coaching sector often ask me how to get going with mentoring and coaching techniques, so the framework below will be a great starting point for you.

Something we used to use in the education sector around structuring mentoring was called the GROW model, created by Sir John Whitmore, and included in his book, Coaching for Performance in 1982 - I hope it helps:

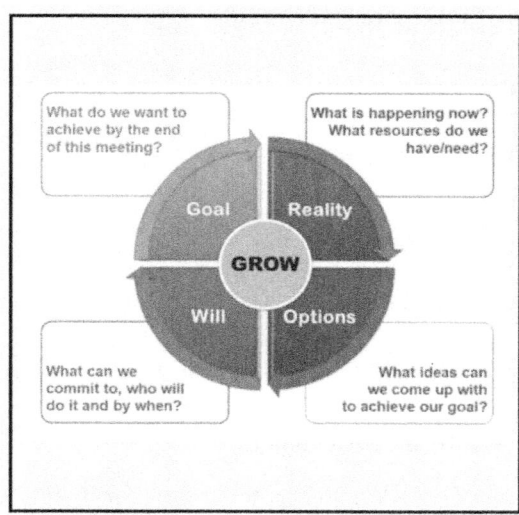

HOW NOT BE A LEADERSHIP D*CKHEAD

Below is a set of questions to help you make a start:

Section 1: What would you like to discuss?

Is there an area you would like to focus on?

Section 2: What would you like the outcome of this session to be?

What are your short, medium, and long-term goals?

When do you plan to achieve your current goals?

Section 3: How much do you want your goal – on a scale of 1 to 10?

If you achieve your goal – how will you feel? How will it look?

How motivated are you to reach this goal?

What would make you more motivated?

What is it exactly that excites you about this goal?

How will you know when you have achieved your goals?

Section 4: What do you feel about the current situation?

What have you already tried?

What problems still remain?

Is your target definitely what you need at the moment?

What choices are you currently making?

HOW NOT BE A LEADERSHIP D*CKHEAD

What other choices are there?

What are your impacts on other people?

What are the future impacts?

How could you play to your strengths?

What could you do if resources (time, money, etc.) were not a limitation?

Section 5: What feels like the natural next step in the process?

Will that next step open doors for you?

How will the options you have chosen move you closer to your goals?

Look back once you have achieved your goals – What were the steps?

Section 6: When will you take each of these steps?

What is the timeline for your progress?

How will you review and measure progress?

What support might you require?

Are these deadlines realistic?

Section 7: What have you learnt from the session?

What may need to be adjusted?

What possible barriers may you reach during your first stage?

HOW NOT BE A LEADERSHIP D*CKHEAD

Is your plan sensible?

In summary:

In addition to the above, use these five basic steps to create an upward trajectory for the performance of teams I support:

1. Stop Start Continue. What do we need to start doing, stop doing, continue doing?
2. Define performance standards with the staff.
3. Create expectations (not rules), I believe rules never work long term!
4. Collaborate on next steps. Write minutes of meetings. Hold people accountable on day one!
5. Follow up, revise, and adjust.

To simplify all of the above:

Plan it, do it, and review it.

In my opinion, one to one support is where the magic happens. These are your opportunities to create gold dust for every single person you lead. With the toolbox I have given you in this book you can start having high-substance, one-on-ones that accelerate progress and performance for your staff.

Reminder:

"People won't let you care about them until they know that you care."

HOW NOT BE A LEADERSHIP D*CKHEAD

Chapter 45

LEADING PROFESSIONAL DEVELOPMENT

"Train people well enough so they can leave, treat them well enough so they don't want to."

Richard Branson

Continuing Professional Development programmes; What are your thoughts?

Question:

"Do enough businesses spend the time and thought to support and improve their staff and align all the various lenses?"

Most of the time I see CPD in most industries as 'off the cuff' from the leaders. I have been involved with many projects around the people development topic, and I've been sat in many boardrooms fighting and challenging peers about what are the best CPD processes to apply with the time available.

There have been lots of disagreements in my time regarding what we do, and why we do it. I have succeeded and failed over the years and consequently, evolved my working practice into a clearer structure. I have named these my **'Top Twelve Tips'** of questions to ask yourself before you create training programmes.

The top twelve tips for effective training programmes:

1. **Stop Start Continue** – What is working? What is not?
2. **Complete the Gallup 12 Survey** – This gives you a great early picture of the staff's headspace.
3. **Reactive versus Proactive** – Are we 'knee-jerk' reacting to current low performance or following the process from our improvement plan set out 6/12 months ago?
4. **Research-based/Evidence-based versus Gut Instinct** - Do we do what we feel? Or what is real? Do we follow what the research says and feedback models to ensure high levels of objectivity and inclusion? or do we get to easily influenced by our belief systems about what is needed for our people?
5. **Happy Hairdryers versus Happy Hoovers** – Do we care about we measuring trait optimism and trait pessimism of staff or High performing teams? Do we need to tell the truth with negativity or are we adopting a positive outlook as the best way to influence? Should we seek out the new and exciting tools for growth? Or focus on brilliant basics and repetition?
6. **Realism versus Idealism** – Some staff still live in the ideal world, with an idealistic mindset. Although this approach can sometimes raise aspiration, it can also hinder the realism required for a pragmatic approach with regards to decision making around what we deliver and why we deliver it.
7. **Perception versus Reality** – As leaders do we trust our perception and lens on the world, or do we have an open mind and embrace new data methods and scientific feedback; do we face the reality of what evidence tells us about our business? Or bury our head in the sand and pretend nothing is wrong.

8. **People versus Process** – Is the process and systems of our training and support affecting the people to perform well or badly? or - Are the people affecting the process leading to over or underperformance?
9. **We or Me?** - Should we make the staff member at the centre of what we do, making them the main focus of the development journey, or is it one size fits all to ensure we make the collective the priority in our models of growth?
10. **Learning versus Performance** - How well are we measuring both? What comes first? Prove the business model or improve the person? How we add value to the individual and the collective is a key question to ask.
11. **Fast Fix versus Future Fit** - Are we the ultimate shortermists? Or are we willing to take short term hits or be more process-driven over the longer term and rely heavily on being KPI led?
12. **Internal versus External** – Do we need a different voice? (An expert hires an expert). Or have we got the super strengths within the building to impart knowhow and support within the current team? As an example, more able staff supporting less able staff.

Summary:
Whatever way you decide to go with CPD, 'staff buy in' at the start is paramount. The reviewing process is equally as important. To many programmes tick boxes and lack rigour. Try these reflection questions to get you going after CPD has taken place:

1. What new knowledge and/or skills did you gain from this learning activity?
2. To what extent did the learning activity affirm or challenge your previous understanding of this topic?
3. How will you implement lessons drawn from this learning activity into your professional practice?
4. How has the learning undertaken guided your future learning on this and/or other topics?

HOW NOT BE A LEADERSHIP D*CKHEAD

Chapter 46

WORKING FROM HOME? GOOD OR BAD? AND JUST SAY YES

"Working from home is morally wrong."

Elon Musk

Whatever your thoughts are regarding working from home, the facts are it is here to stay.

I suppose forgetting the research for the moment, I believe the biggest issue and concern will be summarised by one word.

"TRUST"

Can we as leaders trust our people enough to let them produce the goods without constant supervision. I suppose it is a relatively easy decision though, isn't it? Does the colleague:

1. Deliver increased profit,
2. Add value to the company via objective evidenced-based KPIs
3. Move the team bus in a forward direction or
4. None of the above?

Debate:
Another big issue with the working from home dilemma is also around the "loneliness and laughter debate". What do I mean? It is pretty difficult to:

- Regularly laugh alone at home unless you're a complete weirdo
- Truly connect with people when at home, or

- Spontaneously walk to someone's desk and ask a question regarding a problem you may have.

Reminder:

It is proven that the camaraderie of the workplace will never be beaten when it comes to enhancing our happy hormones and giving us that extra purpose and belonging to the world. The question comes around the effectiveness and productivity of the business I suppose? But has anyone ever studied the productivity versus well-being/freshness/team dynamics conundrum?

Some research from Gleb Tsipursky, CEO of Disaster Avoidance Experts says:

Workers with full schedule flexibility report 29% higher productivity and 53% greater ability to focus than workers with no ability to shift their schedule, according to a just-announced report from Future Forum. But do bosses trust employees to be productive when working out of the office?

Microsoft released a study, where it found that 85% of leaders say that the:

"Shift to hybrid work has made it challenging to have confidence that employees are being productive."

More concretely, 49% of managers of hybrid workers:

"Struggle to trust their employees to do their best work."

This lack of trust in worker productivity has led to what Microsoft researchers named:

'Productivity Paranoia'

This is where leaders worry that lost productivity is due to employees not working, even though:

1. Hours worked

2. Number of meetings, and
3. Other activity metrics have increased.

The above evidence suggests that more questions than answers have to be reviewed here.

Advice:

My advice would be to strategically trial working from home and then measure it to see how your people feel about it. Covid gave us no choice on the matter when working from home was forced upon us, but now the ballpark has changed. We have a new word called HYBRID!

Personally, I would never let my staff work from home every day as that goes against everything I stand for. However, a hybrid model of being both at home and the office would probably keep staff fresher with reduced rigours of the daily commute, and thus they feel more respected and more valued as people. Who knows what works.

So, what does other research say?

Buffer.com in their report called "State of remote report 2020", concluded that 98% of people would like to work from home, some of the time, for the rest of their career. However, when asked:

"What has been your biggest struggle working remotely?"

- 59% of people responded with issues such as loneliness, distractions at home, communication, poor collaboration, and being demotivated.

Food for thought and things to reflect on!

I have mentioned before many times about peoples' lens on the world and staff will undoubtedly have different perspectives on the working from home debate. As the older generation I feel we need to keep one eye:

1. Firmly on old school values as the smart phone kills true and genuine face to face relationships, and
2. The other eye on new ways of thinking.

In summary, my personal lens is I just want people that add value to a business. I don't care how they do it, just get it done, however a balance is needed, and these delicate conversations need to be had in leadership teams.

Reminder:

An elite working culture needs:

A) A set of non-negotiables and
B) To compare these with your desirables/essentials.

It is your job as the leader to ensure that a positive solution is reached with your staff, ie, I'm ok, you're ok.

Advice:

In the first process of the decision-making conundrum: Do you, don't you let people work from home!

JUST SAY YES!

What do I mean?
If someone asks to work from home saying that it suits them.
Your answer should be yes.

Why?

HOW NOT BE A LEADERSHIP D*CKHEAD

1. They perform and excel consistently for 3-6 months whilst working from home and you therefore = you WIN.
2. They don't perform very well with their decision to work from home = you WIN.

I mean, in the short term with option two, you lose productivity of that person.

"But in reality, you win,"
Why?

Shortermists want control and to micromanage. My advice is to therefore do the opposite and trust someone in the first instance and go from there.

This way, you now have this person firmly by the balls forever.

1. You gave them ownership.
2. You didn't use autocratic techniques in the short term in order to fuel your own ego. You gave them ownership and they failed. Building trust is a marathon and not a sprint and a win for you longer term.

This is where many leaders lose their way in terms of their ego being the enemy.

Reminder:

JUST SAY YES TO YOUR PEOPLE AND SEE WHAT HAPPENS.

They might surprise you, and if they don't you can then say goodbye and farewell to them with dignity.

HOW NOT BE A LEADERSHIP D*CKHEAD

Chapter 47

CONCLUSION AND THE SERVANT LEADER

"Twenty-first-century leadership relationship dynamics, are from the bottom up, rather than the top down; from the outside in, rather than the inside out."

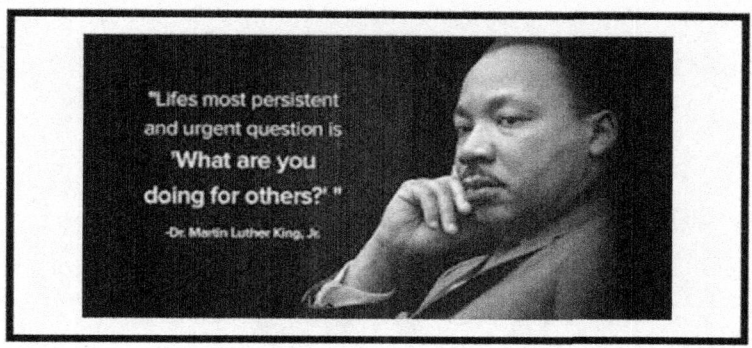

I have left the knowhow of *servant leadership* until the end of this book. Because if you have reached this far, you will undoubtedly be serving your staff very well.

"Servant leadership is a leadership philosophy in which the goal of the leader is to serve. This is different from traditional leadership where the leader's main focus is the thriving of their company or organisation.

A servant leader shares power, puts the needs of the employees first, and helps people develop and perform as highly as possible. Instead of the people working to serve the leader, the leader exists to serve the people."

Mark Robinson (Robbo), the now Chelsea under '23 head coach, is the ultimate servant leader. I was one of his first appointments in first team football management back in February 2021. In the

HOW NOT BE A LEADERSHIP D*CKHEAD

September of the same year we (AFC Wimbledon) reached the third round of the English League Cup and were drawn to play the mighty Arsenal at the Emirates stadium. A whopping 56,276 fans attended the match. Traditionally over decades, past football clubs give ALL of the cup bonuses to the manager and maybe their assistant. Not Robbo!

He distributed over £50,000 - the entire bonus money which he was personally due - to us, his staff. What a guy, and what a human. 'We not me' in its essence. Behaviour like this is so rare in life, so I thought I would share.

Love ya dearly Robbo.

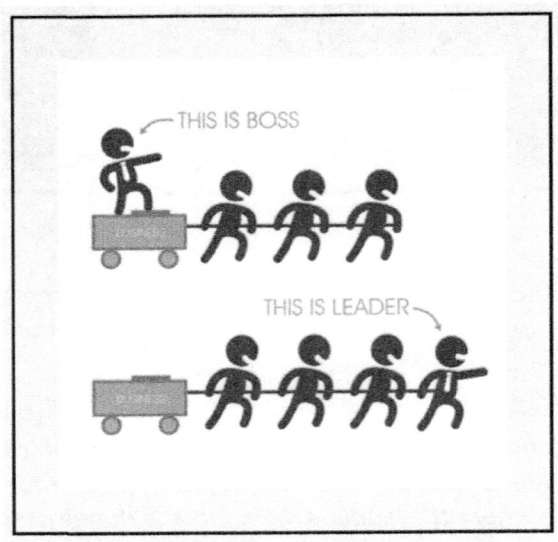

I feel that I have covered nearly every topic, around leadership and high performance and hopefully you have felt deep inside you that these stories were also lived experiences, which I hope, will improve this book's validity and authenticity.

The chapters have been deliberately designed to be short and sweet, with key messages, themes being both theory and practical examples embedded within every chapter.

www.leadershipmindset.uk

Hopefully, I have touched your heart and your mind and upskilled you to greatness with pragmatism and not petty politics.

Please also remind yourself of when to press:

'The less is more button.'

This could be in the form of:

- Keeping your mouth shut when pissed off (People cannot edit what you don't say) or
- Using coaching techniques instead of mentoring ones.

Leadership development is talked about everywhere in the modern day, but it's not always applied and lived. Many leaders around the world still lack the solutions-based 'toolbox' to know when to take a step back (zoom out), from the operational aspects of what they are trying to achieve and stay truly strategic.

Now I appreciate this meta-cognitive strategy depends on what type of work you are involved in as:

"Big businesses work entirely differently to smaller ones."

But the size of the company is partially irrelevant here, because my advice is that staying people focussed is paramount to your success and legacy.

Reminder:

Getting sucked into too many operational aspects (zooming in) of the workplace as a leader isn't going to be effective enough to achieve the best for the people you are employed to serve.

Therefore:

"Strategy + People = Perfection"

Stay Holistic:

This book is here to help you understand that unless you are truly holistic as a leader, you will never achieve the deep internalised spiritual success you want for you, your people, or your business. I want you to grasp your *why* for life as well as the businesses why, because unless the two are working in tandem and heavily aligned, sustained success is less likely to be achieved.

You'll likely steal a few short-term wins, but in the long term you are likely to fail and most importantly create zero life legacy for yourself:

"And if you don't care about that then you're either weird or a selfish prick."

I hope you've learnt and understood the following key principles about modelling the behaviour you want to see as mentioned in both chapters 2 and 43:

The Betari Box explains this nicely:

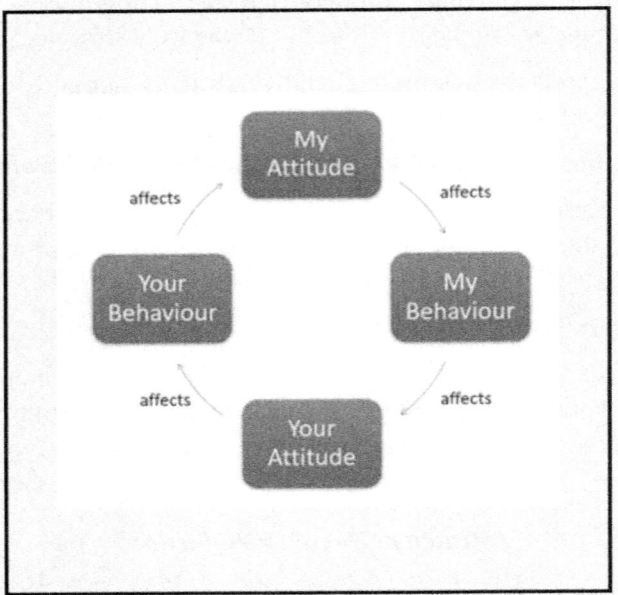

Reminder:

Don't let other people's attitude and behaviour, affect your attitude and your behaviour.

HOW NOT BE A LEADERSHIP D*CKHEAD

Advice:

"Mirror (copy) positive behaviour and don't mirror negative."

I advise you to understand and learn about the process of human behaviour at a greater level and try to understand why people behave like they do, instead of committing to emotionally led 'snap-shot' judgments of people.

Secondly, aim to grasp how elite behaviours can enhance and accelerate learning in your business, and in contrast how bad behaviours merely hinder success for all. Whether you choose to call it behavioural psychology, educational psychology, social psychology, psychology, or just *know how*, the more you know about the behaviours of people, the more you can help and serve them.

"The more you serve them, the MORE they will serve you."

Go and work in a school:

My teaching experiences in schools for three decades, has made me understand far more about both human behaviour and life, than any football club, business, reading a journal or book ever will.

YOU NEED TO LIVE THIS SHIT.

Your understanding of the people over the process is vital in this respect. The core value of society:

Most people I meet do not often spend the time to think about the lens and behaviour of others. So please press the pause button and be sophisticated in your behaviours.

The Character or Calibre debate possibly comes to mind?

The above has previously been mentioned. I have talked about psychological processes, concepts, and opinions, but it doesn't take a rocket scientist to understand that:

> *"Success in business is driven by a culture of learning and self-improvement (improve), and not just centred around profit and loss (prove)."*

Retention of good staff is crucial in order to limit the ball ache of the time-draining recruitment process. All the usual bullshit buzzwords that generally add zero value stuck on walls, are generally blown away by good people.

> *"Good people make you. Bad people break you."*

The Best Leaders:

My great bosses in my teaching years I can still recall now. Robin Field for his wisdom, Jake Reid for his loyalty, Jane Simber for her ability to be normal, Paul Petty for believing in me more than anyone, Vanessa Ogden for her constant calm approach to crisis, Roy Archer for his humour, Jason Morgan for his vision and many more who I have failed to mention.

The Shit Leaders:

As for the shit bosses I have experienced in all industries; Thank you for showing me how not to do it. One of them in particular, can go and fuck himself. Sorry for the aggression but he was a nasty piece of work and the ultimate dickhead leader.

Tips for you to consider:

- The 'why' of your people as early as you can in the process
- What motivates them?
- What gets them out of bed every day?
- What is their current level of performance compared with their actual potential?
- Are they the glue, or the poo?
- Are they energisers or de-energisers?
- Do they thrive or merely survive?
- Are they all about the 'we' or all about the 'me'?
- Do their experiences outweigh others with more experience?

Finally, please, please remember that strengths lie in differences, and not similarities. Too many businesses and leaders have narrow lenses on the world which therefore kills the diversity of their teams, and a lack of diversity can affect long term performance. Ashley Stahl of Forbes magazine wrote:

"Diversity in the workplace means employing people of different ages, genders, ethnicities, sexual orientations, cultural backgrounds, and education levels.

*Not only is diversity crucial for creativity and social justice, but also **research** shows that a diverse workplace is good for the bottom line. In fact, companies with a diverse workforce are 35% more likely to experience greater financial returns than their respective non-diverse counterparts."*

Intelligence is generally seen as the ability to think and learn however, I urge you to think about:

1. Re-thinking your thinking.
2. Unlearning as a major skill for you to succeed.
3. Particularly unlearning your bad habits, beliefs and truths and learning new ones.

With regards to habits, I firmly believe:

"That we first make our habits, then our habits make us."

Reminder:

The world has changed so you have to change with it. Cognitive bias exists everywhere. I have said a million times:

"Shit leaders see what they look for and hear what they listen for."

These leadership dickheads are often the people that laugh at people who have a pair of shoes that look like they are from 1988, when in reality, they are the person who still thinks like it's 1988!

HOW NOT BE A LEADERSHIP D*CKHEAD

They have forgotten that times have changed, and so has society.

Meta-Cognition:

Most humans would prefer to hang on to current ways of thinking rather than challenging their own beliefs with new ways of thinking.

Questioning yourself (meta-cognition) and looking in the mirror isn't easy and can be uncomfortable in a world where we like comfort. We often like listening to people that make us feel good, compared to people that challenge us to make us think hard.

What was once right, may now be wrong and hopefully this book has challenged you to think like that. If not, I have majorly failed you.

Finally, I give you this to use which is an acronym called the CARE model:

The Solutions Mindset 'CARE Model' of Leadership:

- **C**ommitment to your people...
- **A**uthentic with what you say and how you behave...
- **R**esponsibility to serve your staff...
- **E**quality & **E**nvironment... Great Leaders create inclusivity and a genuine 'NO ARMOUR' environment to work in.

LIVE BY THE ABOVE... I TRY TO.

My real legacy I suppose is on the next page...

HOW NOT BE A LEADERSHIP D*CKHEAD

PERFORMANCE AND EXCELLENCE

Abby Harvey
One of the most prominent things you ever said to me which has stayed with me to this day: "Don't be a sheep".

I continually remind myself that I don't owe anyone an explanation for the way I choose to live my life. It's given me the energy to carve my own path, colour outside the lines and challenge the status-quo.

You were a remarkable influence and a very rare teacher.

solutionsmindset.com
We do what you can't...YET

Emma Hamshere
Mr Steve Sallis your legacy grows with us all as we have grown into 30 something year olds. I still speak of you fondly and was talking to my daughter a few days ago she's 6 about how much just one teacher can impact your life and show you the way. You are one of those teachers Sallis and im sure your legacy will live on through us and our children. So much love and thanks for our little shout out. Xx 🖤

Lorraine Tudo...
1 hr

When I was 12, this man basically stopped me from dropping out of school and helped me become who I am today. Now he is doing BITS and I'm all proud of him, like he was the day I finished school! Steve Sallis
#bestteacher #fangirl #doingbits #aosallis

Lorraine Tudo
7 January 2019

Got my copy of Educat right to support him ba The author was my form school and I couldn't be note, it's the cutest! I love copy get onto Solutionsm

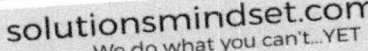
solutionsmindset.com
We do what you can't...YET

Hi Steve, just wanted to personally reach out and thank you for yesterday. All of your delivery was very well received but your guest speaker slot was awesome! You had all of the staff glued 😊
Thanks for the feedback yesterday it was much appreciated. I am very much looking forward to our first session

 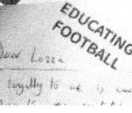

Brad Rushton · 1st   15h ···
Managing Director, SCL Education Group

Thank you **Steve Sallis** for your continued support and helping shape the next generation of leadership within the business. The team are inspired and energised following their sessions with you.

325

www.leadershipmindset.uk

HOW NOT BE A LEADERSHIP D*CKHEAD

HOW NOT BE A LEADERSHIP D*CKHEAD

Acknowledgments

I need to thank my family for their constant love but most importantly for all being achievers. People see, people do, and I really believe this has helped me grow. Dad for being the best dad on the planet, Mum for her unconditional love and Jamie for his wisdom. Step mum Jane, sisters Emma, Harry, and Alfie boy the dog. Plus, RIP Milo. I love you all dearly, Lottie and Tonniaaa you are legends.

My late grandad Sidney Sallis. Finally, my big brother and idol Iain. A Headteacher who I love dearly. He created a little brother with spirit and passion, probably due to him punching me in the back of the head so often it toughened me up.

To the wonderful Karen Stanley and Danii Butler for bringing this book to life for me. Your passion, dedication to my project and professionalism is world class.

To Andy Bate who gave me my first corporate gig in 2018 and believed in me and my work from the off. Other loyal heroes include Jonny Barrett at OTC, Gary Petit at ISM, Craig Hall, Sam Scanlon, Frazer Hutchinson at GRP Connect and Stewart Archibald.

To Doctor Micky Bennett and Ryan and Amani at Orbis, thank you. To the EVC crew Gurpreet and Nick - Thank you for trusting me with your team.

The two Richards at Frankham Group - Both great blokes.

Brad and Becky at SCL for always requiring my work. Love your loyalty.

Thanks to the Scottish Football Association crew who have become genuine friends. Greig Paterson, Andy Gould, Dougie Anderson, Ritchie Wilson, Marion Waddell, Martyn Buckie, Alan Chalky White, Ian Donnelly, Chris Docherty, Catherine Sharp and Tracey Young. What people you are. Love you all to bits and see you all now as my extended Scottish family.

www.leadershipmindset.uk

HOW NOT BE A LEADERSHIP D*CKHEAD

To my educational stalwarts, Eamon Brennan, Charli Napier, Shelley Tuke, Melissa George, Brian Griffen, Hayley Callum, Helen Frances, Julie Richardson, Josh Lampard, Danny Steel, Claire Johnston, Karema Abdalla, Kate Dempster, Jenny Gray, Anna Sheppard, Will Monk, Steve King, Martin Beaumont, Graham Hayes, Rachel Emerson, Emma Legg, Kevin Watson, Bianca Williams, James Whelan, Mel Smith, Dan Portsmouth, Stevie Bramble, Steve Hatton, Peter Marchant and Kat Long. You are all true professionals and are the teachers and leaders every modern school needs. Education needs great authentic leaders which all of you are, end of story.

To my Solutionsmindset.com crew who help me deliver the now trademarked 'My Future Self" schools project. Jonathan Moore, Joe Charm, Tambo, Trevor Elliot MBE, and Mike. Thank you for bringing my content to life.

To all my hundreds of one-to-one clients. Thank you for trusting me with you or your children. These include the Connolly, Griffin, Oliver, Jaiswal, Mead, Irons, Mize, Howell, Wang, Mogal, Smith, Duffy, Perilly, Lameiras, Cooper, Carelton, Gee, Finlayson, Gould, Butler, Manning, Austin, Morrish, Husbands, and Falzon families. Plus many more.

To Dean 'Custard Pie' Austin, for giving me my first chance in 1st team professional football at Northampton Town in 2017 and being a truly brilliant bloke. He welcomed me into his inner circle when he really didn't need to. I love you for this and always will.

To Mark Robinson, for doing the same at AFC Wimbledon and being the ultimate people carrier. To Ben Ryan my token rugby friend who challenged my thinking constantly.

To Steve Morison, for doing the same at Cardiff City and Sutton. One thing we do together is add value even if we see the world differently on occasions. Love you iceman.

www.leadershipmindset.uk

HOW NOT BE A LEADERSHIP D*CKHEAD

Thanks to all the supporters, board members and staff of Sutton United also. We added value in the winter of 2024 even though the outcome wasn't what we wanted.

To Jon Brady my brother from another mother, for our promotion with Northampton Town in the 2022/23 season. I know how hard you work and what this job means to you. You, Teddy, Will, Harriet and Claire have welcomed me into your home and for that I am eternally humbled. Also, to Colin Calderwood, Marc Richards, and the rest of the staff at Northampton Town for being so open about my work during that season.

To Simon Williams at the LFE for generally just being a bloody awesome human being. Also, to Tom Palmer, Ryan White, Gavin Willacy, and Simon Dwight for the same.

To Boyley, Aggy and Tuffsy my non-league partners. Loyalty is what we have, and the Chalk and Cheese metaphor makes us.

To Harry Watling (Tennis Ball Head) for being the best mate anyone could ask for. I cannot wait to see what the future holds for us. You are also my little brother from another mother. A proper human, friend and confidant, who I would run through bricks walls for as a mate. Your wife Cizzarooney is a gem and baby girl Lyla Rose.

The Golfers of the GLB society (Good Looking Blokes). So many laughs, and bullshit stories, every weekend is the best with you lot arguing over handicaps all these years later. So much wisdom, yet so many ultracrepidarians! Never heard a group of blokes talk so much bollocks, but I love you dearly. Del, Tinker, Puffer, Colesy, Paul, Dentist, Two Litre Peter = Beautiful humans.

To football agents, Michael Pryce, Darren Freeman, Dirk Hebel, and Nathan Campbell for trusting me with your clients.

To Chris Gankerseer, Jake Mallen, Mike Cheung for always facetiming me pissed. The New Era crew have been really loyal; Peter Smith, Richard Dunn, Jamie Moralee, Rio and Anton Ferdinand, thank-you for your loyalty.

HOW NOT BE A LEADERSHIP D*CKHEAD

Thanks to all the professional clubs that have believed in the "My Future Self" Project. Alex Carroll, Nick Farrell, Lee Wood, Ross White, Adam Jones, Abby Carrington, John Bitting and many more.

My usual life allies in JJ, OB, Bally, Dinesy, Gary Alex, Sam Thomas, KitKat, Darius, Darren Anslow, Dennis, Covey, Luke Staton, Hicksy, Saul, Dale at Luton Town, Leckie, Bigg Russ, Deaders, cousin Scott, uncle Dave, Hydey, Danny Lee, Murph, Phill, Lee Rogers, Shrooty, Rory, Jack Cassidy, Matt Coleman and his family Lucy, Ollie and Ada, Danny Lee, Livers, Towner, Peters, Charman, Owen, Wattsy, Potbury, Ash Civil, Quinny, Waitsey, Chorley, Michael Turner, Mozza, Tobi H, Rolty, Big Ross, Brenda S, Smithy, Danny Carroll, Whitey and mini lop Oscar, Powelly boy, Sophie, mini-Keith and mini-Sophie. I love you all.

To my business peers and critical friends in Shareen Qureshi, Mark Saville, Thomas Proxa, Nick Bills who speak with wisdom every time I see them.

Thank you to Tony from the Paris Grill, this is the third time you have helped me with your wonderful venue for my book launches.

The final very, very special mention has to go to the amazing and wonderful Megan Carver who I met in 1988 in year 7. She's my best female mate from school and without her I would not be here today writing this book with a platform to sell it on. I genuinely fucking love you MC. What a beautiful human and friend you are. Thank you. You know why. So much loyalty. So much love. So much gratitude. Proper legend you are.

And of course, the WhatsApp group which as mentioned, we still call "The Dickheads".

My uni boys. These Dickheads are: Wheelo, Wilky, Mallin, Terry, Franny aka The Shadow and Sully.

www.leadershipmindset.uk

HOW NOT BE A LEADERSHIP D*CKHEAD

FINAL REMINDER!

Get in Touch:

Email: chiefoperatingofficer@solutionsmindset.com

For resources. www.leadershipmindset.uk

@solutionsmindset

@solutionsmindset

@solutionsmindset

Steve Sallis

@stevensallis

HOW NOT BE A LEADERSHIP D*CKHEAD

ABOUT THE AUTHOR

Author Steve Sallis has appeared on the Netflix Documentary "Sunderland till I Die" supporting Wales international footballer Jonny Williams, spoken on BBC Radio 5 Live, The High Performance Podcast with Jake Humphrey (200 million downloads) and Talk Sport Radio show with Hawksby & Jacobs to several million listeners discussing many topics around "people development".

Steve has worked extensively across business and elite sport including the England U15 National Squad and previously at AFC Wimbledon, Cardiff City, Northampton Town and Sutton United as an assistant to the manager.

Steve has led and supported world class programmes on the Scottish FA, UEFA Pro Licence, along with being the published author of "Educating Football", which received international press and media coverage along with global recognition. It is a book for teachers, coaches, parents and athletes, around mindset, teaching, learning and self-awareness.

Steve has been offered a PhD in sport psychology and is awaiting sponsorship. Steve was Academy Management for four years at Millwall Football Club, south London and is now founder of www.solutionsmindset.com. This entails working in the professional football, education and business industry and being heavily involved in ensuring people fulfil their personal and professional objectives. This includes High Performance support for Elite Athletes, Business Leaders, Headteachers, CEO's Families and Children.

Education and sport are his passions. Steve was a former academy footballer at Brighton & Hove Albion FC, which ended and led to an education career. Steve was short-listed for the National Teacher of the Year Award in 2008 and a Vice-Principal for nine years in 4 failing into aspiring south London comprehensive schools. In addition to this, Steve was a senior lecturer of Physical Education at University of East London for three years.

Steve qualified as an Advanced Skills Teacher in 2006 and specialised in physical education and "behaviour for learning" strategies. This ensured assessment for learning was a key driver to personal growth and institutional change and he helped support the government in an advisory role during this process.

Steve completed his MA in Leadership and Educational Psychology from Kings College London in 2013 and is currently studying a sponsored MBA with the University of Gloucester.

For training and support around High Performing Teams, Athlete Mentoring, Leadership Effectiveness, Group Dynamics, Life Coaching, Mental Health & Resilience, Well-being or Communication.

Steve helps groups become TEAMS.